P9-CDZ-673

DAISY cooks!

DAISY MARTINEZ

with CHRIS STYLER

Daisy cooks!

DAISY MARTINEZ

with CHRIS STYLER

photographs by BUFF STRICKLAND

LATIN FLAVORS
THAT WILL
ROCK YOUR WORLD

HYPERION

NEW YORK

Library of Congress Cataloging-in-Publication Data

ISBN: 1-4013-0160-6

Hyperion books are available for special promotions and premiums. For details contact Michael Rentas, Assistant Director, Inventory Operations, Hyperion, 77 West 66th Street, 11th Floor, New York, New York 10023, or call 212-456-0133.

Design: Hotfoot Studio

FIRST EDITION

10 9 8 7 6 5 4 3 2 1

This book is dedicated to the memory of
my late brother, Joseph R. Martinez

If I could hold a star for every time you've made me smile, I would hold the entire evening sky in the palm of my hand.

—Anonymous

CONTENTS

DAISY cooks!

DAISY MARTINEZ

with CHRIS STYLER

INTRODUCTION

I admit it: I am obsessed with food. I think nothing of driving clear across Brooklyn for the best bagels in a twenty-mile radius, and I've walked from one side of a foreign city to the other in the middle of winter because I heard about a restaurant that serves fantabulous garlic soup. I have never met a dumpling—Chinese, Japanese, American, or other—that I didn't love. When a friend celebrates a birthday or marks a special occasion, I don't spend hours in the mall, I spend days in the kitchen, happily hoppin', poppin', and choppin'!

Of all the food I dream about, cook, sample, order in, or read about, none makes me as passionate as the food I grew up with. My mother and father were both born in Puerto Rico, and the food of that island is closest to my heart because it speaks to me in the same language my mother first taught me to say "I love you." But I have become friends with (and that means cooked with) people from all over Latin America. There are common threads that run through the area's regional cooking and things that make each country's food somewhat different. It is all good.

The palette of Latino food is as varied as the color of its people. We come in every color but share a common past. For most Latino Americans that past is made up of a beautiful blend of Spanish, African, and indigenous peoples. From my grandfather (with white-blond hair and blue eyes) to my grandmother's Tia Leo (who had coppery dark skin with hair as black as ink), the diversity within the same family paints a beautiful mosaic that only today is the world starting to recognize.

Our food has the same common roots and the same diversity. Latino Americans are the fastest growing minority group in the United States, and our numbers are predicted to increase by 35 percent within the next few years. Still, the rest of America has only scratched the surface of our regional cuisines. (Much the same thing has happened with other cuisines in this country. "French cooking" once meant *coq au vin* or *pâté* before Americans began traveling to France and French chefs started arriving on our shores in droves.) Today, almost anyone can tell you what *paella* or *chorizo* is, but words such as *yautia*, *malanga*, and *morcilla* are still bound to draw blank expressions. But the days when "Spanish" food meant tacos and refried beans are numbered.

I wrote this book largely to share these wonderful dishes with you but also in part to clear up any confusion that some of you, such as my childhood friend Rosanne, may have. After running into Roe recently, I invited her to my home for dinner so we could catch up on each other's lives. When I asked what she would like to eat, she was quick to reply, "Spanish food!" I made a beautiful meal of Spanish dishes for her that I was sure would knock her socks off: stuffed mussels (*mejillones rellenos*), chicken braised with figs (*pollo con higos*), and saffron rice. She looked at me, puzzled, and said, "I thought we were having Spanish food. You know, rice and beans and pork chops, like your mom used to make!"

Much of the allure for people discovering Latin cuisine is in what Latinos consider "soul food"—the simple, satisfying dishes that my friend remembered my mother cooking all those years ago. This book is loaded with those treasures—and not just from Puerto Rico and Spain but from Cuba, Santo Domingo, and Central and South America. Every country has its beloved family dishes, and it is my distinct pleasure to bring some of them to you and to show you the diversity in the cuisines of all these countries.

I see evidence of a growing fascination with Latin cuisine everywhere. It's no longer necessary for me to travel to the Essex Street Market on the Lower East Side of Manhattan or the larger market on 125th Street in el Barrio, as I did when I was a young girl. Like Latino culture and music, Latin food has exploded into the mainstream. You can walk into any modern supermarket and find many of the foods of my childhood. I believe you

will have no problem locating the ingredients you need to cook the recipes in this book, but I offer substitutions whenever possible, just in case. Shopping via the Internet is also a possibility (see Sources).

I have spent my adult life sharing the happiness that food brings me with my friends, one barbecue, dinner party, picnic, or buffet at a time. Having an opportunity to share that excitement with many people through this book and the television show that accompanies it is beyond my wildest dreams.

There is everyday food here, and plenty of it. And I mean that literally—food you can prepare and enjoy every day. Take a look at the first few recipes in this book. They include a sofrito—a vegetable puree that brings life to much of my cooking—olive oil seasoned with annatto seeds, and the best damn yellow rice you will ever have. The first two take less than ten minutes (that includes washing out the food processor after you make the sofrito), and the rice takes thirty minutes, for twenty of which you can be reading or buffing your nails. I will tell you in all honesty that the simple act of making sofrito will change the way you cook forever: it will rock your world. With the exception of a few recipes, such as Root Vegetable and Meat Tamales (page 146), most of the dishes are ready in under an hour, and usually much less. If you can season, cook, and dress pork chops and serve them alongside fragrant yellow rice in less than thirty minutes, I can't imagine why you'd eat anything from a cardboard carton. Once you realize that you can *master*—and I mean master—making rice, chicken simmered with plump figs, empanadas stuffed with savory pork filling, and juicy roast pork with crackling-crisp skin will not be far behind.

There are also some recipes for special occasions or for those who are as passionate about good food as I am. These may require a little more time or an extra trip to the market for an unusual ingredient or two, but they are worth the effort.

A word of warning: To this day I have to differentiate between a Daisy serving and a regular serving. My Mami and Abuela would always say the same thing: You should always cook enough so that if someone rings the doorbell while you are eating, you won't have to hide your plates under the table. Instead, pull up a chair for them and make them feel at home. I guess that's the reason I'll never know how to cook for two!

I have organized this book to be as user-friendly as possible. Spend a little time in the kitchen with Daisy's Top Ten Hits (the first chapter). These are the dishes I turn people on to first. I believe you'll find the food so intriguing, delicious, and easy to make that you'll be working your way through the rest of the book in no time—whether it's chicken, seafood, or tamales. I've designed the recipes with busy people in mind; most of them end up on the table in less than thirty minutes. But your friends and family will think that you've been slaving over a stove for days.

Of all the words I can think of to describe myself, "shy" is not one of them. The very same can be said of my food. It's bold, it's sassy, it's colorful, it's full of spice and fun. My favorite way to describe it is that it's a party on your plate. Is it different? Very much so, but not because it relies on exotic or expensive ingredients. Just the opposite is true: I get full flavor out of spices, seasonings, and ingredients that you can find just about anywhere. A little kick here and there from hot chili peppers doesn't hurt, either. Recently my nine-year-old-daughter, Angela, said to me, "Mommy, I have to start building my 'spicy' tolerance!" The child is wise beyond her years! You can develop (or expand) a taste for heat and spice or not. The choice in each recipe is left to you.

Not counting the dance floor, there is no place where I feel as comfortable, as totally in my element, as the kitchen. Very often people ask me, "Daisy, where did you learn how to cook?" My answer is always the same: I went to the French Culinary Institute to learn classical technique, but I am primarily an alumna of the Conchita and Valentina Martinez Cooking Academy. In other words, I learned at my mother's and grandmother's sides. I was a very avid pupil, and my husband, Jerry, can attest to that. If *his* word isn't good enough, you can always ask any of my four children or any one of their numerous friends and cousins who pretty much camp out in my house every weekend partly, I think, for the food!

When I cook with Mami, I still defer to her expertise in the kitchen, although every once in a while she'll call and ask me a question about a certain dish or a recipe. I always answer her the same way: "Ma? Why are you asking me? You were the one who taught me to make it!" Be that as it may, it tickles me no end to have Mami ask me to make something for her. It's the greatest compliment a teacher can give her pupil.

It's a totally different story when I get into the kitchen with my brother, Peter, who is also a chef. When we go at it in the kitchen, there is salsa blaring on the radio, pots and pans clanging, no shortage of laughter and noise, and the results are glorious. We've both taken what our teachers have taught us and given it a very personal interpretation. We both have a blast when I visit Mami's house in Florida, because she invites all her friends and tons of family over and sets Peter and me loose in the kitchen. Papi mans the cleanup detail, and it always translates into a hell of a party! And that's what every trip to the kitchen should be—a big, colorful, and, above all else, flat-out fun party.

DAISY'S TOP TEN HITS

If you look at nothing else in this book, take a careful look at these ten dishes. They are simple, they don't taste like anything you've ever made before, and, most important, they are good enough for company and quick enough to make after you schlep home from work.

These are the recipes my girlfriends ask for and I happily give them. Whenever this happens, the response invariably is something along the lines of "I can't believe it's that simple."

I had a spare moment the other day (we can all agree on what a rare occurrence that is), and I marveled at how complicated life becomes when you're an adult woman. We all wear so many hats—on my hat rack are those of mother, wife, daughter, sister, and friend—it's no wonder I am always looking to simplify my life in any way I can. That being said, and given my love of good food, it shouldn't surprise anyone that while I don't have a lot of time to spend in the kitchen, I certainly do not want to sacrifice delicious meals. This leads me to Daisy's Top Ten Hits, a countdown of the dishes most requested by my family and friends.

These ten recipes are not all for finished dishes. A few of them are little "secrets" (well, not so secret anymore) that will help you get the most out of your time in the kitchen. Take a look at the first two recipes, Sofrito and Achiote Oil. They alone will do nothing short of change your life. Each takes less than ten minutes to make. In these two recipes you will most likely spot a few ingredients that are unfamiliar to you. Take another look and you will see that I have given substitutes here and throughout the book. In the case of the annatto seeds used to make the achiote oil, there really is no substitute, but I bet you will find them, labeled either "annatto seed" or "achiote seed," in the spice aisle of your supermarket.

Something as simple as a roast chicken can be made different in minutes by "daisifying" it—rubbing it with a mixture of spices made in minutes with ingredients you can find in any supermarket. As busy as I get, I am not ready to give up good food. If you try at least one of these recipes, I truly believe you will be inspired to move on to others.

SOFRITO

There is no other recipe I could have chosen to open this chapter, let alone this book. This is the one indispensable, universal, un-live-withoutable recipe. Having said that, it is incredibly easy to make and uses ingredients you can find at the supermarket. If you can't find all the ingredients listed below, see Daisy's Pantry for a simple fix. What sofrito does is add freshness, herbal notes, and zing to dishes. You can do that with the onion, garlic, bell pepper, cilantro, and tomato alone.

In my house sofrito makes its way into everything from yellow rice to black bean soup, sauce for spaghetti and meatballs to braised chicken and sautéed shrimp. Not only that, it freezes beautifully, so in about In ten minutes you can make enough sofrito to flavor a dozen dishes. I'm telling you, this stuff does everything but make the beds. Try out your first batch of sofrito in the recipes you'll find throughout this book or add it to some of your own favorite dishes that could use a little boost. You will change the way you cook. I guarantee it.

MAKES ABOUT 4 CUPS

2 medium Spanish onions, cut into large chunks

3 to 4 Italian frying peppers or cubanelle peppers

16 to 20 cloves garlic, peeled

1 large bunch cilantro, washed

7 to 10 ajices dulces (see Daisy's Pantry; optional)

4 leaves of culantro (see Daisy's Pantry), or another handful of cilantro

3 to 4 ripe plum tomatoes, cored and cut into chunks

1 large red bell pepper, cored, seeded, and cut into large chunks

Chop the onion and peppers in the work bowl of a food processor until coarsely chopped. With the motor running, add the remaining ingredients one at a time and process until smooth. The sofrito will keep in the refrigerator for up to 3 days and can be frozen (see Notes).

DAISY'S PANTRY Ajices dulces, *also known as* cachucha *or* ajicitos, *are tiny sweet peppers with a hint of heat. They range in color from light to medium green and yellow to red and orange. They add freshness and an herby note to the sofrito and anything you cook. Do not mistake them for Scotch bonnet or habanero chilies (which they look like); those two pack a wallop when it comes to heat. If you can find* ajicitos *in your market, add them to the sofrito. If not, increase the cilantro to 1½ bunches and add a pinch of cayenne pepper.*

• *Culantro is not cilantro. It has long leaves with tapered tips and serrated edges. When it comes to flavor, culantro is like cilantro times ten. It is a nice but not essential addition to sofrito.*

• *Cubanelles are thin-fleshed sweet peppers. They are longer and narrower than bell peppers and similar in shape to Italian frying peppers. Cubanelles have a sweet, herby flavor and are found in shades of light green and yellow, with touches of light red.*

• *See Sources for the* ajices dulces *and* culantro.

NOTES: *You can freeze sofrito in ½-cup batches in sealable plastic bags. They come in extremely handy in a pinch. You can even add sofrito straight from the freezer to the pan in any recipe that calls for it in this book.*

• *Recipes that call for Sofrito:*
Yellow Rice (page 13)
Braised Chicken with Little Potato Cubes (page 163)
Rice with Spanish Sausages (page 95)
Daisy's Chicken Diablo (page 161)
Grandma's Spaghetti with Chicken (page 156)
Puerto Rican Pot Roast (page 232)

• *You will also find that sofrito is used liberally in these recipes except in the dessert and beverage chapter—and I'm working on that! As the old disco song said, "Once you get started . . ." Do you make meatloaf? Throw in half a cup of sofrito. Sofrito in minestrone? Why not? And promise me you'll never make a pot of chili con carne unless you brown some sofrito along with the meat.*

ACHIOTE OIL

ACEITE DE ACHIOTE

Annatto seeds, known as *achiote* in Spanish, are small, irregularly shaped, deep-reddish-colored seeds about the size of a lentil. They grow in pods but are sold loose in jars in the spice aisle (or see Sources). Steeping annatto seeds in hot olive oil for a few minutes will do more than give the oil a brilliant orange-gold color: It will infuse it with a nutty, delicate aroma and add a quick kick to whatever you use it in. This incredibly simple technique will become part of your repertoire, not just for the many dishes that call for it in this book but anytime you want a splash of color and a hint of annatto flavor.

MAKES ABOUT 1 CUP

Heat the oil and annatto seeds in a small skillet over medium heat just until the seeds give off a lively, steady sizzle. Don't overheat the mixture, or the seeds will turn black and the oil a nasty green. Once they're sizzling away, remove the pan from the heat and let it stand until the sizzling stops. Strain as much of the oil as you are going to use right away into the pan; store the rest for up to 4 days at room temperature in a jar with a tight-fitting lid.

1 cup olive oil
2 tablespoons annatto (achiote) seeds

NOTES: *In addition to using achiote oil to sauté onions, garlic, and such, you can paint it on fish and poultry headed for the grill or broiler.*
- *Dishes that call for achiote oil:*
  Noodle Paella (page 202)
  *Ecuadorian Fish and Peanut Stew
    (page 86)*
  Yellow Rice (page 13)
  *Braised Chicken with Little Potato
    Cubes (page 163)*
  Red Empanada Dough (page 140)
- *You can also add a spoonful to mashed potatoes, bread dough, or pasta dough. Use room-temperature achiote oil to replace some of the oil in your favorite salad dressing. Take meatballs from gray to fabulous with a tablespoon or two of achiote oil.*

GARLIC SOUP

SOPA DE AJO

Garlic soup is to a Spanish restaurant what apple pie is to an American diner—every menu has one. It is a poor man's soup and may not sound exciting, but it is wonderful. On a cold day it's like a hug from home. On the night I first had this soup in Spain, my boys were off exploring Barcelona. That left just my daughter, Angela, husband, Jerry, and me to fend for ourselves. It was the week of Christmas and was chilly, to say the least. Jerry had spotted the perfect mom-and-pop place earlier in the day and was hell-bent on taking me there for dinner. After much wandering we found Jerry's elusive dream restaurant, only to discover it was closed. We eyed a sweet little restaurant, De Tapa Madre, across the street. It turned out to be a happy accident.

Our waiter, Jose, saw that we were cold and a little stressed, and suggested garlic soup as a way to start our meal. After our first taste we decided Jose could order us whatever else he liked for the rest of the meal.

De Tapa Madre became our favorite restaurant in Barcelona. The restaurant is owned by two women who take turns cooking on alternate days. Both are off on Sundays and the kitchen is run by the sister of one of the waiters. Whenever you go, whoever is behind the stove, the food is fabulous.

Whenever I make this soup at my house for family or friends, it's like getting a delicious, fragrant postcard from my friends in Barcelona.

MAKES 6 SERVINGS

1. Heat the oil in a 4- to 5-quart pot over medium heat. Add the chorizo and cook, stirring, until the oil takes on a bright red color, 2 to 3 minutes. Scoop the chorizo into a bowl with a slotted spoon. Stir the garlic into the seasoned oil, reduce the heat to low, and cook until the garlic is very soft and fragrant, without coloring, about 4 minutes. Scoop out the garlic and add it to the chorizo.

2. Increase the heat to medium, lay the bread slices in the oil, and cook until golden brown, about 3 minutes. Flip and cook the other side. Set the fried bread aside on a plate.

3. Return the garlic and chorizo to the pot and pour in the chicken broth. Add the bay leaf, bring to a boil over medium heat, and adjust the heat to simmering.

4. In the meantime, poach the eggs. Fill a deep skillet two-thirds full of water. Toss in a small handful of salt and add the vinegar. Bring to a boil over high heat, then adjust the heat so the water is at a lively

¼ cup olive oil

2 links (about 6 ounces) chorizo, andouille, or any smoked garlicky sausage, cut in half lengthwise and then into ¼-inch slices

12 cloves garlic, sliced

6 slices (about ½ inch thick) Italian bread

6 cups homemade Chicken Broth (page 155; see Note)

1 bay leaf

Fine sea or kosher salt

1 to 2 teaspoons white vinegar

6 eggs

Freshly ground pepper to taste

NOTES: *This is a quickie soup. To make it even quicker, toast the bread in a toaster while putting the rest of the soup together.*

• I can forgive canned chicken broth in most cases but definitely not here. You need good homemade broth. Also, since they don't use a lot of cilantro in Spain, where this soup is from, you might want to make your broth with thyme instead of cilantro. I don't mind mixing the two flavors; I think they sing a pretty song together.

simmer. Crack the eggs 1 at a time into a teacup, then slide them into the water. Cook until the whites are firm but the yolks are still runny, about 5 minutes.

5. Meanwhile, taste the soup and add salt and pepper if you like.

6. Place a slice of bread in the bottom of each of 6 soup bowls. Remove the eggs with a slotted spoon, letting the water drain back into the skillet. Set one egg on top of each slice of bread. Pour in the soup and serve immediately.

DAISY'S PANTRY *De Tapa Madre was also my introduction to jamón Iberico, one of Spain's contributions to the great foods of the world. In my life I had never tasted a ham with such a wonderful flavor and silky texture. I would pass up foie gras, tenderloin of beef, and even Chinese ribs with hot mustard for a taste of jamón Iberico. It is not yet available in the States but will be shortly.*

YELLOW RICE

ARROZ AMARILLO

You know those packaged rice mixes you can buy with the foil bag of mystery spice? When you taste this rice, you'll forget all about them. This is remarkably easy to make once you have achiote oil and sofrito on hand. Even if you're starting from scratch without those two staples, you can still get this on the stove in fifteen minutes. I have never served this at a party without rave reviews. Guests have often said that they could eat *just* the rice and nothing else. I'm always delighted to tell them how easy it is, but encourage them not to pass on the beans or other accompaniments!

MAKES 8 REGULAR OR 6 DAISY SERVINGS

½ cup Achiote Oil (page 9)
½ cup Sofrito (page 6)
½ cup coarsely chopped alcaparrado (see Daisy's Pantry) or pimiento-stuffed olives
2 to 3 tablespoons salt
1 teaspoon ground cumin
1 teaspoon ground black pepper
2 bay leaves
3 cups long-grain white rice (see Notes)
Chicken Broth, homemade (page 155) or canned, as needed (about 4 cups)

1. Heat the oil in a heavy 4- to 5-quart pot with a tight-fitting lid over medium heat. Stir in the sofrito and cook until most of the water has evaporated. Add the alcaparrado, salt, cumin, pepper, and bay leaves, and stir to combine.

2. When the mixture is bubbling, add the rice, stirring to coat and to fix the color to the rice. Pour in enough chicken broth to cover the rice by the width of two fingers. Bring to a boil and boil until the broth reaches the level of the rice.

3. Stir the rice once, reduce the heat to low, cover, and cook for 20 minutes without opening the cover or stirring.

4. Gently fluff the rice by scooping it from the bottom to the top. Serve hot.

DAISY'S PANTRY *Alcaparrado, a mixture of olives, pimientos, and capers sold in bottles, is widely available. There are versions made with pitted and unpitted olives. Go for the pitted version. If you can't find it, substitute an equal amount of coarsely chopped olives stuffed with pimientos. Throw in a teaspoon of capers if you like.*

• *See Making Rice on page 90 for more pointers on cooking rice.*

TWENTY-MINUTE SHELLFISH SAUTÉ
WITH **PARSLEY GARLIC SAUCE**

MARISCADA EN SALSA VERDE

Although Spanish in origin, this dish is very popular with the Martinez family, especially my mother, who until recently favored traditional Puerto Rican cooking. Mami will ask me to make this dish for her more than once when she comes to visit. There is nothing that makes me happier or prouder than serving a meal I make with my own hands to my parents and watching the happy looks on their faces while they savor it. This is one of my most requested recipes, not just by my parents but by friends as well. The sweetness of the shellfish, the fragrance of the sea, the sparkle of the white wine, and the freshness of the parsley really make this dish sing. Serve with Yellow Rice (page 13) or angel-hair pasta.

MAKES 6 SERVINGS

1. Heat the oil gently in a wide pan with shallow sloping sides (a paella pan works perfectly). Add the garlic and cook 1 to 2 minutes, until soft but uncolored.

2. Stir in the parsley and wine, raise the heat to high, and cook until almost all the wine has evaporated.

3. Stir the cornstarch into the milk in a small bowl until the cornstarch has dissolved. Whisk into the pan.

4. Lower the heat, add the clams, scallops, and shrimp, and cover. Cook, shaking the pan periodically, until the shellfish are cooked through, about 15 minutes. The shellfish should be done perfectly at this point. Check the sauce and adjust the seasonings as you like.

⅓ cup olive oil
6 to 8 cloves garlic, chopped
2 bunches flat-leaf parsley, thick stems removed and leaves washed and chopped
½ cup dry white wine
2 teaspoons cornstarch
⅓ cup milk
12 littleneck clams, cleaned and soaked in a cornmeal bath (see page 179)
1 pound sea scallops, preferably "dry" (see Note)
1 pound large shrimp, shelled and deveined
Kosher salt to taste
Freshly ground pepper to taste

VARIATION: *If you are feeling particularly extravagant, you can add the meat from 1 cooked lobster, cut into serving pieces, when you add the shellfish to the sauce.*

NOTE: *"Dry" scallops are those that haven't been soaked in a preservative solution before coming to market. They are firm, vary a little in color, and are sticky, not wet, to the touch. They're generally a bit pricier but have a much nicer flavor and texture.*

ROAST CHICKEN WITH GARLIC RUB

POLLO ASADO

I know what you're thinking: There can't be anything new to say about roast chicken. Right? WRONG! I can guarantee that you've never tasted roast chicken like this before, and if you have, it's because you have a Puerto Rican friend somewhere. My husband's grandmother, Nanny, always served a beautiful spread for Sunday dinner. All of her family came to visit. It reminded me of my days in Abuela's house—the children running around, the men in the living room watching sports, and the ladies in the kitchen helping out. Nanny was fond of serving a traditional roast chicken dinner, but as big a fan as I was of Nan, I thought her roast chicken needed CPR! When I had the honor of cooking dinner for her, I made her my roast chicken. Her eyes got wide, and she said to me, "I've never tasted chicken like this before." Then, turning to my mother-in-law, she said, "I don't know what she puts into it. It must be those Puerto Rican spices!" Yes, Nan, that's exactly what it is. I'm convinced this will be a staple in your repertoire as well.

MAKES 4 SERVINGS

One 5-pound chicken, washed and patted dry inside and out
Wet Rub for Meats and Poultry (page 19)

1. Preheat the oven to 500° F.

2. Loosen the chicken breast skin by working your fingers gently in between the meat and the skin. Do the same to as much of the legs and thighs as you can without breaking the skin. Flip the chicken over and repeat on the chicken's back. Using a teaspoon, smear the wet rub under the skin all over the chicken and inside the chicken cavity.

3. Truss the chicken with kitchen twine (see page 18) and set on a rack in a roasting pan. Roast for 30 minutes. Lower the heat to 400° F and continue to roast until the juices from the thickest part of the thigh near the bone run clear, about 45 minutes. Alternately, roast until an instant-reading thermometer registers 165° F when inserted into the joint where the thigh meets the backbone. Let rest for 10 minutes before serving.

TO TRUSS A CHICKEN

I truss chickens to make them nice and plump-looking when they come from the oven. It doesn't really affect the way they cook.

Cut a 5-foot length of kitchen twine. Set the chicken on the work surface, breast side up. Drape the center of the piece of twine over the end of the neck that protrudes from the cavity, then bring it underneath the joint that connects the wing to the breast. Run each end of the twine into the creases of the legs, then cross the chicken's ankles and loop the twine around them. Pull gently to secure the legs in place. Tie a single knot, then bring the twine back through the leg creases toward the breast. Wrap the twine around the wing tip joint and flip the chicken over. Tie a knot over the backbone and snip off any excess twine. Keep the twine taut throughout the trussing process.

CUMIN

With the exception of the Spiced Olives on page 42, all recipes in this book call for ground cumin. I prefer to buy whole seeds—they hold up better in the long run—and grind them myself in a little electric spice grinder or coffee mill. Lightly toasting the seeds in a small skillet over low heat for a few minutes before grinding them releases flavor and aroma. Feel free to toast and grind your cumin seeds for any recipe that calls for ground cumin.

Okay, okay, there are really eleven greatest hits in this chapter. But I couldn't decide which rub to include, so I lumped them both under one heading.

WET RUB FOR **MEATS** AND **POULTRY**
ADOBO MOJADO

What is a condiment doing in my Top Ten Hits chapter? You'll hear me say over and over how a simple thing like sofrito will change your life. This is another one of those little life-changing secrets. Adobo, either this wet version or the dry version below, will change the way you make pork, chicken, beef, and even fish. I run the risk of repeating myself, but this is not shy or subtle. It is very much "in your face" food, and I mean that, of course, in a good way.

MAKES ABOUT ½ CUP

Pound the garlic cloves and salt to a paste using a mortar and pestle. Add the peppercorns and oregano, pounding well after each one to incorporate them into the paste. Stir in the oil and vinegar.

12 cloves garlic, peeled
1½ tablespoons fine sea or kosher salt (see Notes)
1 tablespoon black peppercorns
2 tablespoons dried oregano
2 tablespoons olive oil
2 tablespoons white wine vinegar

NOTES: *The salt keeps the garlic from flying all over the place as you pound them together.*

• This wet rub will keep for 5 to 6 days in the refrigerator, which gives you a chance to try it on anything you like, from fish fillets and pork chops to turkey cutlets and steaks.

DRY RUB FOR **MEATS** AND **POULTRY**
ADOBO SECO

MAKES 1 CUP

Mix all of the ingredients together in a small bowl. Store at room temperature in an airtight container.

6 tablespoons salt
3 tablespoons onion powder
3 tablespoons garlic powder
3 tablespoons ground black pepper
1½ teaspoons ground oregano

NOTE: *You can add 1 teaspoon of any or all of the following to customize your dry rub: ground cumin, dried citrus zest (orange, lemon, or lime), saffron, and achiote powder, which can sometimes be found where achiote seeds (see Daisy's Pantry, page 9) are found.*

BEEF STEAK WITH ONIONS

BISTEC ENCEBOLLADO

I'm always looking for things to make my life easier. This recipe, doubled or tripled and paired with a rice or bean dish, can get on the table in 40 minutes and feed my family of six, plus whichever of my sons' friends happen to be hanging out at Daisy's Home for Wayward Boys.

Of the many (and I do mean many) places that serve this in Puerto Rico and the islands, some serve the onions raw, cut in very thin slices. I like mine cooked very lightly—just until they pick up all the beef flavor from the pan and turn crisp-tender. Strip steaks are perfect for dinner, but another great choice is skirt steak, the cut of choice in many *fondas*—restaurants that feature home style cooking.

The usual accompaniment to steak with onions is crispy plantain chips (page 113), but white rice and beans goes very well, too.

MAKES 4 SERVINGS—2 IF YOUR CREW ARE REAL MEAT EATERS

1. Pat the steaks dry. Lay them in a deep bowl and sprinkle enough of the adobo over both sides of the steaks to coat them evenly; don't be shy with the adobo.

2. Pour the vinegar into the bowl and swish it around to coat the bottom. Let the steaks soak up the vinegar until they start to change color on the underside, about 15 minutes. Flip them over and let them stand another 15 minutes.

3. Heat the oil in a heavy skillet (cast iron is great) over medium-high heat. To cook steaks of this size to medium rare, cook 6 minutes on the first side, flip them over and cook 4 minutes on the second side. Take the steaks out, add a little splash of olive oil if the pan looks dry, and add the onions. Cook, tossing the onions around, until they're richly browned but still fairly crisp. Because of the color left in the pan from the steaks, they'll brown pretty quickly, in about 4 minutes. Slice the steaks if you like and serve the onions alongside.

Two 12-ounce strip steaks, each about 1-inch thick
Dry Adobo, homemade (page 19) or store-bought
3 tablespoons cider vinegar
2 tablespoons olive oil
1 large Spanish onion, cut in half, then sliced thin

NOTES: *You can cook the steaks outdoors on the grill (see page 193) or in a grill pan over medium-high heat. Cook the onions in a separate skillet and spoon over the grilled steaks.*

• I like the onions tender-crispy, but if you like softer onions, go ahead and cook them a little more.

GRANDMA'S PORK CHOPS

CHULETAS DE ABUELA

I love pork chops—not dry, underseasoned pork chops, but juicy, flavorful pork chops. There is no better example than these, the pork chops Abuela used to make for us. These were almost caramel colored on the outside, and juicy and delicious when you cut into them. The oranges give them a lovely sweetness, while the vinegar gives them a nice tang. There is just no way I was going to have a Top Ten Hits chapter and not include these.

If you prefer not to panfry, these chops lend themselves beautifully to broiling.

MAKES 6 REGULAR OR 4 DAISY SERVINGS

1. Rub both sides of the chops with the dry rub, coating them generously. Place them in a deep baking dish, overlapping if necessary. Stir the citrus juices, vinegar, and garlic together in a bowl until blended. Pour over the chops and massage into them.

2. Marinate the chops at room temperature for up to 1 hour or in the refrigerator for up to 1 day.

3. Pour enough oil into a large, heavy skillet to film the bottom. (If necessary, work in batches or use two skillets—if you have them and space on the stove to hold them.) Heat the oil over medium heat until rippling. Remove the chops from the marinade and discard the marinade. Add as many chops as will fit in the pan without touching. Cook until the chops are well browned on the underside, about 6 minutes. Turn the chops and cook until they are firm near the bone when you poke them with a finger, about 8 minutes. Keep warm while cooking the second batch, if necessary. Serve immediately.

Six to eight 1-inch-thick loin pork chops
  (3 to 4 pounds) (see Note)
3 tablespoons Dry Rub, homemade
  (page 19) or store-bought
Juice of 3 oranges
Juice of 1 lemon
2 tablespoons cider vinegar
2 cloves garlic, smashed
Canola or other vegetable oil

VARIATIONS: *If you have a source for sour oranges (naranjas agrias; see Note on page 48), substitute two of them for the lemon and one for one of the oranges.*
• Red beans and white rice, side by side, would go nicely here. So would potato salad (yours or Mami's Potato Salad, page 123), Potatoes, Creole Style (page 122), or french fries.

NOTE: *When dealing with thicker chops that need a little extra time, I cook them in a way my grandmother called al vapor—with a little steam. After the chops start to color on the second side, pour about $1/3$ cup of water into the pan and cover the pan. The steam will speed up cooking and keep the chops moist.*

MEXICAN FLAN

FLAN MEXICANO

I first tried this version of flan at a small restaurant in the Cobble Hill section of Brooklyn. I tried to duplicate it by using sweetened condensed milk and cream cheese. My version was good but not quite what I was looking for; it had a slightly grainy rather than a silky smooth texture.

Outside my church, between 9:30 and 12:00 on any given Sunday morning, you will find little stands with people selling long, crispy crullers rolled in cinnamon sugar, griddle cakes filled with beans and pork cracklings, and, always, tamales. The women who sell tamales are Mexican. They laugh when they see me coming; they know I always have a million questions about cooking. When I told them about the flan, they suggested I try something called *Media Crema*, made by Nestlé, for even more wonderful results, so that's what I call for here. I've even seen it in suburban supermarkets in several states, but if you can't find it, use sour cream instead. (See also Sources)

MAKES 8 DAISY OR 12 REGULAR SERVINGS

1. Preheat the oven to 350° F.

2. Make the caramel (see Note): Have ready a 9-inch glass pie plate and a pair of potholders or oven mitts. Pour the sugar into a small, heavy saucepan. Set it over medium-low heat until the sugar starts to liquefy and form clumps. Stir slowly and constantly; the sugar will eventually liquefy completely and then begin to color. Pay careful attention to the caramel at this point; once it starts to color, it will darken quickly. Remove the pan from the heat when the caramel is the color of a bright shiny penny. Scrape all the caramel into the pan, put on the mitts, and grab the pie plate firmly. Carefully but quickly rotate the pan so the bottom and halfway up the sides of the plate are coated with caramel. Set the prepared pan in a shallow roasting pan.

3. Full a teakettle with water and bring to a boil. Meanwhile, combine the evaporated milk, condensed milk, milk, eggs, yolks, and vanilla in a blender jar. Blend on very low speed a few seconds, just until the eggs are blended. Add the Media Crema and blend a few seconds, until smooth. Let stand for 1 minute, then skim off any foam that rises to the surface.

4. Slide the oven rack out halfway and set the roasting pan with the caramel-lined pie plate on the rack. Pour the custard mix into the pie plate. Pour enough water from the teakettle into the roasting

1 cup sugar
One 12-ounce can evaporated milk
One 14-ounce can sweetened condensed milk
¾ cup milk
3 large eggs
3 egg yolks
2 teaspoons vanilla extract
1 cup Nestlé's Media Crema or sour cream

NOTES: *The secret to good caramel is to work slower rather than faster. Use low heat, stir constantly, and be patient.*

• *Be extremely careful when working with caramel. By the time it is brown enough to pour into the mold, it will be very hot—much hotter than boiling water. Handle the pot and pie plate carefully, and when tilting the pan, keep it at arm's length.*

pan to come halfway up the side of the plate. Bake, about 35 minutes, until the center of the flan is set.

5. Remove from the oven and cool to room temperature in the water bath. Refrigerate until completely chilled, at least 2 hours or up to 1 day.

6. To serve, center a large plate over the flan and with one quick flip invert the flan over the plate. Give it a few seconds; the flan will slip right out of the mold and onto the plate. Scrape any caramel left in the mold over the flan. Serve chilled.

I *love* salsa, and I don't mean the tomato-onion variety (although that one is quite good, too). The salsa I'm talking about is Latin music with Afro Cuban roots and rhythms. Salsa comes in through your feet, travels up your legs, grabs you by the hips, and turns you loose! Salsa is music that you can't help dancing to—and I don't mean *move* to, I mean *dance* to. If there is anything that comes a close second to the passion I experience by the stove, it's the passion I experience on the dance floor.

There are home movies of me dancing when I was just a little bit of a thing. Papi always says that I got my love of dancing from Mami (one hell of a dancer), because all he can dance to are merengues and boleros (I guess it's that old "opposites attract" chestnut). I'm not sure where I got it, but I do know that I got it—and good! Whether I'm in the kitchen or on the dance floor, the only thing I need to make me move is my salsa. These are my Ten Top Classic Salsa CDs. Mix up some white sangria, whip up some guacamole, pop one of these into your CD player, and you have the makings of a real fiesta!

1. Willie Colon, *The Best*
2. Orquesta Broadway, *Pasaporte*
3. Celia Cruz, *La Reina de Cuba*
4. The New York Festival, *20 Years of Salsa*, volumes 1 and 2
5. Fania Salsa Classics, *The Best of Fania All Stars*
6. Fania Salsa Classics, *The Best of Eddie Palmieri*
7. Ray Barretto, *Indestructible*
8. Hector LaVoe, *LAVOE*
9. All Great Stars, *60's Gold*
10. El Gran Combo, *40th Anniversario en Vivo*

There you have it. These are sure to get your feet started. Now don't hurt yourself, honey!

Most people don't know the can of worms they open when they ask me what it is about my food that is different and exciting. That conversation usually ends up with me on my feet, gesticulating wildly and practically shouting about how delicious, beautiful, accessible, and relatively unknown Latin cooking is. Invariably, most people end up with a smile on their face because by the time I finish speaking, they are caught up in the passion of my descriptions.

Passion is what it definitely is. My friend once said to me after listening to me wax poetic about a bowl of black bean soup, "You know, Daisy, you are Latin food's biggest fan. Your love of the food really comes through when you talk about it." Well, there is absolutely no doubt about that! I would do anything short of grabbing you by the lapels and shaking you to show you how exciting, fun, and easy this food is. The Top Ten Hits offered here give you a perfect platform to dive into the world of Latin cooking, and that's a small leap when you consider that a third of those recipes are for condiments that you can carry with you into a million other dishes. Do I have your attention yet?

When Jerry and I first got married, I was very concerned with making a good impression on my in-laws. Sunday dinner was a very big event at their house, and the table was literally bowed, being laden with so much food. My father-in-law regularly made Italian marinara sauce with pasta and a meat course (he was a butcher, so meat always figured prominently). My mother-in-law brought out platter after platter of vegetables and side dishes. Just before everyone was about to pass out, the desserts would start to make their way to the table.

I soon found myself in the position of returning their graciousness and hospitality. You might imagine that I found that a bit intimidating, but Jerry assured me that anything I made would be wonderful. I decided to swim in safe harbor, so to speak. I invited the in-laws to dinner and served a simple green salad with avocado (Betty, my mother-in-law, had never had avocado and loved it), and my roast chicken, with red beans and white rice. For dessert, flan. Well, you would have thought I had made a banquet. The food was familiar, but it was made in a manner that was completely new and fresh to them. Betty kept wondering how I managed to get rice that was so loose and fluffy, and my father-in-law, Tom, could not believe how much flavor that simple pot of beans had. And the chicken! What in the world had I done to the chicken? I could not have been happier or more pleased to meet my husband's eyes across the dinner table as he winked me a wink of congratulations.

When they left that night, Betty thanked me once again, and I said, "Stop thanking me! It was nothing special, just chicken." She smiled at me and said, "It's not what you made, it's what you did with it!" I've never forgotten that and would say very much the same thing. It may be just chicken or rice or beans, but it's chicken and rice and beans like you've never done them before! Now do you see why I get so excited?

APPETIZERS AND
LITTLE BITES

BOCADILLOS Y TAPAS

Not long ago my family—husband Jerry, daughter Angela, and sons Erik, Mark, and David—made a trip to Barcelona. It was an eye-opener for me. The food was amazing, the city was vibrant and beautiful, and my kids tried dishes they had never tried before.

One of our favorite things to do was visit tapas bars—those little restaurants that dispense small portions of a remarkable number of foods that can be as simple as local cheeses and hams, seasoned olives, and anchovies, or as sophisticated as snails in garlic butter and baby octopus sautéed with oil, garlic, and paprika. Spaniards make a night of it, going from one bar to another, depending on which serves their favorite version of a particular dish. I can also tell you that sherry, wine, and hard cider are involved as well.

This is a fun way to eat, too. And if you're watching your weight, it's likely you'll eat less picking from several plates than you would if you sat down to a single main course, appetizer, and dessert. People in the United States are starting to realize that a couple of bites of potato, a few shrimp, and a bit of steak can make a meal. I love to do this when I entertain, starting with a half dozen or so dishes that can (even should) be made ahead, to ease up last-minute stress. The dishes in this chapter, whether they're inspired by the tapas bars of Spain, pulled from Latin American cooking, or are products of my own imagination, lend themselves well to that kind of treatment. Feel free to pull together meals like this from the recipes in this chapter, doubling or tripling the recipes for a larger crowd. The recipes here also do well as a standard leadoff for a more traditional meal.

TOMATO SALAD

ENSALADA DE TOMATES

I left the door wide open for the type of tomato to use here. In season they can be big, juicy beefsteak or heirloom tomatoes that you grow or buy at the market. Out of season stick to cherry tomatoes or the kind you find on the stem.

None of this is written in stone. If you like more garlic, add it, and the same with the onion and cilantro. This sounds like a lot of olive oil, and it is, but it mixes with the juices from the tomato and makes the most delicious sauce—perfect for dunking pieces of crusty bread.

You can make this just before you serve it, but it's better if you make it at least a few hours beforehand. It is truly miraculous the day after it's made. For me, in peak tomato season this salad with a hunk of bread is lunch.

MAKES 6 SERVINGS

Core the tomatoes and cut them into 1-inch wedges. If you're using cherry tomatoes, just cut them in half. Put them in a bowl, add the remaining ingredients, and toss everything together. If you're going to serve the salad right away, check the seasoning and add additional salt or pepper if you think it needs it. If not, let the salad sit for up to a few hours and taste just before serving.

2 pounds ripe, juicy tomatoes
3 cloves garlic, finely chopped
½ small red onion, cut into thin strips
1 teaspoon fine sea or kosher salt, or as needed
Freshly ground black pepper to taste
1 cup olive oil
2 big sprigs of cilantro, thick stems removed and thin stems and leaves finely chopped (about ¼ cup loosely packed)

AVOCADO AND TOMATO SALAD

ENSALADA DE TOMATE Y AGUACATE

In Puerto Rico this is "salad." You can, of course, use your favorite type of lettuce.

MAKES 6 SERVINGS

1 head iceberg lettuce
1 Hass avocado
1 lime, cut in half
Garlic-Anchovy Dressing (see below)
2 ripe medium tomatoes, cored and
  sliced horizontally ¼-inch thick
Fine sea or kosher salt to taste
Freshly ground pepper to taste

1. Remove any wilted or yellow outer leaves from the lettuce. Cut the lettuce in half through the core. Remove the core and cut the lettuce into ½-inch ribbons. Wash and dry, preferably in a salad spinner.

2. Cut the avocado in half and remove the pit. (See the box on page 34.) Peel the avocado halves and slice them lengthwise about 1 inch thick. Squeeze the lime halves over the avocado slices to prevent them from darkening.

3. To serve, in a medium bowl toss the lettuce and enough dressing to coat it lightly. Arrange the lettuce ribbons on a platter. Season the tomato slices with salt and pepper, and place them and the avocado slices decoratively on top of the lettuce. Pour thin ribbons of the remaining dressing in a pretty pattern over the whole salad platter.

GARLIC-ANCHOVY DRESSING

ALIÑO

MAKES ABOUT 1½ CUPS

3 flat anchovy fillets
2 cloves garlic
¼ teaspoon salt, or more to taste
Juice of 1 lemon
1 cup olive oil
¼ cup white wine vinegar
½ cup (loosely packed) finely chopped
  cilantro or parsley
Freshly ground pepper to taste

1. Pound the anchovy fillets, garlic, and ¼ teaspoon salt to a paste using a mortar and pestle. Stir in the lemon juice.

2. Gradually whisk in the oil and vinegar, alternating so the dressing doesn't separate. Stir in the cilantro. Taste and add pepper and, if you like, additional salt. The dressing will keep in the refrigerator for about 2 days.

VARIATION: *You can also make this in a blender, working in the same order. Add the vinegar and oil with the motor running. Dressing made in a blender will really homogenize—not a bad thing if that is what you like. It also turns creamy and a bright green color.*

SHRIMP AND **AVOCADO SALAD** WITH **COCKTAIL SAUCE**

ENSALADA DE CAMARONES Y AGUACATE
CON SALSA DE CÓCTEL

This is one of my favorite early autumn salads when the tomatoes and avocados are perfect and the shrimp are sweet. The tartness of the cocktail sauce and the bite from the horseradish frame the buttery avocado like a masterpiece. It is always a hit at parties.

MAKES 6 SERVINGS

1. Heat 2 quarts of water in a large saucepan or pot. Cut a 6-inch square of cheesecloth. Place the bay leaves, lemon, parsley, and peppercorns in the center. Gather the ends of the cheesecloth and tie them securely with kitchen twine. Drop the cheesecloth bag into the water, bring to a boil, and cook for 15 minutes. Fill a bowl halfway with ice water and set it near the sink.

2. Add the shrimp to the pot and boil for 3 to 4 minutes, until pink and cooked through. Drain and plunge the shrimp into the ice water to stop the cooking. Drain again and chill until ready to serve.

3. Halve the avocado and remove the pit (see page 34). Cut the avocado into 1-inch cubes and toss with the lime juice in a small bowl to prevent darkening. Drizzle the oil over the avocado and toss gently. Season with salt, pepper, and cilantro.

4. Toss the avocado with the chilled shrimp, dot with the cocktail sauce, and toss again.

5. To serve, divide the lettuce among 6 serving plates. Top with the shrimp and avocado. Drizzle whatever dressing remains in the bowl over the salad.

2 bay leaves
1 lemon slice
5 sprigs of flat-leaf parsley
½ teaspoon black peppercorns
2 pounds very large (fewer than 15 per pound) shrimp, peeled and deveined
1 large Florida (not Hass) avocado (see Note)
Juice of 3 limes
½ cup olive oil
Fine sea or kosher salt to taste
Freshly ground pepper to taste
Chopped fresh cilantro to taste
Bottled or homemade cocktail sauce, to taste
2 cups romaine lettuce, washed, dried, and cut into thin ribbons

NOTE: *Hass avocados are the fist-size avocados with pebbly green skin that turns blacker as they mature. They are creamy, firm, green with a trace of yellow near the pit, and slightly soft when ripe. They should not be confused with Florida (sometimes called Duerte) avocados, which are larger, smooth-skinned, and lighter green. Florida avocados have a flesh that is more watery than creamy, which is more suitable to some dishes.*

GUACAMOLE

My friend Edgar says it all the time: Garlic is not an ingredient in authentic Mexican guacamole. I know it isn't, but I like it, so here it is. If you prefer, omit it. Serve this with your favorite taco chips or some crispy tostones (page 117). I even love it as a side to grilled Seafood Skewers (page 194) or to plop a dollop on my Cuban Black Bean Soup (page 81).

MAKES ABOUT 2 CUPS, ENOUGH FOR ABOUT 8 AS A DIP

Pit and peel the avocados (see below). Cut the avocados into rough chunks and toss them in a bowl with the lime juice. Add the cilantro, tomato, onion, jalapeño, and garlic, and mash with a fork until everything is evenly distributed and the guac has a nice, chunky texture. Season with salt and pepper. Serve immediately, preferably, but if you are making it ahead of time, refrigerate up to 4 hours with a piece of plastic wrap pressed directly on the surface to prevent discoloration.

4 to 5 small Hass avocados
Juice of ½ lime
1 cup chopped fresh cilantro
1 plum tomato, cored, seeded, and chopped
1 small Spanish onion, finely chopped
1 jalapeño, cored, seeded, and finely chopped
2 cloves garlic, finely chopped
Fine sea or kosher salt to taste
Freshly ground black pepper to taste

WORKING WITH AVOCADOS

The easiest way to pit and peel an avocado involves a little practice. Lay the avocado flat on your cutting board. With a good-sized knife, cut from the stem down to the pit. Work the knife around the pit to cut the avocado in half. Twist the two halves apart. With a folded kitchen towel in your hand, hold the half of the avocado with the pit. Give the pit a firm whack with the knife. The knife should stick firmly enough in the pit to allow you to twist out the pit. Discard the pit. Working with a paring knife to get you started, remove the peel in strips. (Unless you'd like to keep the halves intact, peeling is easier to do if you cut each half in half again lengthwise.) Cut or slice the avocado as called for in the recipe. If you are not using the peeled avocados immediately, rub or toss them with a cut lemon or lime to prevent them from turning black.

CHILEAN TOMATO SALAD

ENSALADA DE TOMATES CHILEÑA

Simple, right? Made with tomatoes at their peak, and with that pricey bottle of olive oil that your best friend gave you for Christmas, this can turn into the start of a truly memorable meal.

MAKES 4 SERVINGS

Arrange the tomato and onion slices overlapping on a serving platter. Spoon some of the spicy pepper sauce, including some of the vegetables if you like, over the tomatoes and onions. Drizzle the oil over the salad and season with salt and pepper. Serve immediately.

4 large, ripe tomatoes, cored and
  sliced ½ inch thick
2 small red onions, thinly sliced
Spicy Pepper Sauce (see below)
Olive oil to taste
Fine sea or kosher salt to taste
Freshly ground pepper to taste

SPICY PEPPER SAUCE

AJI (AH-HEE)

Aji is the ketchup of much of Latin America. It goes on vegetables, into soups and stews, and over grilled meats and poultry. You will find a million uses for it once you have a batch sitting around. It will last up to five days or so. Start with the fresh hot chili peppers of your choice—"bird" peppers, habaneros, cayenne, or even jalapeño. The more kick the pepper has, of course, the zippier the finished condiment. You can also adjust the level of heat by finely chopping some of the peppers, seeds and all. The more you chop, the more heat in the aji. Leaving all the peppers whole will make a milder sauce. Take the amount of peppers you pick and put them in a glass jar with a tight-fitting lid. (Remember to chop some of them if you like spice.) Squeeze enough lime juice to cover the peppers. Add finely chopped red onion and finely chopped garlic to taste.

The details are up to you, but here's a suggestion: For 2 cups of chilies use 1 small red onion, 6 cloves of garlic, and about 2 cups of lime juice.

ROMAINE, BEET, AND BLUE CHEESE SALAD

ENSALADA DE LECHUGA, REMOLACHA, Y QUESO CABRALES

The dressing for this salad doesn't contain as much vinegar as I usually use for salad dressing. I like the fruitiness of the olive oil to dominate. If you have fresh thyme on hand, chop a small handful and add it to the dressing.

Talk about a perfect match: This salad features crunchy green romaine, earthy-sweet beets, and the piquant twang of blue cheese, all bound together with fruity olive oil.

MAKES 4 LUNCH OR 6 FIRST-COURSE SERVINGS

1. Cut off the beets' stems, peel the beets, and cut them in half. Place the beets in a medium saucepan, cover with plenty of cold water, and toss in a small handful of salt. Bring the water to a boil, then adjust the heat so it is boiling gently. Cook until the beets are tender but not mushy, 20 to 35 minutes, depending on the beets. Drain the beets and let them stand until cool enough to handle but still a little warm.

2. While the beets are cooling, prepare the lettuce: Separate the head into leaves and remove any thick ribs from the leaves. Tear the leaves into 2-inch pieces. Wash and dry the leaves, preferably in a salad spinner.

3. Cut the beets into ½-inch dice. Toss the beets with the sherry vinegar and a kiss of oil. Place the lettuce in a bowl large enough to hold it comfortably. In a separate small bowl, whisk the white wine vinegar into ½ cup of oil. Season with salt and pepper to taste. Pour the dressing over the lettuce and toss until it is coated. Scatter the beets and cheese over the top.

DAISY'S PANTRY *Cabrales, a semisoft blue-veined cheese from the Asturias region of Spain, is my cheese of choice for this. It is a fairly mild cheese made from a mix of goat's, sheep's, and cow's milk, and is worth searching for.*

2 medium beets (about 12 ounces) (see Note)
Fine sea or kosher salt
1 head romaine lettuce
2 teaspoons sherry or other vinegar
½ cup olive oil, plus a little more for the beets
1 tablespoon white wine vinegar
Freshly ground black pepper
4 ounces blue cheese (see Daisy's Pantry), crumbled (about 1 cup)

NOTE: *If your beets have bright, bushy leaves, use them instead of (or along with) the chard to make Chickpeas and Swiss chard on page 132.*

ORANGE, RED ONION, AND OLIVE SALAD

ENSALADA VALENCIANA

1. Remove any wilted or yellow leaves from the head of romaine. Separate the head into leaves and trim the thick center ribs from the leaves. Tear the leaves up into bite-sized pieces. Wash and dry the leaves, preferably in a salad spinner. You can prepare the lettuce up to a few hours before serving it; refrigerate it in the serving bowl covered with a damp towel.

2. Cut a small sliver off the top and bottom of the oranges. Remove the skin and as much of the white pith as you can without cutting into the orange. Remove the orange sections from between the membranes with a paring knife. Work over a medium bowl to catch any juice from the oranges and let the orange segments drop into the bowl. Set the orange segments aside in a small bowl.

3. Whisk together the collected orange juice, vinegar, honey, and thyme. Whisk in the oil in a thin stream until blended. Add salt and pepper if you think the dressing needs them.

4. Toss the lettuce, onion, and olives together with the dressing in a serving bowl. Scatter the orange segments over the salad and serve.

1 head romaine lettuce
2 navel oranges
¼ cup white wine vinegar
1 tablespoon honey
1 teaspoon chopped fresh thyme
¾ cup olive oil
Salt and pepper to taste
1 medium red onion, cut in half and then into ¼-inch slivers
1 cup pitted kalamata, oil-cured, or Sicilian olives

Tapas, little plates of food, are one of my favorite ways to eat. If you have ever looked at a restaurant menu and been unable to make up your mind what to order, you'll know why. Serving tapas means you don't have to decide: You can have them all!

I went out to dinner with my girlfriends one night, and we couldn't decide what to order. Loni came up with a great idea: "What if we each order two or three appetizers for dinner and then share them all?" Let's see: Two or three appetizers times four girls equals a tapas party! It was a total blast. We ordered a beautiful bottle of wine, had little tastes of lots of different things, and still managed to have room for dessert.

It occurred to me that this is the way Europeans eat. The bulky or heavy meal is eaten in the afternoon so that you have ample time for digestion. Then later in the evening people eat lighter and do not go to bed with that "heavy" feeling. The next time my girlfriends were over for dinner, I did just that! I set out little casseroles of clams, Serrano ham, cold asparagus, salads, olives, cheese, and potato chips, and made a big carafe of sangria. We dined like Spanish royalty, giggled like schoolgirls, and broke out the salsa records. (Watch out for those two left feet, Roe!) Tapas have definitely become our favorite way to eat on Girls' Night Out!

ASPARAGUS WITH SERRANO HAM AND MANCHEGO CHEESE

ESPÁRRAGOS CON JAMÓN SERRANO Y QUESO MANCHEGO

This makes a wonderful side dish, too. I placed it here and not in the vegetable chapter because you will find something like it in just about every tapas bar in Spain. Take it easy with the salt here because you get salt from the ham and cheese—but that's not all you get: The ham adds smoke and aroma and the cheese adds a peppery tang, all of which goes beautifully with the crisp green asparagus.

MAKES 6 SERVINGS

1. Remove the tough part from the bottom of the asparagus stems, about 2 inches or so. Peel the stalks up to about 1 inch from the tip. Lay the asparagus about 2 deep in a skillet that fits them comfortably. Pour in enough water to fill the pan about ¼ inch. Pour the oil over the asparagus and bring the water to a boil. Cook until the water has evaporated and the asparagus begins to sizzle in the oil, about 5 minutes. The asparagus will be bright green and crisp-tender.

2. While the asparagus is cooking, roll the ham slices up tightly and cut the roll crosswise into thin ribbons. When the asparagus starts to sizzle, scatter the ham over the asparagus. Toss just until the ham is mixed around the asparagus and starts to frizzle. Taste and add salt if necessary.

3. Scoop the asparagus onto a serving plate. While it is still hot, grate enough cheese over the asparagus to coat it evenly. Serve hot or at room temperature

DAISY'S PANTRY *By now most of you are familiar with the wonder of Prosciutto di Parma, the classic Italian ham. Well, you may think me a bit biased, but I think Serrano ham gives Prosciutto a good run for its money! Serrano ham has a delicate buttery flavor with a hint of sweetness and smoke that makes my knees weak. The texture is intoxicating as well. It has real "tooth" to it without being tough, and it has a gorgeous medium rose color with ribbons of white. Please, please, please don't pass up an opportunity to try a slice of Serrano, and if you're lucky enough to score the shank bone from one of these hams, know that your next bowl of sauce, pot of beans, or soup is going to make history!*

1 pound medium-thick asparagus
2 tablespoons olive oil
6 slices Serrano, prosciutto, or any good-quality ham
Fine sea or kosher salt to taste
Piece of Parmesan or Manchego cheese

NOTE: *Manchego is a firm, fairly sharp cow's milk cheese that can be grated like Parmesan, although it's not quite as crumbly. If you can't find it, use Parmesan or even a milder pecorino Romano.*

POTATO CHIPS

PATATAS FRITAS

Any tapas bar you walk into in Spain has potato chips as an offering. They are substantial, like these, not ultra-thin like the ones Americans are used to.

Russet potatoes, peeled
Vegetable oil
Salt

ONE MEDIUM RUSSET POTATO (7 TO 8 OUNCES) YIELDS ABOUT 20 CHIPS

1. Peel the potatoes and cut them on a mandoline or, if you have a blade thin enough, in a food processor. The slices should be very (but not paper) thin—about the thickness of a credit card.

2. Swish the slices around in a large bowl of cold water, then drain them. Lay them out on a double thickness of paper towels and blot them completely dry.

3. Pour enough oil into a deep, heavy pot to fill about 3 inches. Heat over medium heat until the tip of the handle of a wooden spoon gives off a lively sizzle when dipped into the oil (about 375° F).

4. Slip as many of the potato slices as float freely (6 to 8) into the oil. Fry, turning them with a slotted spoon, until deep golden brown, about 1 minute. Remove and drain on paper towels. Repeat with the remaining potatoes. Adjust the heat as necessary so the potatoes give off a nice sizzle and brown evenly without burning. Sprinkle the potato chips with salt to taste.

SPICED OLIVES

ACEITUNAS CON ESPECIAS

This makes a large batch—enough to get you through a couple of parties. If you like, cut the recipe in half. In my house, however, there are never enough of these. I can make a meal of just these olives and a piece of crusty bread.

Cook the garlic in boiling water for 1 minute and drain. Place the olives in a 1-quart jar or container with a tight-fitting lid. Add the garlic, oregano, and cumin seeds. Pour in enough oil to barely cover the olives. Cover the jar and shake well to distribute the spices. Place the jar in the back of the refrigerator for at least 3 or 4 days. They are better after a week. Bring to room temperature before serving.

4 cloves garlic, crushed with a knife
1 pound of your favorite olives (see Note)
1 tablespoon fresh or dried oregano
1 teaspoon cumin seeds, toasted
1⅔ cups, or as needed, olive oil

NOTE: *I like large green Spanish, Italian Cerignola, or black Greek olives for this. Their meaty texture absorbs the flavor of the marinade.*

SWEET AND SPICY ALMONDS

ALMENDRAS DULCES Y PICANTES

My very good friend Liz Montez is more than a chocolate maven; she is a passionate student of the importance of cocoa and chocolate in Mexican history. She also runs a company in Portland, Oregon, called Sahagún that specializes in exquisite chocolates seasoned with chilies, coriander, and other Latin spices. Liz developed this recipe for hazelnuts, which abound in her neck of the woods, but you can use just about any nut with its skin on—the spices will stick better. When I make these at my house, I put my daughter Angela on "almond rolling" detail. Then we both pick up the delicious bits that stick to the bottom of the pan and treat ourselves to a chef's snack.

This recipe can easily be doubled or tripled for a crowd.

MAKES ABOUT 3 CUPS

1 tablespoon ground toasted cumin seeds
2 teaspoons ground coriander
1 teaspoon fine sea or kosher salt
½ teaspoon ground cayenne pepper
½ teaspoon ground cinnamon
1 pound dark brown or piloncillo sugar (see Daisy's Pantry)
1 cup water
¾ pound unpeeled almonds (about 2½ cups)
⅔ cup unsweetened cocoa powder
¼ cup confectioners' sugar

1. Preheat the oven to 300° F. Stir the cumin, coriander, salt, cayenne, and cinnamon together in a medium bowl.

2. Heat the brown sugar and water together in a medium saucepan over medium heat, stirring, until the sugar is dissolved. Add the almonds and stir until coated. Scoop them out with a slotted spoon, letting them drain over the pan, and then add them to the bowl with the seasonings. Stir or toss until the nuts are evenly coated with the seasonings.

3. Spread the seasoned almonds on a baking sheet and bake for 10 minutes. Rotate the pan and bake until the nuts are fragrant, about 10 minutes more.

4. While the nuts are baking, stir the cocoa and confectioners' sugar together on a baking sheet.

5. Roll the almonds, still hot from the oven, in the cocoa mix until well coated. The coating will cake up a little, but that's fine. Cool completely in the coating, shaking them every so often. Scoop the nuts out with a wire skimmer and store them in a container with a tight-fitting lid.

DAISY'S PANTRY *Piloncillo is a type of brown sugar sold all over the Latin American and Spanish world. It has a rich, molassesy aroma and flavor. It is usually sold in dome-shaped pieces that range in size from about 1 ounce to several pounds. If you'd like to try it, using it in place of the brown sugar called for here is a good place to start. Find the smaller pieces; they are easier to use.*

POTATO AND EGG OMELET

TORTILLA ESPAÑOLA

Who doesn't love potatoes and eggs? Certainly the Spanish do. This thick omelet is the quintessential tapa. You will find it everywhere you go in Spain. You might find the term *tortilla* a bit confusing. Here in the United States we associate that term with the round, flat corn or flour breads of Central America. In other parts of Latin America and Spain the term *tortilla* describes an omelet or frittata-type dish. Traditionally, potatoes for a tortilla are cut into very thin slices and browned. This recipe uses potato cubes because they are much easier to prepare.

Serve this omelet hot, cold, or even at room temperature. It is delicious for breakfast, lunch, and dinner.

MAKES ABOUT 20 TAPA-SIZED PIECES OR 8 LUNCH SERVINGS

1. Pour enough cold water over the potatoes in a large saucepan to cover them generously. Bring to a boil over high heat. As soon as the water comes to a boil, drain the potatoes and let them air-dry while you cook the onion.

2. Heat the oil in a large (at least 12 inches) nonstick or seasoned cast iron skillet over medium-low heat. Add the onion and thyme, and cook, stirring occasionally, just until the onion starts to color, about 10 minutes. Stir in the potatoes and cook, stirring gently, until the potatoes are coated in oil. Continue cooking, stirring occasionally, until the potatoes are tender and lightly browned, about 10 minutes.

3. Spread out the potatoes and onions in an even layer. Pour in the eggs and cook a few minutes, until they start to set around the edges. Push the set eggs very gently toward the center of the pan, letting some of the raw egg from the top of the omelet run down to fill in the empty spaces around the edge. Continue until there is no more uncooked egg running from the top. The omelet tells you when it is ready to turn: It will slide easily across the bottom of the skillet when you shake the pan.

4. Choose a plate that is an inch or two larger than the skillet or a flat baking sheet (with no sides). Remove the skillet from the heat. Cover it with the plate or baking sheet. Wearing oven mitts, clamp the skillet and plate together with one hand on each side and invert the omelet onto the plate. Return the skillet to the heat and slide the omelet, cooked side up, back into it. Reduce the heat to low and continue cooking until the bottom is set, about 10 minutes. Serve hot, warm, or at room temperature. These are delicious chilled, too.

3 large Idaho potatoes (about 2 pounds), peeled and cut into 1-inch cubes (see Note)
2 tablespoons olive oil
1 medium Spanish onion, thinly sliced
4 sprigs of fresh thyme
6 eggs, well beaten

NOTE: *If you're not using the potatoes right away, keep them covered in cold water at room temperature for up to an hour or in the refrigerator for up to 8 hours. Drain thoroughly before using.*

TIP: *There is no time when a tortilla is out of place. Serve it for breakfast with country bread and butter or marmalade of Seville oranges. Serve it for lunch with really good Spanish ham, such as Serrano. Serve it for dinner with a crisp green salad, some asparagus, or a delicious tomato salad.*

DAISY'S PANTRY *Olive oil is (or was) not a staple in the cooking of Latin America and the Spanish-speaking Caribbean the way it has been in Spain. Lard or dende (palm) oil were the fats of choice. With better education about nutrition, that is changing.*

While I have used and like Italian and Greek olive oils, my choice is Spanish oil. Goya makes an excellent mellow, fragrant, fresh-tasting, slightly nutty Spanish olive oil at a terrific price that I use for everyday cooking. If I'm frying or cooking at a high heat, it's vegetable or canola oil all the way. I save olive oil for gentle cooking, lower heat browning, or drizzling over dishes at the table. The high temperature required for frying breaks down olive oil in no time flat.

CLAMS IN CILANTRO BROTH

ALMEJAS EN CALDO DE CILANTRO

These ended up in the appetizer chapter, but they can be served as a main meal, especially if you serve a crusty piece of bread and a salad. Or beef it up even more by stirring in a handful of cooked rice or thin egg noodles.

MAKES 4 APPETIZER OR 2 MAIN-COURSE SERVINGS

1. Heat the oil in a large, heavy skillet over medium heat. Add the garlic and cook, shaking the pan once or twice, just until it starts to turn golden, about 3 minutes. Add the hot red pepper and wine. Add the clams, bring the liquid to a boil, and cook for 2 to 3 minutes.

2. Stir in the cilantro, cover the pan, and cook, shaking the pan, until the clams are open, about 4 minutes. Ladle the clams and broth into shallow bowls and serve immediately, discarding any clams that don't open.

½ cup olive oil
6 cloves garlic, sliced
½ teaspoon hot red pepper flakes
½ cup white wine
3 dozen littleneck clams or other small hard-shell clams, soaked in cornmeal and water (see page 179)
1 bunch cilantro, thick stems and roots, if any, removed, and leaves and thin stems coarsely chopped

CRAB SEVICHE

SEVICHE DE CANGREJO

I discovered lump crabmeat at my local big-box store that comes in pasteurized one-pound cans. It's cheaper than most, has nice big chunks (which is important to this recipe), and, best of all, never contains pieces of shell or cartilage in my experience.

Lime juice usually cooks the seafood in a seviche. In this case the crab is already cooked, so there is considerably less juice than in the shrimp seviche on page 48.

MAKES 6 SERVINGS

Empty the crabmeat into a serving bowl large enough to mix the seviche and serve it comfortably. Pick over the crabmeat and remove any pieces of shell or cartilage, but do it carefully to keep the crab in pieces as large as possible. Add the remaining ingredients, toss gently, and season with salt. You can make the seviche up to a few hours in advance and keep it in the refrigerator. Bring it to room temperature about 15 minutes before serving.

1 pound lump crabmeat
2 tablespoons fresh lime juice
½ habanero chili or chili of your choice, very finely minced
½ yellow bell pepper and ½ red bell pepper, cut into fine dice (see Note)
1 tablespoon fresh lime juice
Fine sea or kosher salt to taste

NOTE: *To make perfect strips or dice of yellow or red pepper: Cut the pepper in half through the core. Cut off the stem and opposite ends. Remove the white ribs. Cut the large pieces of pepper into strips. Bunch a few strips together and cut crosswise into dice. Save the pepper scraps for soups, salads, or, of course, Sofrito (page 6).*

GRILLED CALAMARI WITH SOUR ORANGE MARINADE

CALAMARES A LA PARILLA

You can grill the calamari on top of the stove in a grill pan or, of course, on your outdoor gas or charcoal grill. In the summer my son Erik loves to man the grill. I make the marinade, Erik throws the calamari on the grill, and everybody else licks their fingers and smacks their lips! It used to be hard to find cleaned squid at a fish store; now it's hard to find them uncleaned. (Good for us!) Either way, don't wait for an excuse to try these because they are that fabulous.

1. Remove the fins from the calamari bodies; you can peel them off easily with your hands. (If you like, don't bother with this step.) Pour the marinade over the calamari. Squish the calamari around a little to coat it completely with the liquid.

2. Scatter the chilies and oregano over the calamari and season them with salt and pepper. Marinate at room temperature for 30 minutes to 1 hour, but no longer because the acid in the citrus juice will "cook" the squid.

3. Heat your grill to high or build a very hot charcoal fire. Grill the calamari, turning only once, until opaque and browned in places, about 3 minutes on the first side and 2 minutes on the second. Serve right away.

2 pounds cleaned calamari (squid)
⅓ cup bottled sour orange marinade (see Note) or the juice of 1 lemon and 1 orange
1 habanero or hot chili pepper of your choice, stemmed and minced
2 teaspoons chopped fresh oregano
Fine sea or kosher salt to taste
Freshly ground pepper to taste

NOTE: *Sour orange marinade is made with the juice of sour oranges (naranja agria; see note on page 48), oranges, onions, and seasonings. Goya makes a good one that you can find in any supermarket with a decent Latin foods section. Sour orange marinade is a very handy item to have on the pantry shelf.*

VARIATION: *If you don't want to venture outdoors, grill these in a grill pan on the stove top. They'll dance around a little when they hit the heat, so weigh them down lightly at first—with a lightweight skillet or heat-proof plate—just until they lose their dancing shoes.*

SHRIMP "COOKED" IN CITRUS JUICE

SEVICHE DE CAMARONES

All over South America people "cook" fish by soaking it in citrus juice. After marinating for several hours, the seafood turns opaque and firm, and has a texture halfway between sushi and traditionally cooked fish. Seviche goes fast at a party—especially in the summer when the citrusy fresh bite feels especially right. There is a lot of room for improvisation here: Buy whichever type of sweet peppers look good, play with the proportion of citrus juices, and control the heat with your choice of hot peppers.

Like Sofrito (page 6), there are a million variations on this theme. Use this very simple recipe as the base for your own.

MAKES 6 SERVINGS

1. Toss the shrimp, yellow and red peppers, onion, cilantro, salt, and chili pepper together in a bowl to mix them thoroughly. Pack into a nonreactive container (see Notes; a 2-quart glass jar works well). Squeeze the citrus, strain out any seeds, and pour over the shrimp and vegetables. There should be enough juice to cover the shrimp and vegetables; if not, add more. Seal the container and refrigerate until the shrimp is opaque, 12 hours to 1 day.

2. To serve: Drain, discard most of the liquid, and pile the shrimp and vegetables in a serving bowl.

DAISY'S PANTRY *Ninety-nine percent of the shrimp you see in the market are frozen or previously frozen. There is nothing wrong with that as long as they have been handled properly. I buy my shrimp in bulk from the local big-box store and thaw them as I need them to make sure they're in prime condition. If you find fresh shrimp, go ahead and buy them, but there is nothing wrong with frozen or defrosted shrimp.*

1½ pounds large (about 20 per pound) shrimp, shelled and deveined (see Daisy's Pantry)
1 yellow bell pepper, cored, seeded, and cut into thin strips about 2 inches long
1 red bell pepper, cored, seeded, and cut into thin strips about 2 inches long
½ small red onion, cut into thin slivers
1 small bunch cilantro, thick stems removed and the rest chopped coarsely
1 tablespoon plus 1 teaspoon fine sea or kosher salt
1 Scotch bonnet, jalapeño, or hot chili pepper of your choice, stemmed and minced
12 lemons, or as needed
8 limes, or as needed
4 oranges, or as needed (see Notes)

NOTES: *Sour oranges (naranjas agrias) are lumpy greenish oranges that are full of pits. Their juice is very sour, so I usually pair them with regular oranges to tone them down a bit. Sour oranges are used extensively in Latin American and Caribbean cooking. If you can find them in a Latin market, substitute two of them for the lemon and one of the oranges.*

• A nonreactive container in this case means anything but aluminum, which will react with the citrus juice and lend the seviche an off flavor, or plastic, which may do the same.

VARIATION: *You can substitute bay scallops for the shrimp.*

CANNELINI BEANS WITH CLAMS

HABICHUELAS BLANCAS CON ALMEJAS

On the last night of our trip to Spain we walked into a restaurant that we had been eyeing for a few nights, but it had been booked completely. I told the maitre d' that we were leaving the next morning for Madrid and would hate to miss the opportunity to eat at their restaurant. He asked me if we could finish in forty-five minutes because the only table they had that could accommodate our family was reserved for then. I quickly assured him we would. This was one of the dishes we shared, and it was love at first taste. The sweetness of the clams mixed with the smoke of the bacon and the creaminess of the beans make for a truly celestial combination in Spain, in Brooklyn, and in your house, too!

MAKES 6 SERVINGS

8 ounces slab bacon, in one piece, or ham steak
One 16-ounce bag of cannelini beans (see Note)
6 cups water
2 bay leaves
Three to four 8-ounce bottles of clam juice
¼ cup olive oil
5 cloves garlic, sliced
2 dozen littleneck clams, scrubbed and soaked in a cornmeal bath (see page 179)
Fine sea or kosher salt to taste
Freshly ground pepper to taste
2 tablespoons chopped fresh flat-leaf parsley

1. Remove the rind from the bacon (see Note on page 171). Place the bacon in a small cold skillet over low heat. Cook, turning as necessary, until golden brown on all sides. (See Note if using ham.)
2. While the bacon is rendering, place the beans in a large pot. Add the water and bay leaves. Bring to a boil, then adjust the heat so the beans are simmering. Skim the foam off the top from time to time. When the bacon is brown, add it to the beans in one piece.
3. When the level of water has reached the beans, begin adding the clam juice. Add 2 bottles at first and continue cooking until the level of the liquid reaches the beans again. Add another bottle, and if the beans still aren't tender by the time the level of the liquid reaches them, add the last bottle. All in all, the beans should take about 2 hours to cook.
4. When the beans are tender, heat the oil in a large shallow pan with a tight-fitting lid. Add the garlic, and when it starts to color, scoop all but 1½ cups of the beans out of the pot with a slotted spoon or skimmer and into the pan. Reduce the heat to low and add 2 cups of the cooking liquid from the beans. Bring to a boil.
5. Drain the reserved 1½ cups of beans and puree them in a food processor. Add to the beans in the pan and stir to mix. Remove the bacon from the bean pot and cut it into 1-inch slices and then crosswise into ½-inch strips. Stir them into the bean mix. (The recipe can be prepared to this point up to 1 day in advance. Refrigerate the beans, then heat them to simmering before continuing.)
6. Increase the heat to medium-high. Stir in the clams, cover the pot, and cook until the clams open, about 10 minutes. Add salt and pepper if you like and sprinkle with the parsley.

NOTE: *You can make this with drained and rinsed canned beans because the sauce from the clams will doctor up the beans. But please try it once with dried beans to see the gold standard.*
• To substitute ham steak for the bacon, just add a little oil to the pan or spray the pan with vegetable oil cooking spray and proceed.

SPANISH FLAT BREADS

COCAS

Think of *cocas* as thin-crusted Spanish pizzas. And just as there is a pizzeria on every corner in New York City, you will see *cocas* piled high, one atop the other, in tapas bars all over Spain. And why not, given the crispy-chewy crust and the endless varieties of toppings that are possible.

Traditionally, *cocas* are rectangular, but the *coca* police won't come knocking if you make them round or any other shape you like.

As with pizza, there is virtually no end to the ways you can top a *coca*. Following the recipe for dough are two toppings to get you started. Also delicious would be the Sautéed Spinach with Pine Nuts and Raisins on page 130.

DOUGH FOR FLAT BREADS

MASA PARA COCAS

There is usually something bubbling away on my stove, so when I make dough, I put it on a corner of the stove, away from direct heat, and let it rise there. If you like, you can bring a large pot of water to a simmer, turn off the heat, and set a cooling or oven rack over the pot. Set the dough in its bowl on this rack, cover with a kitchen towel, and the dough will rise very quickly.

MAKES ENOUGH DOUGH FOR ONE 13 × 18-INCH FLAT BREAD

1²⁄₃ cups warm (110° to 115° F) water
1 envelope dry yeast
2 teaspoons sugar
1 tablespoon olive oil
1 tablespoon white wine or other vinegar
4 cups all-purpose flour, or as needed
2 teaspoons salt
Vegetable oil
Coarse cornmeal

1. Stir the water, yeast, and sugar together in a small bowl until the yeast and sugar are dissolved. Let stand in a warm place until the liquid starts to foam, about 10 minutes.

2. Pour the yeast mixture, oil, and vinegar into the bowl of an electric mixer fitted with the paddle attachment. Add the flour and salt, and mix at low speed until the dough is smooth and somewhat sticky. Switch to the dough hook attachment and continue mixing until the dough is smooth and elastic, about 3 minutes. Add flour if the dough sticks to the bowl and attachment. Turn the dough out onto a lightly floured surface, knead it into a smooth ball, and place it in an oiled bowl. Turn the dough to oil it on all sides, cover the bowl with a kitchen towel, and let it rise in a warm place until doubled in bulk, from 30 minutes to 1½ hours.

> **VARIATION:** *Check your local bakeries or pizza places. Chances are one of them will sell you balls of pizza dough. They are a great resource to have on hand. Take them right from the freezer to an oiled bowl, cover it with a kitchen towel, and let rise.*

3. Sprinkle the bottom of a 13 × 18-inch jelly roll pan with the cornmeal. Roll the dough out to a rectangle an inch or two larger on all sides than the pan. Fit the dough into the pan, tucking it into the corners. Don't worry if the edges of the dough are a little uneven. Poke the dough with a fork at 1-inch intervals and let the dough rise in a warm place until it starts to puff, about 30 minutes.

VEGETABLE FLAT BREADS

COCA CON VERDURAS

Not a carnivore? Not a problem! Cocas lend themselves beautifully to vegetables. Peppers, onions, asparagus—all translate well into coca toppings. More suggestions? How about spinach seasoned with garlic, pine nuts and raisins (page 130), or sliced fresh figs with Las Tinajas cheese? If that doesn't make your eyes cross, I'd check your pulse!

MAKES ENOUGH TO TOP A 13 × 18-INCH FLAT BREAD

Dough for Flat Breads (page 50)
1 each red and yellow bell pepper, cored, seeded, and cut into ¼-inch strips (see Note)
5 cloves garlic, thinly sliced
¼ teaspoon dried oregano
Olive oil
Fine sea or kosher salt to taste

NOTE: *Letting the seasoned vegetables stand while the dough is rising makes a better tasting topping.*

1. Make the dough.
2. While the dough is rising for the second time, toss the bell peppers, garlic, and oregano together in a bowl. Drizzle in the oil until the vegetables are lightly coated. Season lightly with salt. (They will cook down quite a bit, and you don't want to end up with oversalted peppers.)
3. Preheat the oven to 400° F. Spread the pepper mixture in an even layer over the dough, leaving a small border around the edges. Bake until the dough is well browned and crisp, about 20 minutes. Cool for 10 minutes before serving or serve at room temperature.

SAUSAGE FLAT BREAD

COCA CON LONGANIZA

MAKES ENOUGH TO TOP A 13 × 18-INCH FLAT BREAD

1. Make the dough.

2. While the dough is rising for the first time, prepare the sausages: Put the sausages in a medium skillet, poke them all over with a fork, and pour in about ½ inch of water. Bring to a boil over medium heat. Cook the sausages until they turn color on the bottom, about 3 minutes. Flip the sausages and cook until the water evaporates and the sausages start to brown in their own fat. Adjust the heat to low and cook until the sausages are browned on all sides, about 5 minutes. Remove and let stand until cool enough to handle.

3. Stir the onions into the fat in the pan. Cook, stirring, until wilted and crisp-tender, about 5 minutes. Season with salt and pepper.

4. Meanwhile, preheat the oven to 400° F. Spread the dough with an even layer of the onions, leaving a border of about ½ inch around the edges. Cut the sausages into ½-inch slices. Dot the onions with the sausages. Bake until the dough is well browned and crisp, about 20 minutes. Cool for 10 minutes before serving or serve at room temperature.

DAISY'S PANTRY *Longaniza is a Spanish-style fresh sausage, meaning it's not a cooked or smoked sausage like chorizo. It is seasoned with garlic and spices, and sometimes it is flavored and colored with achiote oil (see page 9). It is sold in long spirals, much like the Italian sausages flavored with parsley and cheese. You will find it sweet and hot, just like Italian sausages, which you can use if you can't find longaniza.*

Dough for Flat Breads (page 50)
1 pound longaniza (see Daisy's Pantry) or sweet Italian sausages
3 large Spanish onions, sliced ½ inch thick
Freshly ground pepper to taste
Fine sea or kosher salt to taste

CRISPY OPEN-FACED SANDWICHES

TOSTADAS

In Spanish there is a saying, "So-and-so is a piece of bread!" That means a person is as good as good can be. After all, what's better than a good piece of bread? A good piece of bread with a marvelous topping, of course! You can easily make a meal out of any or all of these and a salad. Add a pitcher of sangria or hard cider (see Note on page 272), and you're on a sidewalk café in Madrid, looking and feeling über-fab!

Each of the following toppings makes enough to cover one half of a long (about 18 inches) loaf of Italian bread or baguette. For a big party make all three or double any of the following to top both halves of the loaf.

ROASTED GARLIC-ANCHOVY TOPPING

ADEREZO DE AJO ASADO CON ANCHOA

1. Drain the oil from the anchovies. Separate the anchovy fillets, put them in a small bowl, and pour in enough cold water to cover. Let stand for 15 minutes.

2. Preheat the oven to 350° F.

3. Meanwhile, squeeze the garlic pulp from the cloves into a small bowl. Mash to a paste with a fork. Brush the cut side of the bread with the oil, then spread the roasted garlic paste evenly over it. Drain the anchovies and pat them dry with paper towels. Make X's with the anchovies down the length of the baguette. Bake until the bread is crispy, about 10 minutes.

One 2-ounce can flat anchovies (see Note)
1 head roasted garlic (see page 129)
2 tablespoons olive oil
½ loaf (cut lengthwise) Italian bread or wide baguette

NOTE: *In Spain and Italy, and maybe other parts of Europe, you will find meaty white anchovy fillets. The flavor is more delicate than the canned anchovies we're all used to. If you find them (see Sources), use them here.*

TO PEEL AND SEED TOMATOES

If you cook tomatoes without peeling them, the skins will curl up and get hard and nasty. And when you remove the seeds, you remove not only that grainy texture but lots of excess liquid as well, which comes in handy when you want to cook something down such as a thick sauce. No matter what kind of tomatoes or how many of them you're cooking, the procedure is the same:

Heat a large pot of water to a boil. Fill a bowl that is large enough to hold the tomatoes comfortably halfway with ice cubes. Pour in just enough cold water to cover the ice. Remove the cores from the tomatoes with a paring knife. Cut an X in the end opposite the core. (That will make it easier to peel them later.) Slip four or five tomatoes into the boiling water and cook them just long enough for the skin around the X to curl. The time will depend on the type of tomato you're using and how ripe they are—usually from thirty to sixty seconds. Scoop them out with a slotted spoon and slip them into the ice water. Repeat until all the tomatoes are done. Drain the tomatoes and peel off their skins. Cut the tomatoes in half (cut plum tomatoes lengthwise and rounder tomatoes along the "equator"). Squeeze out the seeds and the liquid around them.

TOMATO "JAM" TOPPING

ADEREZO DE TOMATES Y AJO

Prepare a double batch of this recipe. The unused half, kept in the refrigerator covered with a thin layer of olive oil, will last at least one week. Use it to season soups, pasta dishes, and anything else that would benefit from a dash of tomato flavor, such as a hamburger, vegetable sandwich, or omelet.

1. Heat 2 tablespoons of the oil in a wide skillet over medium heat until rippling. Add the garlic and cook just until it begins to change color, about 1 minute. Stir in the tomatoes and bring to a simmer. Cook, stirring often, until the water given off by the tomatoes has evaporated, about 20 minutes. Watch the tomatoes, especially near the end of cooking, so they do not stick and scorch. Stir in the oregano and season with salt and pepper. Cool to room temperature before using.

2. Preheat the oven to 350° F.

3. Spread the remaining 2 tablespoons of oil on the cut side of the bread. Spread the tomato jam in an even layer over the oil. Bake until the bread is crispy and the tomato is heated through, about 10 minutes.

4 tablespoons olive oil
5 cloves garlic, chopped
2 pounds ripe plum or vine-ripened tomatoes, cored, peeled, and seeded (see box on page 56), coarsely chopped (about 4 cups)
1 teaspoon chopped fresh oregano
Fine sea or kosher salt to taste
Freshly ground pepper to taste
½ loaf (cut lengthwise) Italian bread or wide baguette

BLUE CHEESE TOPPING

ADEREZO DE QUESO CABRALES

1. Preheat the oven to 350° F.

2. Spread the cut side of the bread with the oil. Cut the blue cheese into slices about ¼ inch thick. Line the slices on the oil. Bake for 10 minutes, until the bread is crispy and the cheese is softened.

3. Heat the broiler and broil the tostadas about 4 inches from the heat until the cheese is bubbling. Serve hot.

½ loaf (cut lengthwise) Italian bread or baguette
2 tablespoons extra-virgin olive oil
¼ pound Cabrales (see Daisy's Pantry on page 36) or other blue cheese, softened (bring to room temperature about 1 hour before using)

STUFFED YUCCA FRITTERS

ALCAPURRIAS

Versions of this simple fritter made with grated yucca abound throughout the world of Latin cooking. You will find them filled with beef or pork picadillo (page 60) or even leftover chicken or seafood. Underneath the crispy, golden, delicious crust is the satiny yucca. If that's not enough, there is a completely different texture when you get to the center.

Not feeling the meat thing? How about a chopped olive salad or a delicious piece of Valdeon or Tetilla cheese? Whichever way you decide, just make sure you make them.

YUCCA FRITTER DOUGH

MASA PARA ALCAPURRIAS

If you're not up to speed on yucca, check out the information on page 110.

MAKES ABOUT 16 FRITTERS

1. Peel the yucca and grate it coarsely. Stir in the oil, salt, and pepper. Use right away.

2. To form alcapurrias: Scoop ¼ cup of the batter into the palm of your hand. Work the dough into an egg shape, then make an indentation in the dough with your thumb. Spoon about 1 tablespoon of filling into the indentation, then work the dough around the filling to encase it completely. Set the alcapurria on a baking sheet and repeat with the remaining dough and filling.

4 pounds uncooked yucca (see Note)
½ cup Achiote Oil (page 9)
2 tablespoons fine sea or kosher salt
½ teaspoon freshly ground black pepper

NOTE: I swear, life keeps getting better. Not long after I spotted frozen peeled yucca in the freezer section of my supermarket, I discovered grated uncooked frozen yucca. It is perfect for making these fritters; just thaw and use.

CRAB FILLING FOR YUCCA FRITTERS

SALMOREJIO DE CANGREJO

On a recent trip to Puerto Rico, my cousins took me to an adorable restaurant in Guajataca, overlooking the ocean. My cousin Jose Ramon knows the chef, who made a delicious meal for us of the crab filling (*salmorejio*) with fluffy yellow rice and crispy fried plantain chips. We sat at the back of the restaurant with its alfresco views of the beach, the sound of the surf crashing, the sweetness of the sea in the air. I took my first forkful of *salmorejio* and had to dry the tears from my eyes. It was so good!

MAKES 1¼ CUPS, ENOUGH TO FILL 16 FRITTERS

Heat the oil in a medium skillet over medium heat until rippling. Add the sofrito and cook, stirring, until the liquid has evaporated and the sofrito starts to sizzle. Stir in the alcaparrado, tomato sauce, and crabmeat. Bring to a boil, adjust the heat so the sauce is simmering, and cook just until lightly thickened, about 4 minutes.

DAISY'S PANTRY *I am a firm believer in good-quality convenience foods, and Spanish-style tomato sauce, which comes in small 8-ounce cans, is a fine example. Unlike tomato sauces meant for pasta, Spanish-style tomato sauce is very lightly seasoned—more like a tomato puree, really—so it doesn't add any unwanted flavor to a dish.*

2 tablespoons Achiote Oil (page 9)
¼ cup Sofrito (page 6)
¼ cup coarsely chopped alcaparrado or pimiento-stuffed olives (see Daisy's Pantry on page 13)
¼ cup canned Spanish-style tomato sauce (see Daisy's Pantry)
½ pound special or lump crabmeat

PORK PICADILLO

PICADILLO DE CERDO

You may have heard of *picadillo,* ground beef or pork cooked with seasonings (think Latin Sloppy Joes). *Picar* means to cut, and *picadillo* means to chop fine. Whether it's pork, beef, or a mix of the two, it's usually a filling for something like alcapurrias or empanadas or stuffed vegetables. The filling is left rather simple so the saltiness of the olives and the flavor of the pork come through.

MAKES ABOUT 2½ CUPS, ENOUGH TO FILL ABOUT 32 FRITTERS

1. Heat the oil in a large skillet over medium-high heat until rippling. Add the sofrito and alcaparrado, and cook, stirring, until the liquid has evaporated and the sofrito starts to sizzle, about 5 minutes.
2. Add the pork and cook, stirring to break up any lumps, until the pork is cooked through. The pork will give off a lot of liquid. Keep cooking, stirring once in a while, until the liquid has evaporated. Stir in the tomato paste and cook 1 to 2 minutes. Taste and add salt and pepper if you like. Cool before using. The pork filling can be made up to 2 days in advance.

2 tablespoons Achiote Oil (page 9)
¼ cup Sofrito (page 6)
¼ cup alcaparrado or coarsely chopped pimiento-stuffed olives (see Note on page 13)
1 pound ground pork
1 tablespoon tomato paste
Fine sea or kosher salt to taste
Freshly ground pepper to taste

VARIATIONS: *Make a beef picadillo by substituting an equal amount of beef for the pork. Everything else stays the same.*
• *Although this is usually a filling, it is sometimes eaten on its own with white rice.*

CHEESE PUFFS

BUÑUELOS DE QUESO

In Spain they fry these little puffs and make them more of a fritter. I like them baked.

In Puerto Rico they make these with cheddar cheese (*queso de papas*). The cilantro is my own addition—it adds a little color and a subtle flavor. Once you get the dough down pat, you can add whatever you like, really. Just make sure that the ingredients are fine enough to blend into the dough.

MAKES ABOUT 3 DOZEN PUFFS

1. Bring the water, butter, and salt to a boil in a medium saucepan over high heat. Stir for 1 to 2 minutes, until the butter has melted. Adjust the heat to medium-low, add the flour all at once, and stir like mad until the dough is nice and smooth and pulls away from the sides of the pan. Stir for another 1 to 2 minutes to dry out the dough.

2. Remove the pan from the heat. Add the eggs, 1 at a time. Beat well enough after each addition that the dough, which won't want to absorb the egg at first, becomes smooth again. Stir in the cheese.

3. Preheat the oven to 425° F. Line a baking sheet (2 if you have them) with parchment paper; this is not necessary if you're using a nonstick baking sheet. Scoop up a teaspoonful of the batter. Nudge the batter onto the sheet with a second spoon to make a rough ball about 1½ inches in diameter. Don't worry about making perfectly round balls; they should be a little rough around the edges.

4. Bake for 15 minutes. Turn the oven down to 375° F. Bake until puffed and golden, about 30 minutes. (You can make the dough up to a few hours before baking the puffs. Cover and refrigerate until needed.) Serve warm.

1 cup water
8 tablespoons (1 stick) unsalted butter, cut into 4 pieces
1 teaspoon fine sea or kosher salt
1 cup all-purpose flour
3 large eggs
1 cup grated *queso de freir* (see Note), cheddar, Gouda, or any semi-firm cheese

NOTE: Queso de freir, *or frying cheese, is a firm-textured, mild-flavored white cheese that is available in Latin markets.*

VARIATION: *If you're having a party, divide the dough in half. Bake one half like this and add to the other half a little diced hot pepper and/or finely diced chorizo that has been cooked for a minute or two (see step 3 of Mami's Potato Salad, page 123).*

SALT COD FRITTERS

BACALAITOS

Make these fritters when you find yourself with odds and ends of soaked and cooked salt cod—for example, after making Salt Cod Salad (page 189) or Salt Cod with Eggplant (page 189). The pieces of cod have to be finely shredded anyway, so it doesn't matter if you're working with bits of fish pulled from the belly or tail, say, of the fish. On the other hand, it seems you can never make enough *bacalaitos*, so you may want to soak and cook some salt cod just for these. Add grated onion or minced garlic to taste to the batter if you like. You can also load these up with more salt cod for a richer flavor. Any way you make them, they will disappear as quickly as you can fry them.

MAKES ABOUT 3 DOZEN

2 cups all-purpose flour
1½ teaspoons fine sea or kosher salt, or more to taste
2 teaspoons baking powder
2 cups water
1 cup finely shredded cooked salt cod (see page 188)
⅓ cup very finely chopped fresh cilantro
Vegetable oil

1. Stir the flour, salt, and baking powder together in a large bowl. Add the water and stir until no lumps remain. Stir in the salt cod and cilantro. Let the batter sit while the oil heats.

2. Pour enough oil into a large, deep skillet to fill 1 inch. Heat over medium heat until the tip of the handle of a wooden spoon gives off a lively sizzle when you dip it in the oil (about 375° F). Taste the batter and add a little more salt if you think it needs it.

3. Scoop up a mounded tablespoon of the batter and slip it carefully into the oil. Fry as many fritters at one time as will bob around freely in the skillet. If you fry too many at one time, the temperature of the oil will drop, and you'll have soggy, not crispy fritters. Fry until cooked through and deep golden brown, about 4 minutes. Drain on paper towels and serve hot. Repeat with the remaining batter.

CHICKEN LIVERS WITH ROSEMARY

HIGADOS DE POLLO CON ROMERO

This is very Spanish, very tapas bar, and very classical (the last you can tell by the rosemary). Nobody in the islands or Central or South America would recognize this beautiful piece of the puzzle that is Latin cooking. The livers are creamy and rich, the sauce has a little bit of smoke from the bacon yet is still sweet, and the rosemary adds a gorgeous fresh green sparkle. Good gravy! I'm making my own mouth water!

MAKES 6 TO 8 SERVINGS

1. Make the sauce, adding the rosemary along with the broth.

2. Cut the livers in half where the two lobes meet. Trim as much fat and connective tissue as possible from the liver, most of which you will find around the area where you cut the livers in half. Rinse them and pat dry thoroughly with paper towels.

3. Heat the oil in a large skillet over medium-high heat. Season the flour with salt and pepper, dredge the livers in the flour, and shake off the excess. Carefully slip as many of the chicken livers into the oil as will fit without crowding. Cook, turning once or twice, about 5 minutes, until they are firm, are crisp around the edges, and are light pink in the center. Drain on paper towels as they are done. Repeat with the remaining livers if necessary.

4. Place the toast slices in the bottom of 6 to 8 shallow soup bowls. Divide the livers among the bowls and pour a ladle or two of sauce over each mound. Sprinkle with parsley and serve.

4 cups Rich Brown Sauce, Daisy Style (page 171)
4 sprigs of fresh rosemary
2 pounds chicken livers
3 tablespoons olive oil
1 cup all-purpose flour
Fine sea or kosher salt to taste
Freshly ground pepper to taste
6 to 8 slices of Italian bread, toasted
Chopped fresh flat-leaf parsley

VARIATION: *You can make a main course of this dish by serving it with fluffy white rice and a vegetable such as String Beans with Roasted Garlic (page 129).*

SOUPS AND
ONE-POT MEALS

SOPAS Y COCIDOS

There may be a lot of things I could give up if I had to, but soup will never, ever make that list. I love soup. Forget ice cream and potato chips, cookies and cakes, or anything else for that matter. There is no food that says "comfort" to me as much as a bowl of soup. Whenever I got sick as a child, Mami made me special broths, not too highly seasoned. She would explain to the poultry man, and he usually gave her a little bag of "unhatched" eggs that she would float in my soup. She made delicious pigeon soup or chicken soup and served it with some noodles or a bit of rice, and always one of the wings, because she knew how I loved them.

When I started college, I moved in with Abuela. I eagerly looked forward to going home on the first day it snowed because I knew she would have a big pot of *sancocho* bubbling on top of the stove. I only had to open the door downstairs to smell it, and I would take the stairs two at a time to get to the mouthwatering, steaming bowl she had set out for me. I asked her a million questions about why her soup was so good and how to make it. She would laugh and say, "Ay, *nena*, stop talking so much and eat your sancocho. It's going to get cold!"

Today I am the one making the soups that I love for family and friends. Nothing says "welcome" like a big pot of bubbly soup, brothy or thick, full of vegetables or meat. I love serving sancocho on the first day it snows, as well as tending a nice big pot of it when my girl-friends are over or when one of my own kids is under the weather.

KALE and CHORIZO SOUP

CALDO VERDE

I first had this soup on a vacation to Cape Cod. There is a large Portuguese community, mostly fishermen, in Provincetown on the tip of the Cape. Kale is not a shy green; it likes to be cooked well. If you can find Portuguese sausage (linguica), use it here. If not, go with the chorizo or kielbasa. With canned broth this is a quick fix for dinner, giving you more time to enjoy with your family.

MAKES 6 SERVINGS

1. Place the sausage in a cold Dutch oven and then set it over medium heat. Cook until the sausage starts to render its fat and sizzle. When nicely browned, remove with a slotted spoon to a plate lined with paper towels.

2. Stir the sofrito into the fat in the pan. Cook until the water has evaporated and the sofrito starts to sizzle. Stir in the broth and potatoes, and bring to a gentle boil. Cook until the potatoes are tender, about 15 minutes.

3. Meanwhile, clean the kale. Fill a clean sink with cool water. Trim the stem ends and any wilted or yellow parts of the leaves. Remove the thick stems from the leaves. Chop the remaining leaves coarsely and, if you like, cut the stalks crosswise into ½-inch strips. (Otherwise, discard them.) Swish the chard and stems (if using) around in the water, then let them sit for a bit so the dirt settles to the bottom of the sink. Scoop the chard out into a colander and drain thoroughly.

4. Add the kale and sausage and adjust the heat so the soup is simmering. Cook, partially covered, until the kale is tender, about 10 minutes. Taste and add salt and pepper.

4 links well seasoned garlicky sausage such as linguica, chorizo, or kielbasa, skins removed, and cut into ½-inch dice

½ cup Sofrito (page 6)

3 quarts Chicken Broth, homemade (page 155) or canned

6 large potatoes, preferably Yukon Gold (about 3½ pounds), peeled and cut into 1-inch cubes

1 small bunch kale

Fine sea or kosher salt to taste

Freshly ground pepper to taste

GAZPACHO

On a recent trip to Florida, during one of the hottest summer weeks, it was hard to imagine getting excited about food. But hungry I was, and when I came across a cute little restaurant, I was as excited about getting out of the heat as I was about eating. I opened the menu and saw gazpacho. That was as far as I needed to look. Cool gazpacho, almost like a liquid salad, not only refreshed me but perked up my taste buds as well. After that, I felt so good, I could have given salsa lessons in the back of the restaurant!

MAKES ABOUT 2 QUARTS (8 SERVINGS)

1 pound ripe tomatoes, peeled and seeded (see page 58)
1 large red bell pepper, roasted (see box below), cored and seeded, or 1 large bottled fire-roasted pepper
1 English (hothouse) cucumber, peeled, cut in half lengthwise, seeded, and then cut into 1-inch chunks
½ cup roughly chopped Spanish onion
½ cup loosely packed chopped fresh cilantro
1 clove garlic
2 cups bottled tomato juice
1 tablespoon sherry vinegar
1 teaspoon ground cumin
2 teaspoons fine sea or kosher salt
¼ cup olive oil
Freshly ground pepper to taste

1. Process the tomatoes in the work bowl of a food processor until chopped. Add the roasted pepper, cucumber, onion, cilantro, and garlic one at a time and process until you have a thick, soupy puree. Add the tomato juice, vinegar, cumin, and salt, and pulse the processor until incorporated. With the processor running, slowly add the oil. Chill.

2. Check the seasonings and add additional salt, if necessary, and pepper. Serve in chilled mugs or bowls. You can make this the day before you plan to serve it. The flavor will only get better. Store it in the refrigerator for up to 3 days.

TO ROAST PEPPERS

Roasting peppers until the skins turn black and then peeling them intensifies their sweetness and adds a smoky note. Whichever method you choose, life will be easier if you start with square-sided, thick, meaty peppers. They'll blacken more evenly and hold up better. In a pinch, bottled roasted peppers will do. Just make sure they say "fire-roasted" somewhere on the label.

Using a gas stove: Turn on as many burners as needed to high (figure 2 peppers per burner). Rest the peppers on the grate over the flame. Keep an eye on them and turn as necessary, just until all sides and crevasses are black and blistered.

Using a broiler: Set the oven rack about 5 inches from the broiler and preheat the broiler. Broil the peppers, turning as necessary, until blackened on all sides, about 8 minutes.

Wrap each pepper in damp paper towels and cool to room temperature. Remove the paper towels and pull the pepper apart into strips. Scrape off the seeds and blackened skin with the back of a knife.

A FESTIVE GAZPACHO PRESENTATION

These ingredients make enough to serve 8 first-course servings or 4 main-course servings. Make more or less depending on who's hanging around at the moment.

8 large shrimp, peeled and deveined
½ cup Spicy Pineapple Vinegar (page 218)
2 tablespoons olive oil
Fine sea or kosher salt to taste
Freshly ground pepper to taste
1 ripe avocado
Lime juice

1. Toss the shrimp with the vinegar, oil, salt, and pepper. Let stand at room temperature for at least 30 minutes or refrigerate up to 2 hours, tossing occasionally.

2. Meanwhile, soak 8 wooden skewers in enough water to cover.

3. Just before serving, heat a gas or charcoal grill. Skewer the shrimp on the soaked skewers (1 shrimp per skewer for a first course, 2 shrimp per skewer for a main course).

4. Cut the avocado in half and remove the pit (see page 34). Make avocado balls using a melon baller, dropping them gently into a small bowl as you go. Sprinkle with lime juice and toss gently.

5. Grill the shrimp, turning to cook evenly, until cooked through, about 3 minutes. When the shrimp are cooked, add an avocado ball or two to each skewer.

6. For first-course servings, ladle gazpacho into martini or other glasses and suspend a shrimp and avocado skewer on the top of each.

7. For main-course servings, place the gazpacho in a shallow bowl and suspend 2 shrimp and avocado skewers over it.

PIGEON PEA SOUP WITH GREEN BANANA DUMPLINGS

SOPA DE GANDULES CON BOLLOS DE GUINEITOS

Did I tell you that I love dumplings in any shape or form? Mami's and Abuela's dumplings are delicious enough to qualify as a religious experience! I'm willing to bet that *these* dumplings, made with green bananas and love, are something you've never had before. I hope you remedy that very soon.

Pigeon peas are smooth, oval, green beans—sort of like a flattish, overgrown green pea. They are high in protein and taste a little like black-eyed peas. Also known as Congo peas, *feijao guandu*, and *frijol de palo*, pigeon peas are eaten fresh—in other words, without having been dried—in India, Southeast Asia, parts of Africa, and the West Indies. You will most likely find them canned or frozen in grocery stores.

SERVES 6–8 AS A MAIN COURSE

1. Rinse the pigeon peas in a colander under cold water. Drain and place in a heavy 5- to 6-quart pot. Add the water, neck bones, and bay leaves, and bring to a boil over high heat. Adjust the heat so the liquid is at a soft bubble. Cook for 30 minutes, skimming off any foam that rises to the top.

2. Stir the celery root, carrots, and sofrito into the pot. Bring back to a simmer, cover, and cook until all the vegetables are tender, about 20 minutes.

3. Meanwhile, make the dumplings: Grate the green bananas using the finest side of a box grater. Stir the cilantro, salt, oil, and pepper into the batter, working quickly so that the batter does not darken.

4. Slide a tablespoon of batter gently onto the surface of the soup. Continue until all the batter is used. Make sure that the heat is super low—a bubble coming up to the top here and there—or your dumplings will break apart. Partially cover the pot and cook until the dumplings are firm, 15 to 20 minutes. Ladle one out and check that it is cooked through.

5. To serve, scoop 2 dumplings into each shallow bowl and ladle soup around them.

FOR THE SOUP

1 pound pigeon peas, fresh or frozen
6 cups water
1 pound smoked pork neck bones or turkey wings
2 bay leaves
1 small (about 10 ounces) celery root, peeled and cut into 1-inch cubes (about 2 cups)
3 carrots, trimmed and cut into ½-inch slices
½ cup Sofrito (page 6)
Fine sea or kosher salt
Freshly ground pepper

FOR THE DUMPLINGS

4 green bananas (see page 116 and Note), trimmed and peeled
1 tablespoon minced fresh cilantro
1½ teaspoons fine sea or kosher salt
1 teaspoon Achiote Oil (page 9)
¼ teaspoon freshly ground black pepper

NOTE: *If you do not plan to use the green bananas immediately after peeling them, soak them in a bowl of cold salted water to prevent them from darkening.*

VARIATION: *A little splash of Spicy Pineapple Vinegar (page 218) brings this to a whole other level.*

PERUVIAN MINESTRONE

MINESTRA PERUANA

Mami's good friend Christina is a fabulous woman. Her family owns a white asparagus farm in Peru, where her father was a chef of great renown. Christina is no stranger to good food, and good Peruvian food in particular. She is so passionate about the wonderful cuisine of Peru that I was motivated to visit her country with my family last Christmas. Machu Picchu? Forget it! Minestrone is truly the jewel of Peru! Thick, chunky, aromatic, and soul satisfyingly delicious. Get the picture? Good. Now try the soup!

MAKES 6 MAIN-COURSE SERVINGS

1. Heat the oil in a 5- or 6-quart heavy pot over medium heat until rippling. Add the bacon and cook, turning as necessary, until lightly browned on all sides and the bacon begins to render its fat, about 10 minutes.

2. Add the sausages and cook until brown and crusty, about 5 minutes. Stir in the celery root, onion, and garlic. Keep stirring to free the brown bits stuck to the pan. Add paprika and cook until fragrant.

3. Add the broth, potatoes, cheese rind, and bay leaves. Cook until the potatoes are tender, about 30 minutes.

4. Cut the bacon into ½-inch slices. Cut the slices crosswise into ½-inch strips. Add to the soup. Stir in the corn pieces and season with salt and pepper. Cook until the corn is tender, about 3 minutes. Remove the cheese rind and bay leaves, and serve the soup in warm bowls.

1 tablespoon olive oil

½ pound slab bacon, rind removed (see page 171)

10 ounces longaniza (see Note on page 53) or thin Italian sausages, cut into 1½-inch lengths

One small celery root (about 10 ounces), peeled and diced (about 2 cups)

1 large Spanish onion, chopped (about 2 cups)

4 cloves garlic

1 teaspoon paprika, preferably smoked or hot paprika (see page 211)

One 64-ounce can chicken broth

2 medium potatoes, peeled and cut into 1-inch pieces

Piece of rind from hard cheese such as Parmesan or zamorano (optional; see Note)

2 bay leaves

2 ears corn, cut crosswise into 1-inch rounds

Fine sea or kosher salt to taste

Freshly ground pepper to taste

NOTE: *If you don't have the rind from a piece of cheese in your refrigerator, don't sweat it. But it does add salt and flavor to all soups like this. Don't ever throw that rind out. You paid good money for that cheese, and you may as well use all of it.*

VARIATION: *There are as many recipes for minestrone in Peru as there are Peruvian mothers. Let your appetite guide you and make this soup your own by adding some beef or chicken or even little meatballs!*

LITTLE PASTA SHELLS WITH HAM AND PEAS

CARACOLITOS DE PASTA CON JAMÓN Y GUISANTES

I make this so it is halfway between a soup and a pasta dish, but you can add as much or as little broth as you like to make it as soupy or as dry as you like. This is another staple in our house because I have most of the ingredients kicking around. Feel free to use elbow noodles or whatever shape you like.

MAKES 4 LARGE PORTIONS OR 8 FIRST-COURSE SERVINGS

1. Make the soup or sauce: Heat 2 tablespoons oil in a large, heavy saucepan over low heat. Add the ham and cook, stirring occasionally, until the ham starts to color and is fragrant. Add the sofrito and cook until most of the liquid has evaporated. Stir in the tomato sauce, broth, oregano, cayenne, and bay leaves. Bring to a boil, then adjust the heat so the liquid is simmering.

2. Cook the shells in a medium pot of boiling salted water until al dente. Add the cooked peas to the sauce.

3. Drain the pasta and empty it into a deep serving bowl. Toss with enough oil to coat lightly. Spoon the sauce over the pasta to coat and cover (it should be brothy). Add salt and pepper to taste. Scatter the cilantro over the top and serve immediately.

2 tablespoons olive oil, plus more for dressing the pasta
1 pound ham, cut into ½-inch dice (see Notes)
1 cup Sofrito (page 6)
One 28-ounce can tomato sauce
2 cups homemade Chicken Broth (page 155) or canned
1 teaspoon dried oregano
½ teaspoon ground cayenne pepper or to taste
2 bay leaves
Fine sea or kosher salt
1 pound small pasta shells
2 cups fresh or frozen peas (see Notes)
Freshly ground pepper to taste
Chopped fresh cilantro

NOTES: *I like to use Serrano ham, but you can use prosciutto or even a cooking ham such as Hatfield. Cooking ham is how I refer to boiled (not smoked) ham, such as the ham steaks you can buy in a supermarket. At a Spanish butcher shop they cut it right off the ham, so it is a little drier than what you get in the supermarket.*

• If you are using shelled fresh peas, cook them in boiling water for 2 minutes and drain them before using.

LENTIL SOUP

SOPA DE LENTEJAS

This is a good place to use leftover baked ham, cut into chunks if there is enough meat left on the bone, or just the bone itself in place of meat. I never throw out ham bones; they're worth their weight in gold in my kitchen. In fact, I think I would throw Jerry out before I threw out a ham bone. (Just kidding, honey!) Use the larger quantity of lentils if you like a thicker soup. (That's what I do.) The smaller amount will give you a brothier soup, which is nice, too.

1. Heat the oil in a large saucepan over medium-high heat. Add the ham and cook 1 or 2 minutes, just until it changes color. (This is not necessary if you're using the ham bone or ham hock.) Add the celery, carrots, onion, and garlic, and cook until the vegetables are softened, about 3 minutes. Stir in the sofrito and cook, stirring, until the liquid from the sofrito has evaporated and the sofrito starts to sizzle.

2. Add the lentils and stir until they're coated with sofrito. Pour in enough broth to cover the lentils by 1 inch. (The amount will vary depending on how many lentils you're using.) Add the bay leaves, bring to a boil, and then adjust the heat so the liquid is simmering. Cook until the lentils are tender, about 45 minutes. Keep an eye on the soup as it cooks. The level of the liquid should stay more or less constant. Add broth (or water if you run out) to keep the level constant.

3. Add a little more broth if you like a brothier soup. Season with salt and pepper. Serve hot, passing the pineapple vinegar separately if you are using it.

⅓ cup olive oil
2 cups diced smoked ham or 2 ham hocks or a ham bone
3 stalks celery, trimmed and chopped
3 medium carrots, peeled and very finely chopped (so they melt into the soup)
1 medium Spanish onion, chopped
3 cloves garlic, chopped
½ cup Sofrito (page 6)
1 to 1½ pounds lentils (2 to 3 cups)
6 to 8 cups (or as needed) Chicken Broth, homemade (page 155) or canned
2 bay leaves
Fine sea or kosher salt to taste
Freshly ground pepper to taste
Spicy Pineapple Vinegar (page 218; optional)

If I ever had to state which one dish says "love" to me, I would have to say fresh chicken soup. It has fared so prominently in my memories that I don't think there is anything else I could cook or eat that would make me feel so safe, cozy, and happy.

I love to entertain, and when I do, it's usually for a large group. My husband, Jerry, and I are both the first of five children, so the house was always bursting at the seams when we had both families over, leaving little room for our friends. This caused me some stress, especially around Christmas time when I literally regress and become a little kid again. I love to decorate the house so it says Christmas everywhere! I have the three wise men prominently featured. *El Dia de Los Tres Reyes*—when the magi arrived with gifts for baby Jesus—is still very important in the Latin community. There are garlands of pine, bunches of mistletoe, and a Christmas village straight out of Dickens set up from one wall to another!

I came up with a way to have all of our family at the house during the holiday season. After discussing it with Jerry, we decided that we would create a new tradition. Since Christmas Eve is very important to the Puerto Rican side of the family, we would celebrate that day in our house with my family. There would be the traditional Puerto Rican Roast Pork Shoulder, Rice with Pigeon Peas, coquito, and pasteles (pages 212, 94, 273, and 146), but I would also make seafood so that the traditions of the Italian contingent were represented as well. Our children experience both sides of their culinary and cultural roots. Okay, that took care of the Martinez side—but what to do about the Lombardo side —who have since become big fans of the Latino kitchen thanks to yours truly?

Jerry, the kids, and I have always made a family day out of driving up to a tree farm in Connecticut and chopping down our tree, after which we always have a little tailgating party in the parking lot complete with "Santa Claus Is Coming to Town" blaring in the CD player, steaming mugs of hot chocolate, and thermoses full of hot soup. Hauling the tree back to Brooklyn, I said, "Why don't we have a tree-trimming party? Everyone can bring an ornament, help decorate the tree, and build Christmas memories with us." Why not, indeed? So a new tradition was born.

What to make? This situation lends itself readily to tapas, but decorating is hard work, so what else? After much thought I decided on soup and a sandwich! I make three huge pots of soup and three different types of sandwiches. (Cuban Sandwiches [page 215] are the most requested!) I usually have a seafood soup, a vegetable soup, and I always serve fresh chicken soup dressed with fresh chopped cilantro and thin fideos (love in a mug). Add to that menu family, friends, and a little coquito—rummed-up Puerto Rican eggnog, my mother-in-law Betty's personal favorite—and we have a wonderful tree-trimming party every year.

CHICKEN SOUP WITH THIN EGG NOODLES

SOPA DE POLLO CON FIDEOS

I always keep canned chicken broth on hand and rely on that most of the time. Having said that, there are a few places where canned broth will not do, and this is one of them. This soup is all about the delicious flavor of homemade broth. The chicken broth is already flavored with cilantro, bell pepper, onion, and garlic. These diced fresh vegetables freshen up the flavor, and the saffron gives a beautiful color and undernote of flavor. Then when you mash the pepper in the bottom of the bowl, it puts the whole thing over the top. You might not feel the magic in the first spoonful, but you will after a few. Pick your pepper according to the heat you like—my weapon of choice is the ultra-spicy habanero—and leave it in there until the spiciness is where you want it to be.

MAKES 8 SERVINGS

1. Heat the broth to a simmer over medium heat. Add the celery, bell pepper, and saffron, and cook until the vegetables are softened and the broth takes on a rich color from the saffron, about 5 minutes. Stir the chicken into the broth.

2. Bring a large pot of salted water to a boil. Stir the noodles into the boiling water. Cook, stirring gently, until the noodles are tender, 5 to 6 minutes.

3. I like to mash half (or less) of a hot chili pepper, such as a Scotch bonnet, at the bottom of each bowl. You can control the heat by the choice of pepper and by removing the seeds and ribs. Divide the noodles among the bowls and ladle the hot soup over the noodles and pepper. Sprinkle some of the chopped cilantro over each.

10 cups Chicken Broth (page 155)
1 celery stalk, cut in half lengthwise and then into ½-inch pieces
1 red bell pepper, cored, seeded, and diced (½ inch)
1 teaspoon saffron threads
1 cup shredded cooked chicken, reserved from making the broth
Salt
1 pound very thin egg noodles, such as Spanish *fideos* or angel-hair pasta
Hot chili peppers such as Scotch bonnets, habaneros, jalapeños, or serranos
Chopped fresh cilantro

PUERTO RICAN WHITE BEAN SOUP

SOPA DE HABICHUELAS BLANCAS

In Puerto Rico this would be made with fresh white beans shelled just before making the soup. This is a big favorite of my mother's and one of the first things she asks for when visiting the island. Once, on a trip to Puerto Rico, my mother, father, brother Pete, and I drove around visiting places even my parents hadn't been to before. The whole time Mami and I sat in the backseat and shelled white beans. We brought them to my aunt's house, which is always filled with people, and made big potfuls of this delicious soup.

White beans in the shell are impossible to find in the States, but this version made with dried white beans is also delicious. One more little change: When my mother makes it in Puerto Rico, she adds a big handful of beans still in the pod. I add a small amount of string beans to approximate the taste and texture of those whole pods. This is one of those recipes that should be made with homemade broth, but if you don't have it, use canned.

MAKES 6 TO 8 MAIN-COURSE SERVINGS

1 pound dried navy beans

1 bay leaf

1 red bell pepper, cored, seeded, and cut into 1-inch dice

3 stalks celery, trimmed and coarsely chopped

8 cups (or more to taste) Chicken Broth, homemade (page 155) or canned

½ cup Sofrito (page 6)

1 pound calabaza or butternut squash (see Notes), rind removed, and flesh cut into 1-inch cubes

1 pound ditalini pasta, thin egg noodles, or macaroni (see Notes)

1 pound string beans, topped and tailed, and cut into 1-inch lengths (about 3 cups)

½ cup (loosely packed) chopped fresh cilantro

1. Cook the beans according to the directions on page 96, seasoning them with the bay leaf. You can cook the beans up to a day before you make the soup. Cover and refrigerate.

2. When the beans are tender, stir in the red pepper and celery. Pour in the broth, raise the heat to high, and bring to a boil. Stir in the sofrito and cook until the vegetables are soft, about 15 minutes. Skim off any foam that rises to the top as the soup cooks.

3. Stir in the squash and cook until tender, about 15 minutes. While the squash is cooking, boil the pasta in a large pot of salted water.

4. Stir the string beans and cilantro into the soup and cook until the string beans are tender, about 10 minutes. Drain the pasta and add to the soup.

DAISY'S PANTRY *Calabaza is a firm-fleshed squash with orangey flesh and a streaky yellow-green rind. You will find them, usually cut into manageable pieces, in Latin markets and in an increasing number of supermarkets. If you cannot find them, pumpkin or butternut squash will work just as well. If you opt for pumpkin, choose a "pie" or "sugar" pumpkin, not the large size that are more suitable for carving than cooking.*

NOTE: *Stir the pasta into the soup only when you plan to serve it. If you are serving only a portion of the soup, cook and stir the appropriate amount of pasta into the soup you are serving and refrigerate or freeze the rest of the soup. If you refrigerate or freeze soup with pasta in it, the pasta will swell and absorb all the liquid.*

VARIATION: *You can add a ham hock to the beans if you like.*

"SPANISH MARIA'S" BEEF AND VEGETABLE SOUP

CALDO GALLEGO

This recipe came to me from Mami's friend Maria, one of the most amazing women I have ever met. (Because there are a number of "Marias" among our family and friends, we distinguish her by calling her Maria la Española or Spanish Maria.) She's from Madrid, stands about five feet tall, and is a spitfire of a woman. There is absolutely nothing that this woman cannot do! Whenever I saw her car parked in front of my house, I knew she was visiting my mother and something was going on inside, though I never knew what. From laying down a tile floor and reupholstering the furniture to sewing new draperies and whipping up traditional Spanish dishes, nothing was out of reach when these two got together!

I loved watching them as they cooked. Maria told me stories about her teenage years in Spain and taught me how to flirt with Spanish guys. Mami would always poke her in the ribs, telling her I had no need for those kinds of lessons, but that never seemed to deter Maria!

Mami and I learned how to make this delicious soup from her saucy friend.

MAKES 8 SERVINGS

1. Place the chuck, bacon, ham hock, and bay leaf in a large (about 8-quart) pot. Add enough broth to cover the meats, bring to a boil over high heat, and adjust the heat so the broth is simmering. Cook until the meats are tender, about 2 hours. Keep an eye on the meats as they cook; they should remain covered with liquid. If not, add broth or water as necessary.

2. While the meats are cooking, clean the chard. Fill the sink with cool water. Trim off any wilted or yellow leaves and trim the stem ends. Cut the leaves and stems into 1-inch pieces. Swish them around in the water and then drain them in a colander.

3. When the chuck starts to get tender—after about 1½ hours— remove the bacon and chuck from the broth. Cut the chuck into 1-inch cubes. Trim as much of the fat as you like (or, if you're like me, trim none at all) and cut the rest of the bacon into pieces about as wide as your pinky. Stir them into the soup and cook until the chuck is tender, about 30 minutes.

4. Stir in the potatoes and cook until almost, tender, about 10 minutes. Stir in the chard leaves and stems and chickpeas. Cook until the chard and potatoes are tender, about 5 minutes. Season with paprika, salt, and pepper, and ladle into warm bowls.

1½ pounds boneless chuck
1 pound slab bacon
1 smoked ham hock or 1 pound andouille or other spicy, garlicky sausage
1 bay leaf
4 quarts (or as needed) Beef Broth (page 233) or three 46-ounce cans reduced-sodium beef broth
1 pound Swiss chard or kale
1 pound small (about 1½ inches) yellow potatoes, cut into quarters
Two 14-ounce cans chickpeas, drained
1 teaspoon Spanish paprika
Fine sea or kosher salt to taste
Freshly ground black pepper to taste

VARIATIONS: *This is my workaday version of caldo gallego, and it is absolutely delicious. If you have the time—and the money, where the Serrano ham is concerned—here are a few things to consider:*

• *Soak 1½ cups of chickpeas in plenty of cold water the night before you make the soup. Drain them and add them at the start of the soup along with the chuck and bacon.*

• *If you can find it, and don't mind paying for it, substitute a chunk of Serrano ham for the slab bacon and carve it up with the other meats.*

• *Homemade beef broth adds richness. If you have some in the freezer, use it here even if only a portion of the stock is homemade.*

• *This is the kind of thing to put up on the stove when you have a little work to do around the house. Once you get everything together in the pot, the soup more or less takes care of itself. You'll have time to get a lot of work done while the meats tenderize in the simmering liquid.*

CUBAN BLACK BEAN SOUP

SOPA DE FRIJOLES NEGROS AL ESTILO CUBANO

I like a little heat in my black bean soup, so I add a tiny piece of Scotch bonnet chili pepper, as I do in the Chicken Soup with Thin Egg Noodles on page 76. If you don't, leave it out. This is such a favorite of mine that a bowl of this and a little crusty bread is a meal. I also think of this as my "ice cream sundae" soup: Fill bowls with the soup and let people top them as they like.

MAKES 6 TO 8 SERVINGS

1. Make the black beans.

2. Stir the chicken broth, sofrito, tomato sauce, alcaparrado, salt, pepper, and chili pepper into the black beans. Bring to a boil over medium-high heat. Skim off any foam that rises to the surface. Continue boiling until the soup is nice and thick and has just enough liquid to cover the beans. Remove the pot from the heat and let it sit for 5 to 10 minutes so the beans soak up a little more of the liquid. Serve hot, ladled into warm bowls, and pass the toppings you have prepared.

Black Beans (page 98)
Two 14½-ounce cans chicken broth
½ cup Sofrito (page 6)
½ cup canned Spanish-style tomato sauce
3 tablespoons alcaparrado or chopped pimiento-stuffed olives (see Daisy's Pantry on page 13)
1 tablespoon fine sea or kosher salt
Healthy dose of freshly ground black pepper
¼ Scotch bonnet or jalapeño pepper (optional)

TOPPINGS (PICK WHICHEVER YOU LIKE)

Cooked white rice
Chopped red or white onion
Chopped cilantro
Sour cream
Olive oil
Spicy Pineapple Vinegar (page 218) (optional)

THICK DUCK STEW

SECO DE PATO

It doesn't get homier than this. It's worth commuting home from work in the middle of a harsh New York City winter when a bowl of this is waiting for you. The duck has a sweetness that you don't find in chicken. You can serve this with anything you like, but my favorite is yucca because you can sop up the sauce with it—and, believe me, you don't want to miss a drop. Serve a nice salad and a piece of melon for dessert, and that'll wrap things up.

MAKES 6 TO 8 SERVINGS

1. Pat the duck pieces dry and toss them with the wet rub in a large bowl until the duck is coated. Cover the bowl (or transfer the duck to a sealable 1-gallon plastic bag) and refrigerate at least 1 hour or up to 1 day.

2. Pour just enough oil into a large skillet, preferably nonstick, to film the bottom. Heat over medium-low heat. Wipe the wet rub from the duck pieces (see Notes). Add as many of the duck pieces, skin side down, as will fit without touching. Cook, turning often, until medium brown on all sides, about 15 minutes. Transfer the duck pieces to a bowl as they are browned.

3. Spoon off all but a tablespoon of the fat from the pan. Stir the onion and garlic into the pan. Stir to remove the little browned bits from the pan. Add the ajíces dulces, if using, chili peppers, and cumin.

4. Strain the tomatoes and reserve the liquid; you may use some of it later. Crush the tomatoes with your hands and add them to the pan. Raise the heat to high and bring to a boil. Stir in the beer, add the bay leaf, and return to a boil. Tuck the duck pieces into the sauce. Cook at a lively boil for 15 minutes, turning the pieces of duck in the sauce from time to time.

5. Adjust the heat so the sauce is simmering. Cover the casserole, leaving the cover a tiny bit ajar, and cook until the duck is tender, about 1 hour.

6. After the duck has been cooking for 45 minutes, cook the yucca according to the directions on page 110.

7. Stir in the string beans and as many of the smaller pieces of yucca as fit without crowding the pot. Cover and cook until the string beans are tender and the duck is very tender, about 15 minutes. Stir in the cilantro. Transfer the remaining yucca to a large serving platter or individual rimmed soup bowls. Spoon some of the duck, sauce, and vegetables over the yucca. Serve hot.

One 5-pound duck, cut into 10 pieces (see page 164)
Wet Rub (page 19), preferably made with Achiote Oil (page 9)
Canola oil
1 large Spanish onion, cut into fine dice
4 cloves garlic
4 ajíces dulces (see Daisy's Pantry on page 6; if you cannot find ajíces dulces, increase the amount of cilantro to ¾ cup)
2 fresh cayenne chili peppers or chili peppers of your choice
1 teaspoon ground cumin
One 28-ounce can whole tomatoes in liquid
1 cup amber beer
1 bay leaf
3 pounds yucca (see Variation)
½ pound string beans, topped and tailed, cut into 1½-inch lengths (about 1½ cups)
¼ cup coarsely chopped fresh cilantro

VARIATION: *In Peru they add a handful of asparagus tips to a seco. Chileans and Ecuadorians add green peas along with corn on the cob, cut into neat circles.*

This version of duck seco calls for yucca, but you can use potatoes or cooked white rice, either stirred into the seco at the end or served on the side. Or, in a completely nontraditional move, boil up a chunky pasta shape, drain it, and put it onto a platter. Spoon the duck, vegetables, and sauce over it.

NOTES: *The duck will have a tendency to burn if you're not careful. Keep the heat moderate and turn the duck often.*

• Cilantro added at the end keeps its bright green color and adds a note of real freshness.

These next few recipes are soup, but they can easily be meals.

SEAFOOD STEW

SANCOCHO DE PESCADO

This is an all-seafood version of the meatier *sancocho* on page 84. My father loves this dish, and so do I. The salty-sweetness of the fish works really well with the earthiness of the root vegetables. The practice of cooking with coconut milk traveled from Africa to the Caribbean and South America, where it is still alive and well. Here is an interesting thing: Back in the day, my grandmother (who made her own coconut milk from grated coconut and coconut water) used coconut milk as an economical alternative to broth in rice dishes. Now her granddaughter, who uses coconut milk from a can, likes it for its unmistakable flavor and richness.

MAKES 6 TO 8 SERVINGS

1. Wrap the achiote seeds in a 4-inch square of cheesecloth. Tie securely with a length of kitchen twine.

2. Heat the olive oil in a large Dutch oven over medium heat. Add the sofrito and cook until the water has evaporated and the sofrito begins to sizzle. Add the cumin and bay leaves, and cook for 1 to 2 minutes. Pour in the clam broth, add the packet of achiote seeds, and bring the broth to a boil. Adjust the heat so the broth is simmering and cook until the broth has a rich yellow-orange color, about 15 minutes. Skim off any foam that rises to the surface while the broth cooks.

3. Take a look at the monkfish. It may be covered with a thin silvery red membrane. Working with the tip of a paring knife, cut away as much of it as you can. Cut the fillets into 1½-inch lengths. Cut the halibut into similar size pieces.

4. Season the fillets with salt and pepper. Dredge them in flour to coat all sides, then tap off any excess. Pour enough canola oil into a heavy, large skillet to fill about ½ inch. Heat over medium-high heat until the tip of the handle of a wooden spoon gives off a lively sizzle. Slip as many of the coated fish fillet pieces into the oil as will fit without touching. Fry, turning once, until golden brown on both sides. Drain on a baking sheet lined with paper towels.

5. Add the taro, ñame, and yucca to the broth. Cook until tender, about 30 minutes.

6. Stir in the fish and coconut milk. Cook gently just until the fish is heated through. Taste the broth and add salt and pepper to taste.

1 tablespoon achiote (annatto) seeds
3 tablespoons olive oil
½ cup Sofrito (page 6)
1 teaspoon ground cumin
2 bay leaves
9 cups bottled or canned clam broth
1½ pounds monkfish fillets
1½ pounds halibut fillets
Fine sea or kosher salt
Freshly ground black pepper
All-purpose flour
Canola oil
1¼ pounds taro root (*yautia*; see page 110) or Yukon Gold potatoes
2 pounds ñame (see page 110) or acorn or butternut squash, peeled
1 pound fresh yucca, peeled, or defrosted frozen yucca
One 13-ounce can coconut milk

VARIATIONS: *Any thick, firm-fleshed white fish, such as shark and swordfish, will work here. It's nice to mix at least two types, but if the best you can do is one, then that'll do.*

• If you want a real upscale version, buy a boiled lobster (or boil one yourself), remove it from the shell, and cut it into bite-size pieces. Stir the pieces into the soup just before serving.

• Aside from yucca, yautia and ñame are my two favorite viandas *(root vegetables), which is why I'm using them here. You can use hard squash, yucca, and your favorite type of potato in place of any of the vegetables you cannot find.*

BEEF AND **ROOT VEGETABLE STEW**

SANCOCHO

This is my dream version of a traditional South American stew. (This dish is familiar to the Caribbean as well.) It's a dish that is as beautiful to look at as it is good to eat. I know that many people are not fans of tripe, and that the root vegetables listed in the ingredients may be tough for some people to find, so I listed several suggestions below. As always, it is the spirit of a dish I want you to enjoy, and no matter how you configure this one, enjoy it you will.

MAKES 8 LARGE SERVINGS

1. Place the tripe in a large bowl and pour enough cold water over it to cover completely. Pour in the vinegar and squeeze in the juice from the lemon. Refrigerate for at least 30 minutes or up to overnight.

2. Rinse the calves' feet under cold running water and put them in a large stockpot. Add the onions, garlic, bay leaves, and achiote sachet. Pour in enough cold water to cover, then bring to a boil over medium-high heat.

3. Rinse the tripe and cut it into pieces 1 inch by 2 inches or in narrow strips if you prefer. Add to the calves' feet with additional water to cover if necessary. Bring to a boil. Adjust the heat to a gentle boil and cook for 1 hour, skimming off any foam that rises to the top.

4. After 1 hour, remove the achiote sachet. Add the beef chuck, sofrito, culantro, and *ajices dulces* to the pot. Add salt to taste and cook for 45 minutes.

5. If you haven't already done so, peel and cut the ñame, yucca, and yautia. Add them to the pot. Cook until they are tender, 15 to 20 minutes.

6. Taste and add salt and pepper to taste. Serve in wide, shallow soup bowls sprinkled with cilantro.

1½ pounds honeycomb tripe (see Notes)
½ cup white vinegar
1 lemon
1½ pounds calves' feet, split (see Note)
2 large Spanish onions
2 whole heads of garlic
2 bay leaves
1 teaspoon achiote (annatto) seeds (in a cheesecloth sachet; see Seafood Stew, page 83)
One 1-pound piece of beef chuck (cut into 1 × 2 × ½ inches)
1 cup Sofrito (page 6)
4 culantro leaves (see Note on page 6) or ½ cup chopped fresh cilantro
5 *ajices dulces* (see Note on page 6) or 1 medium cubanelle pepper, quartered
Fine sea or kosher salt
1 pound ñame (see page 110) or purple potatoes, peeled, quartered lengthwise, and cut into 1-inch pieces
1 pound yucca or Yukon Gold potatoes, peeled, halved lengthwise, and cut into 1-inch lengths
1 pound yautia or new potatoes, peeled, halved lengthwise, and cut into 1-inch lengths
Freshly ground pepper
Chopped fresh cilantro

NOTES: *Sancocho is always better the next day. This is enough for 8 servings, with enough for a lucky somebody to have leftovers for lunch the next day!*

• *If you don't care for tripe, omit it and increase the beef by 1½ pounds.*

• *Here are three vegetables you can use if you are having trouble finding the root vegetables listed: Yukon Gold potatoes, orange sweet potatoes, and butternut squash. Substitute a pound of one of them for whatever it is you can't find. Even if you substitute these three ingredients for those called for in the recipe, your sancocho will still be delicious.*

NOTE: *Veal trotters, also known as calves' feet, add flavor and texture to soups and broths. If you can find them, ask your butcher to split them; if you can't, make this dish anyway.*

"SOUPY RICE" WITH CHICKEN

ASOPAO DE POLLO

This isn't really a rice dish or a soup; it's sort of halfway between. In South America, dishes such as this are called *secos*, meaning dry, a reference to the fact that they are a rather dry soup. Brothy soups are referred to as *aguado*, or "watered." My mother makes this with an old hen, which she insists tastes better. (My father teases her that she says that only because she's no spring chicken herself anymore.) You can make this as thick or as thin as you like simply by cooking it less or more. I love it the next day, too, when almost all the liquid has been absorbed by the rice.

MAKES 6 SERVINGS

1. Heat the oil in a 5- or 6-quart Dutch oven or heavy pot over medium-high heat. Add the chicken pieces, skin side down, and cook, turning as necessary, until well browned on all sides, about 10 minutes. Remove to a plate.

2. Stir the sofrito, alcaparrado, and cumin into the oil. Cook until the liquid has evaporated and the sofrito starts to sizzle. Add half of the can of broth and the bay leaves, and bring to a boil. Return the chicken to the pot, add salt if necessary, and stir in the rice. Bring to a boil, give it a big stir so the rice doesn't stick to the bottom, and lower the heat. Partially cover the pan and cook until the rice is very tender and the chicken is cooked through, 30 to 40 minutes. Check the liquid from time to time, adding broth as necessary to keep the mixture creamy.

3. Ladle into warm bowls and serve.

¼ cup Achiote Oil (page 9)
6 to 7 chicken legs, cut in half at the joint, or 4 pounds drumsticks and/or thighs
1 cup Sofrito (page 6)
½ cup alcaparrado or coarsely chopped pimiento-stuffed olives (see Note on page 13)
2 teaspoons ground cumin
One 46-ounce can chicken broth
2 bay leaves
Fine sea or kosher salt (optional)
2 cups long-grain rice

VARIATIONS: *When my mother makes this version, she adds a little heat in the form of chopped hot peppers. She also serves it with chilled sliced avocado—a match made in Puerto Rican heaven.*

• You may substitute an equal amount of duck or turkey pieces for the chicken.

• There is also a world of seafood asopaos, *including those made with assorted shellfish, shrimp, salt cod, or lobster. To make any of these, prepare the rice as described above without the chicken. Stir the seafood into the rice shortly before it is finished.*

ECUADORIAN FISH AND PEANUT STEW

BICHE DE PESCADO

Similar to the Seafood Stew on page 83, this is peasant food, made with whatever fish are brought home or found in the market. (It is also related in its roots, too: Cooking with peanuts traveled to the New World from Africa.) In that spirit, make it with whatever kind of fish you like. I like to start with a pound of firm white fish and then dress it up with a little of this and a little of that—such as a handful of shiny black mussels, a dozen shrimp, and some bay scallops. I love this with corn bread, which I make from the recipe on the bag of cornmeal and add a few extra pinches of sugar.

This is a great dish for a party because the soup base tastes better when it's made a few hours or even a day in advance. Fry the fish up to an hour or two before and add it to the hot soup at the last minute with the rest of the seafood.

What you're doing here is making a finely chopped version of sofrito instead of the pureed version on page 6. It adds the same fresh flavor to foods as the sofrito you make in a blender, but it also adds texture to the finished dish.

MAKES 6 TO 8 SERVINGS

1. Cut the fish fillets into pieces about 1½ inches in length. (If you're using monkfish as one of your choices, see Notes for trimming and cutting directions.) Season them with salt and pepper. Spread the flour out on a plate and dredge the seasoned fish in it, then shake off the excess flour.

2. Pour enough vegetable oil into a large skillet to fill it ½ inch. Heat over medium heat until the tip of the handle of a wooden spoon gives off a lively sizzle when dipped into the oil. Add as many pieces of the fish as fit without touching. Cook, turning once, until golden brown on both sides, about 10 minutes. Remove to a plate lined with paper towels. (If you choose to add shellfish, it's not necessary to brown them first.)

3. Heat the olive oil in a heavy 5- to 6-quart pot over medium heat. Add the onion, pepper, leek, cilantro, ajices dulces, garlic, and cumin. Cook until the garlic is fragrant and the vegetables are wilted, about 4 minutes. Stir in the alcaparrado.

4. While the sofrito is cooking, blend the peanuts and milk at low speed until smooth.

5. Pour the clam broth and water into the pot and bring to a boil. Skim off any foam and fat that rises to the surface.

1 pound firm white fish fillets, either one kind or a mix such as halibut, sea bass, monkfish, or swordfish

Fine sea or kosher salt

Freshly ground black pepper

All-purpose flour

Vegetable oil

1 tablespoon olive oil

1 large Spanish onion, diced (about 2 cups)

1 red bell pepper, cored, seeded, and finely diced (about 1 ½ cups)

1 leek, white and light green part only, cleaned (see box opposite) and finely chopped

½ cup chopped fresh cilantro

2 ajices dulces, finely chopped (see page 6; also see Notes)

4 cloves garlic, chopped

1 teaspoon ground cumin

¼ cup alcaparrado or coarsely chopped pimiento-stuffed olives (see Note on page 13)

1 cup salted or unsalted peanuts (see Notes)

¾ cup milk

4 cups bottled clam broth

2 cups water

1 yucca (about 12 ounces)

2 green plantains, peeled (see page 113) and cut into 1½-inch lengths

12 ounces calabaza or butternut squash, peeled (see page 78), seeded, and cut into 1½- to 2-inch pieces

2 ears corn, shucked and cut crosswise into 1½-inch rounds

Various shellfish (optional; see Note)

6. Peel the yucca and cut it in half crosswise. Cut the thicker end into quarters lengthwise and the thinner end in half lengthwise. Cut all the yucca pieces crosswise into 1-inch pieces. Add the yucca, green plantains, and calabaza to the broth. Cook, partially uncovered, until the vegetables are tender, about 20 minutes.

7. Stir the corn into the soup and then add the peanut mixture. When the broth returns to a simmer, stir in the fish. (If you're adding shellfish, do so now.) Cook until the fish is heated through and the corn is tender, about 4 minutes.

8. Ladle the soup into warm bowls and serve immediately.

NOTES: *If you don't have ajices, use a few tablespoons of finely chopped cubanelle pepper.*

• You can use peanut butter (start with about ⅓ cup) in place of the peanuts. Stir into the soup at the point you would add the peanut-milk mixture. Don't salt the stew until after you add the peanut butter.

• Feel free to experiment with your choice of shellfish. I love to use mussels and shrimp because, in addition to flavor, they add gorgeous color and contrast to the stew. Substitute clams and/or scallops or even lobster if you like.

• Monkfish tails are coated with a thin silvery membrane. Cut along both sides of the bone to remove the fillets. With a thin sharp knife remove the membrane from the surface of the fillets. Cut the trimmed fillets into ½-inch slices.

TO CLEAN LEEKS

Cut off the root end and the dark green tops, leaving only the white and yellow/light green parts. Split the leek lengthwise and rinse under cool water, separating the layers to be sure you remove all the dirt from between them. Shake the leek dry and cut as directed.

RICE AND BEANS

ARROZ Y FRIJOLES

I can't talk about beans without talking about rice, and vice versa. In my house, whether it's family or friends at the table, rice and beans are usually eaten together and very often cooked together. They are for me the highlight of a meal, but for many of my friends they remain off limits. Rice is tricky to cook, they say, and beans, between the soaking and the cooking, are a pain in the neck. Very often I have to tell them they've been going at it all wrong. Nothing makes me happier than when friends come back to me after their first batch of rice or beans done "à la Daisy" and tell me how easy it was and how delicious it tasted.

Rice, for me and many Latinos, is really the centerpiece of a meal, outranking whatever meat, fish, or poultry is served. One of the recipes that is a staple at my table and at my parties is the Yellow Rice on page 13. It is the recipe that friends request most from me and the one I find easiest to make. If you're rice-averse, start with the Basic White Rice that follows, which is a simple introduction and a real eye-opener. The technique may look a little odd, cooking the rice in oil first and eyeballing the amount of water, but it works every time.

Beans, contrary to popular opinion, are a rather forgiving group. I approach their cooking differently from most cooks and friends I know. With the exception of chickpeas (garbanzos), I don't soak beans—ever. I just plunk them in a pot with some water and add whatever seasonings I like, usually bay leaves and a ham hock, but no salt. When they come to a boil, I skim them and check on them from time to time to make sure there is enough water to cover them. That's it. Once done, beans can be pushed to the back of the stove for a few hours and reheated when needed.

Rice and beans make great party food. People love them individually or together, and they are cheap, colorful, nutritional, and easy to make in large quantities—all the things I love in a party dish.

One more note: You can use brown rice in any of these dishes. Follow the same directions and double the cooking time.

MAKING RICE

I use long-grain rice (such as the Carolina brand). Short-grain rice has a different taste and texture; it is chewier. Some people rinse their rice one or more times before cooking it. I never do, and it seems to come out just fine. Storing rice is never an issue in our house; we go through it so fast that it is not a problem. If you are keeping it, make sure it is in a cool place in a tightly covered container.

If you look at these recipes, you'll see different seasonings but always the same techniques. Here they are in brief:

- Cook the rice in oil over fairly high heat, with or without seasonings, until the rice turns chalky.
- Pour in enough water or liquid to cover the rice by the width of two fingers — about 1 inch. I have never used the "two parts liquid to one part rice" rule, and until I wrote this book, I never thought about it at all. When I started measuring things in the process of writing this book, it turned out that I use a good deal less water than two times the amount of rice. I put quantities of water or broth in the recipes as a guideline only; the amount of liquid you add will actually depend on the size and shape of your pot. My favorite rice pot holds 6 quarts and measures about 10 inches wide by 4 inches high. Yours can be any size, but it should hold the finished rice comfortably and should be wider than it is tall.
- Bring the liquid to a boil and boil until the level of liquid meets the top of the rice.
- Give the rice a big stir, turn the heat to low, and cover the pot.
- Set the timer to 20 minutes and walk away. Do not uncover, think about, or, most definitely, stir the rice.
- Uncover and fluff. You can leave the rice covered in a heavy pot, and it will stay hot and in good shape for about an hour.
- To reheat rice that has been refrigerated, I prefer the microwave. Put the rice in a bowl, sprinkle a little water on top, cover the bowl with plastic, and cook until hot. You may also reheat rice in a skillet with a tight-fitting lid. Add a few tablespoons of liquid and cook over very low heat until hot.

BASIC WHITE RICE

ARROZ BLANCO

When I was young, I always took "plain" white rice for granted because we ate it so often. But when I was a teenager and ate at friends' houses, I realized how awful rice can be if you don't treat it right. There is nothing easier (see Making Rice, opposite) and in some ways more satisfying than good white rice. Trust me on this one.

MAKES 8 SERVINGS

½ cup canola oil
4 cups long-grain white rice
3 tablespoons salt
Water or broth to cover the rice (about 5 cups)

1. Heat the oil in a Dutch oven, or a smaller vessel with a heavy bottom, over medium-high heat. Add the rice and salt, stirring to coat the rice with oil. When the rice starts to appear opaque and chalky, add enough cold water to cover it by the width of two fingers, about 1 inch. Bring to a rapid boil and boil—without stirring!—until the water level reaches the level of the rice.

2. Stir the rice once and reduce the heat to low. Cover the pot and cook until the rice is tender and all the liquid has been absorbed, about 20 minutes. Stir the rice gently from the bottom to the top to fluff it and serve. Perfect rice!

THE EXTENDED FAMILY OF
YELLOW RICE DISHES

I love yellow rice so much that I included it as one of my "Top Ten Hits" (see page 13). Once you have that incredibly simple technique mastered, there are a thousand things you can add. Here are five of them.

YELLOW RICE WITH CORN

ARROZ CON MAIZ

Follow the recipe for Yellow Rice (page 13), adding 2 cups of corn kernels to the sofrito mixture.

YELLOW RICE WITH CRAB AND COCONUT

ARROZ CON CANGREJO Y COCO

Follow the recipe for Yellow Rice (page 13), substituting coconut milk for the broth. Add 1 pound of lump crabmeat (picked over for bits of shell and cartilage) to the rice after the rice has been stirred into the oil.

YELLOW RICE WITH SHRIMP

ARROZ CON CAMARONES

Add 1½ pounds of large shrimp that have been peeled and deveined to Yellow Rice (page 13) along with the sofrito mixture. Proceed with the basic recipe, substituting bottled clam broth for the water.

YELLOW RICE WITH SALT COD

ARROZ CON BACALAO

Soak, cook, and shred 2 pounds of salt cod (see page 188). Add the salt cod to Yellow Rice (page 13) along with the alcaparrado.

RICE AND RED BEANS

ARROZ JUNTO

1. Place the beans, ham hock, and bay leaves in a 3-quart saucepan. Pour in enough water to cover the beans by 2 inches. Bring to a boil. Skim off the foam that rises to the surface and then adjust the heat so that the liquid is simmering. Cook the beans until tender, adding water as necessary to keep the beans submerged as they cook, about 2 hours. Add less water during the last half hour or so of cooking. The idea is to end up with tender beans and just enough liquid to cover them. See Beans on page 96 for more pointers on cooking them.

2. Heat the oil in a 5-quart pot over medium heat. Stir in the sofrito and cook until the liquid has evaporated and the sofrito begins to sizzle. Stir in the alcaparrado and cumin. Add the rice, salt, and pepper and stir until the rice is coated with oil and seasonings and turns chalky.

3. Drain the beans, saving ½ cup of liquid if you like. Stir the beans and culantro into the rice and then pour in the reserved cooking liquid, if using, and enough chicken broth to cover by the width of two fingers. Bring to a boil over high heat and boil without stirring until the level of the liquid reaches the rice. Give the rice a big stir, turn the heat to very low, and cover the pot. Cook until the liquid has been absorbed, about 20 minutes.

4. Uncover the pot, give the rice a big stir, bringing the rice on the bottom to the top, and serve.

One 16-ounce bag red kidney beans
1 smoked ham hock
2 bay leaves
6 cups water
¼ cup vegetable oil
1 cup Sofrito (page 6)
¼ cup alcaparrado or coarsely chopped pimiento-stuffed olives (page 13)
1 teaspoon ground cumin
4 cups long-grain rice
2 tablespoons fine sea or kosher salt
Freshly ground pepper to taste
Chicken Broth, homemade (page 155) or store-bought, as needed (5 to 6 cups)
4 culantro leaves (see Note on page 6) or ½ cup chopped fresh cilantro

RICE WITH PIGEON PEAS

ARROZ CON GANDULES

There is never a holiday or celebration with my family or friends without rice and pigeon peas. Lee, the nice Jewish boy from across the street, asks me for this all the time. This is a traditional holiday dish, so this recipe is for a large batch. Feel free to cut it in half for everyday use.

If you can't find smoked pork neck bones, a ham hock works fine—even better if you can get your butcher to split it.

The banana leaf lends the rice a wonderful flavor and perfume, but please don't pass this up if you can't find banana leaf. It is wonderful either way.

MAKES 10 TO 15 SERVINGS AS A SIDE DISH

1. Heat the oil in a heavy 5-quart pot or Dutch oven over high heat until rippling. Stir in the sofrito, alcaparrado, salt, pepper, and cumin. Cook until the sofrito stops boiling and starts to sizzle, about 5 minutes.

2. Add the pork bones and stir until they are coated with oil. Stir in the rice until everything is mixed together and the rice is coated with oil. Stir in the pigeon peas and enough broth and/or water to cover the rice by the width of two fingers. Top with the banana leaf, folding it up as necessary to fit over the rice. Bring to a boil and boil without stirring until the level of liquid meets the rice. Remove the banana leaf, give the rice a big stir, and put the leaf back on top. Reduce the heat to low, cover the pot, and cook until the water has been absorbed and the rice is tender, about 20 minutes.

3. Remove the banana leaf, give the rice a big stir, and fluff it with a fork. Serve hot.

DAISY'S PANTRY *Banana leaves and/or plantain leaves are large, pliable, dark green leaves that are used quite a bit in Latin American cooking. In Rice with Pigeon Peas they lend the rice a subtle flavor. In Sole Baked in a Banana Leaf on page 198 they lend flavor and protect the delicate fish from overcooking if grilled. They are available, usually frozen in 1-pound packages, in Latin markets and in some specialty stores. Also see Sources.*

½ cup Achiote Oil (page 9)

1 cup Sofrito (page 6)

3 tablespoons alcaparrado or coarsely chopped pimiento-stuffed olives (see Daisy's Pantry on page 13)

3 tablespoons fine sea or kosher salt

1 tablespoon cracked black pepper

2 teaspoons ground cumin

1½ pounds smoked pork neck bones or smoked turkey wings, or 1 smoked ham hock

6 cups long-grain rice

One 13-ounce bag frozen pigeon peas or one 15-ounce can pigeon peas, drained

Beef Broth, homemade (page 233) or store-bought and/or water as needed (about 8 cups)

1 banana leaf (optional)

RICE WITH SPANISH SAUSAGES

ARROZ CON CHORIZO

Fabulous and simple as this is, it never fails to bring the house down. Rice has such a mellow flavor that it can frame whatever goes in it. In this case the paprika and garlic from the chorizo perfume the rice. Rice in our house is always a side or accompaniment, but this dish is so satisfying that it can be a meal for me.

MAKES 10 REGULAR OR 8 DAISY SERVINGS

1. Place the chorizo in a cold 4- to 5-quart heavy pot and set the pot over medium heat. When the chorizo has rendered some of its fat and is sizzling, stir in the sofrito. Cook until the water has evaporated and the sofrito begins to sizzle.

2. Stir in the alcaparrado, cumin, and salt. Cook 1 or 2 minutes, then stir in the rice. When the rice is chalky, pour in enough broth to cover by the width of two fingers. Bring to a boil and cook until the level of liquid meets the rice. Add the culantro leaves and give the rice a big stir. Reduce the heat to low and cover the pot.

3. Cook until the liquid has been absorbed and the rice is tender, about 20 minutes. Stir the rice and serve.

1 pound chorizo, andouille, or any smoked garlicky sausage, cut in half lengthwise and then crosswise into ¼-inch slices

½ cup Sofrito (page 6)

¼ cup alcaparrado or coarsely chopped pimiento-stuffed olives (see Daisy's Pantry on page 13)

1 teaspoon ground cumin

2 tablespoons fine sea or kosher salt

4 cups long-grain rice

Chicken broth, homemade (page 155) or store-bought, as needed (about 5½ cups)

4 fresh culantro leaves (see Daisy's Pantry on page 6) or ¼ cup finely chopped fresh cilantro

Piece of banana leaf (optional)

BEANS

When I was a little girl, you couldn't get me to look at a bean. Now I like beans so much that a bowl of them can be a dinner for me—alone or with a chunk of bread or some leftover chicken shredded into them.

Let's face it, beans are cool. You can keep them in the cabinet until you need them, and while they may not be ready in five minutes, you can put up a big pot of them with hardly any fuss.

Everybody and their mother talks about soaking beans. If that is how you're used to cooking them, then keep on going. I rarely know what I'm having for dinner the next day, so I can't get the soaking thing together. I take beans right out of the bag, place them in a potful of cold water, and cook them straight through. What I'm left with is whole, evenly cooked beans that are done in 2 hours, give or take 10 minutes.

Here's how to do it:
Rinse the beans in a colander under cold running water. Remove anything that isn't a bean. Pour the beans into a roomy, heavy pot (I use a 6-quart enameled cast-iron pot most of the time). Pour in 6 cups of water or enough to cover them by 2 inches. Don't add salt at this point. Toss in a couple of bay leaves and a ham hock or a couple of smoked turkey wings, a half-pound of ham steak cut into cubes, or diced salchichon (Dominican pepperoni) if you like. Bring the water to a boil, then adjust the heat so there is a happy bubble, not a full boil. Start skimming off the foam that rises to the top. The beans will take about 2 hours to cook. During the first 1½ hours, keep half an eye on them. They should be covered by about 1 inch of water as they cook; add more water to keep them covered if necessary. At that point the beans are almost tender. Lower the heat to a simmer. You can start to season them with ½ cup Sofrito (page 6), if you like, canned Spanish-style tomato sauce, alcaparrado, and salt and pepper. You can also add (as I do) a peeled potato cut into 1-inch pieces. Keep cooking until the beans are tender, adding less and less liquid; when there is barely enough liquid, it is like a nice, thick gravy covering the beans. You can leave the beans on the stove for a few hours and reheat them gently when it is time for dinner.

Canned beans: In my experience, especially with four kids, you have to be prepared for any eventuality, so I always keep canned beans in the pantry. Don't beat yourself up too bad for using canned beans because you can really doctor them up, especially if you have some sofrito on hand. But please remember to drain and rinse them before cooking with them.

PINK BEANS WITH HAM

HABICHUELAS ROSADAS CON JAMÓN

Put a plate of this in front of my friend Miguelina and stand back. She loves it, and you will, too. Cooking dried beans is practically part of my daily routine, but if I ever get caught short, I have emergency canned beans on the shelf. I've used canned pink beans in this recipe with wonderful results.

MAKES 6 TO 8 SERVINGS

1. Place the beans and bay leaves in a medium saucepan and add enough water to cover them by 2 inches. Bring the water to a boil, then adjust the heat so it is boiling gently. Cook the beans until near tender, about 1½ hours. Keep an eye on the beans; they should always be covered by liquid. When the liquid meets the level of the beans, add cold water to cover by 1 inch or so.

2. Add the broth, recaito, alcaparrado, tomato sauce, potato, ham, and salt and pepper. Continue cooking until the beans and potato are tender, about 30 minutes.

1 pound pink beans
2 bay leaves
One 14½-ounce can chicken or vegetable broth
½ cup Recaito (page 99)
½ cup alcaparrado or coarsely chopped pimiento-stuffed olives (see Daisy's Pantry, page 13)
½ cup canned Spanish-style tomato sauce
1 russet potato, peeled and cut into 1-inch pieces
½ pound cooking ham (see Note on page 73), cut into ½-inch cubes (about 1½ cups)
Fine sea or kosher salt to taste
Freshly ground black pepper to taste

NOTE: *You can make a quick version of this dish using canned beans. Drain and rinse three 15-ounce cans of pink beans. Combine all ingredients in a pot and bring to a boil. Adjust the heat so the liquid is simmering and cook until the potato is tender, about 20 minutes.*

BLACK BEANS

FRIJOLES NEGROS

From this simple recipe come a lot of dishes that are in heavy rotation in our house. It is the base for Cuban Black Bean Soup (page 81) and the "Moors and Christians" on page 102.

Most people soak their beans before cooking them—my mother always got it together to soak hers the night before—but I don't. It takes longer to cook them, but they are still delicious. If you want to soak your beans before cooking them, go ahead.

1 pound black beans
1 smoked ham hock
2 bay leaves

MAKES ABOUT 4 CUPS

1. Place the beans and ham hock in a medium saucepan and pour in enough water to cover them by 2 inches. Toss in the bay leaves and bring the water to a boil, then adjust the heat so the water is boiling gently. Cook the beans, skimming off any foam that rises to the top, until tender, about 2 hours. Keep an eye on the beans; they should always be covered by liquid. When the liquid meets the level of the beans, add ½ inch or so of cold water.

2. Toward the end of cooking, ease up on the liquid you add. The goal is to have the beans barely covered with liquid by the time they are tender.

RECAITO

There really is no translation for this mixture of onion, garlic, peppers, and green herbs. *Recao* is culantro (see below) in Puerto Rican–speak, so this seasoning is nicknamed *recaito*, or "little culantro." I use recaito for such dishes as Cuban black beans and Puerto Rican Pot Roast (page 232), where you don't want the color or extra liquid that you have in Sofrito (page 6). Culantro is the defining flavor.

Recaito, like sofrito, can get you out of any kitchen emergency. It pays to make extra (which this recipe does) and portion it out for the freezer.

MAKES ABOUT 1½ CUPS

Place the onion and garlic in the work bowl of a food processor fitted with the metal blade. With the motor running, add the remaining ingredients, one at a time, and process until the mixture is smooth. Set aside the amount you need for the recipe you're preparing. Pack the remaining recaito in ½-cup portions in sealable plastic bags and store in the freezer.

1 medium Spanish onion, cut into big chunks

8 cloves garlic, peeled

6 *ajices dulces* (see page 6) or 1 cubanelle pepper, cored, seeded, and cut into chunks

4 leaves culantro (see Note)

6 big sprigs cilantro, stems and all, coarsely chopped (about 1 cup packed)

NOTE: *If you can't find culantro, increase the amount of ajices dulces or cilantro by half.*

"BLOND MORO"
(RICE COOKED WITH WHITE BEANS)

MORO RUBIO

"Moro" is the nickname given to beans cooked together with rice. I often cook rice and white beans together, hence the nickname "blond moro."

MAKES 6 TO 8 SERVINGS

1. Heat the oil in a heavy 4- to 5-quart pot over medium heat. Add the sofrito and alcaparrado, and cook, stirring, until the water has evaporated from the sofrito and it begins to sizzle. Stir in the salt, cumin, pepper, and bay leaves.

2. Add the beans to the pot and stir gently to color the beans. Add the rice and stir to fix the color to the rice.

3. Pour in enough broth to cover the rice by width of two fingers. Bring to a boil and cook without stirring until the level of the broth reaches the level of the rice. Give the rice one big stir, reduce the heat to low, and cover. Cook over low heat until the water has been absorbed and the rice is tender, about 20 minutes. Fluff with a fork.

½ cup Achiote Oil (page 9)
1 cup Sofrito (page 6)
½ cup alcaparrado or coarsely chopped pimiento-stuffed olives (see Daisy's Pantry on page 13)
2 tablespoons fine sea or kosher salt
1 teaspoon ground cumin
1 teaspoon freshly ground pepper
2 bay leaves
One 15½-ounce can white beans, such as cannellini, drained and rinsed
4 cups long-grain rice
Chicken Broth, homemade (page 155) or canned, as needed (about 5 cups)

WHITE BEANS WITH CALABAZA

When I whip up a batch of Chicken with Rice (page 105), these are the beans I like to serve alongside. But then my girlfriend Rosanne, a Sicilian's Sicilian, turned me on to *pasta e fagioli* (known as "pasta fazool" in my neck of the woods), and a light went off in my head. Why couldn't I add a little pasta to my favorite bean dish? If I don't get around to the chicken part of dinner, I boil up short macaroni such as ditalini, stir it into the beans right at the end, and serve the whole thing with a little salad. That's dinner.

MAKES 6 TO 8 SERVINGS

1. Rinse the beans and place them in a pot with the ham hock and bay leaves. Add enough water to cover by 2 inches. Bring to a boil, then adjust the heat so the liquid is at a soft bubble, not a furious boil. Cook for 90 minutes, adding more water as necessary to keep the beans submerged.

2. After 90 minutes, add the sofrito, cumin, and cinnamon. Continue cooking, adding broth to keep the beans submerged, partially covered, for 15 minutes.

3. Add the cubed squash and enough broth to cover. Continue simmering until the beans and squash are tender, 30 to 45 minutes. Once the squash is tender enough, mash a few of the pieces into the beans with the back of a spoon to thicken the beans.

4. Taste and add salt and pepper if necessary. Serve with white or yellow rice if you like.

One 16-ounce bag small white navy beans
1 smoked ham hock
2 bay leaves
½ cup Sofrito (page 6)
1 teaspoon ground cumin
Pinch of ground cinnamon
Chicken Broth, homemade (page 155) or canned, or canned vegetable stock as needed (about 3 cups)
¾ pound *calabaza* (see Daisy's Pantry on page 78), acorn squash, or butternut squash, peeled and cut into 1-inch cubes
Fine sea or kosher salt to taste
Freshly ground pepper to taste

"MOORS AND CHRISTIANS"

MOROS Y CRISTIANOS

The Moors had a tremendous influence on the architecture, the language, and certainly the food of Spain and therefore the rest of the Spanish-speaking world. There is no politically correct way to get around this classical Spanish dish of black beans and white rice. It is a direct reference to the blending of cultures during the Moorish occupation of Spain. In this dish the black beans and white rice are cooked separately and then served side by side. See the box on Moro, below, for more info on mixing beans and rice.

MAKES 8 GENEROUS SERVINGS

Black Beans (page 98)
Basic White Rice (page 91)
½ cup Recaito (page 99)
1 tablespoon fine sea or kosher salt
Freshly ground black pepper
3 tablespoons alcaparrado or coarsely chopped pimiento-stuffed olives (see Daisy's Pantry on page 13)
½ teaspoon ground cumin
2 to 3 leaves culantro (optional)

1. Prepare the black beans.

2. When the beans are done, start the rice.

3. After covering the rice, stir the recaito, salt, a healthy amount of pepper, the alcaparrado, cumin, and culantro, if using, into the beans. Bring to a simmer and simmer until the rice is finished.

4. Serve the rice and beans side by side on a large, deep serving platter. Or, if you like, gently tamp the finished rice into a 10-inch bundt pan and invert it onto a large serving platter. Fill the center with the black beans and either spoon the remaining beans around the edges of the bottom of the rice ring or pass them separately.

MINGLING RICE AND BEANS (MOROS):

Moros y Cristianos is the name given to black beans and white rice served side by side. This shouldn't be confused with the generic term moro, which is used throughout Spanish-speaking Caribbean countries to mean any dish where rice and beans are cooked together in the same pot. This means that the Rice with Pigeon Peas (page 94), the "Blond Moro" (page 100), and Rice and Red Beans (page 93) are all examples of "moros."

PAELLA

Paella, one of the best-known dishes in Spanish cooking, has a reputation as a daunting dish to prepare. That just isn't true—it's fairly quick and lots of fun to make. Try it the next time you have people over for dinner.

The vessel best used for making paella is, of course, a *paellera*—a very wide (about 16 inches) pan with shallow sloping sides. Any pan of that description will allow the rice to cook uniformly despite all the chicken and shellfish that is tucked into it.

Traditionally, saffron is added to paella to lend flavor and color. But nobody ever accused me of being traditional. I love achiote oil and actually prefer the taste to the much more expensive saffron. The color achiote lends to food is more intense than that of saffron, and the flavor is subtler. If you're from Valencia or Madrid and view this as sacrilege, make yours with saffron in the traditional manner.

Clam juice is more predictable than shellfish liquid.

MAKES 6 DAISY SERVINGS

1. Heat the oil in a paellera or similar pan over medium-high heat until rippling. Season the chicken with salt and pepper and add to the pan as many pieces, skin, side down, as fit without touching. Cook, turning as necessary, until well browned on all sides, about 10 minutes. Remove pieces as they are done and set aside. Adjust the heat under the pan, especially after you start removing chicken, so the chicken browns without the oil darkening.

2. Add the chorizo to the pan and cook, stirring, until lightly browned. Add the sofrito, alcaparrado, salt, and pepper. Raise the heat to high, add the shrimp, and cook, stirring, until they change color, 1 to 2 minutes.

3. Stir in the rice until coated with oil. Return the chicken to the pan, pour in enough clam juice to cover the rice by ½ inch (the shellfish will contribute more liquid), and bring to a boil. Cook over high heat until the level of liquid reaches the rice. Nestle the shellfish into the rice in and among the chicken pieces. Adjust the heat to low, cover the pan, and cook until the rice is tender, the liquid has been absorbed, and the chicken is cooked through. Timing will vary depending on your pan; check after 20 minutes.

4. Scatter the peas and roasted red peppers over the top, give the paella a big stir, and serve immediately.

¼ cup Achiote Oil (page 9)
One 3- to 4-pound chicken, cut into 10 pieces (see page 164)
Fine sea or kosher salt
Freshly ground black pepper
6 chorizo, andouille, or any smoked, garlicky sausages (about 1¼ pounds), cut into ½-inch slices
½ cup Sofrito (page 6)
¼ cup alcaparrado or coarsely chopped pimiento-stuffed olives (see Daisy's Pantry on page 13)
1 pound large (about 20 per pound) shrimp, shelled and deveined
4 cups long-grain rice
Bottled clam juice or Chicken Broth, homemade (page 155) or canned, or water, as needed (about 4 cups)
1 dozen littleneck clams, cleaned and soaked in a cornmeal bath (see page 179)
1 pound mussels, scrubbed
One 10-ounce package frozen peas, defrosted and drained
½ cup diced (½ inch) roasted red peppers, homemade (page 67) or store-bought

VARIATIONS: *Chicken with rice (arroz con pollo) can be made by omitting the shrimp, clams, and mussels, and using chicken broth instead of clam juice.*

• *Paella can be made to suit one's taste. You can replace the chicken with rabbit. Add chucks of firm, white-fleshed fish such as halibut or sliced, cleaned calamari. Make a completely seafood version, paella marinera, with shrimp, lobster, scallops, clams, and mussels.*

NOTE: *As mentioned in the chicken chapter, a paella pan comes in handy for a lot more than paella. Inexpensive ones are widely available.*

VEGETABLE PAELLA

PAELLA DE VERDURAS

This vegetarian version of paella is remarkably full of flavor. It makes a satisfying and delicious dish for a party whether or not your guests are vegetarians.

1. Heat the oil in a paella pan or other wide, shallow pan. Stir in the sofrito and cook until the liquid has evaporated and the sofrito begins to sizzle. Stir in the alcaparrado and cumin, and cook for 1 to 2 minutes.

2. Stir in the artichokes and cook for 1 to 2 minutes to evaporate some of the water.

3. Add the mushrooms and string beans, and cook until the mushrooms are wilted, about 5 minutes.

4. Add the rice and stir until yellow and coated with oil. Pour in enough broth to cover the rice by the width of two fingers. Bring to a boil and cook until the level of liquid meets the rice. Give the rice and vegetables a big stir, reduce the heat to low, and cover the pan. Cook until the liquid has been absorbed and the rice is tender, about 20 minutes.

5. Scatter the peas over the top of the rice, stir well, and serve immediately.

½ cup Achiote Oil (page 9)

1 cup Sofrito (page 6)

½ cup alcaparrado or coarsely chopped pimiento-stuffed olives (see Daisy's Pantry on page 13)

1 teaspoon ground cumin

One 14-once can artichoke hearts, drained and cut into quarters, or fresh baby artichokes (see Note)

½ pound cremini or white mushrooms, wiped clean and cut into thick slices

6 ounces string beans, topped and tailed, cut into 1½-inch lengths (about 1½ cups)

3 cups long-grain rice

4 cups Chicken Broth, homemade (page 155) or canned, or canned vegetable broth

1 cup frozen peas

VARIATION: *You may add strips of roasted red peppers, store-bought or homemade (see page 67), or a handful of olives. In short, whatever is in your vegetable drawer or garden. If you choose something that takes longer than 20 minutes to cook, such as a handful of diced carrots, boil them for a few minutes and drain them before stirring them into the paella.*

NOTE: *To use fresh baby artichokes: Choose 10 to 12 baby (about 1 inch) artichokes. Fill a medium saucepan halfway with cool water. Squeeze in the juice of a few lemons and drop the lemon halves in, too. Peel the stem down to the pale green interior using a vegetable peeler. Snap off the outer leaves until you reach the completely yellow leaves. With a paring knife, trim off the base of the leaves you've just snapped off to reveal the white artichoke bottom. Cut the trimmed artichokes into quarters and scrape out any choke and purple leaves with a small teaspoon. Drop the prepared artichokes into the water as you go. Bring the artichokes to a boil and cook for 4 minutes. Drain and proceed as in the recipe.*

As I've grown older, I've found myself looking more and more for the company of women—not only in my friends, but in my family as well. My mother-in-law's sister, Aunt Muriel, lives in upstate New York, and her daughter, Lorraine, lives next door to her. One of my favorite things to do is make Latin food for the "other" side of my family, especially since they are *so* unaccustomed to it. A few years ago during dinner with Susan, another of Jerry's cousins, we toyed with the idea of getting together for a "hen's party." (The only spring chicken there would be my daughter, Angela!) As the idea took shape, we decided that an evening was certainly not going to be time enough, so we stretched the event into a weekend and decided to drag Aunt Muriel and Lorraine into it as well! They were totally game, and the date was set.

I painstakingly planned the menu and paired the wines, did the shopping and packed the car. With Angela safe in the backseat, Susan and I took off with navigation instructions in hand. (We did really well, too, and got lost only once.) Once we arrived at Aunt Muriel's, we went out for a lovely dinner (Angela tried raw oysters) and made the final plans for the dinner I would prepare the following evening. I couldn't wait.

The next morning, after a light breakfast, the hens gathered at Aunt Muriel's and prepared to go shopping and for lunch. I planned to make guacamole with tortilla chips to start, a lovely green salad, and Twenty-minute Shellfish Sauté with Parsley Garlic Sauce with yellow rice (page 14). Lorraine's daughter, Rachel, was going to get married soon after our weekend together and was lamenting her lack of prowess in the kitchen. I told her that the kitchen is made out to be a much more intimidating place than it really is, and I was going to show her how easy it was to make a pear tart. She was skeptical, to say the least.

The dinner started without a hitch. The wine was flowing, and everyone was oohing and aahing about the guacamole. The yellow rice raised some eyebrows, but I begged the hens to bear with me and they would reap the rewards soon enough. The tart went into the oven; Lorraine arranged the salad; Susan set the table; and Aunt Muriel surveyed the scene with the proud eyes of a matriarch. Everything came together at the same time. Perfect timing!

Now for my favorite time of the evening: when I get to watch everyone else's face as they taste this food for the first time. Oh, joy! Oh, rapture! Second helpings are passed, more wine flows, giggles everywhere. We felt so generous, we even let Rob, Lorraine's husband (who is a dead ringer for George Pataki, so we call him Guvnah), join in the festivities. Then we called my mother-in-law to tease her about missing the fun with our flock of hens.

This has clearly become an instant tradition, one that no one looks forward to more than our little spring chicken, Angela. And, yes, Twinkie, if you eat all your vegetables and all the right food, you will one day grow up to be a fabulous hen, too.

STARCHY FRUITS,
ROOT VEGETABLES,
AND TUBERS

VIANDAS

*V*ianda is a difficult word to translate. It encompasses a wide assortment of starchy fruits, root vegetables, and tubers that serve as staples in the diet of the Spanish-speaking Caribbean and Latin American countries. They range from tubers such as yucca, taro root, and sweet potato (not the one you're thinking of) to actual fruits with starchy textures such as breadfruit and plantains. Some of them may be familiar—you've seen green bananas in the grocery store, I'm sure—and some may be names you've never heard before, such as *yautia* and *malanga*. They vary depending on which you choose and how you prepare them, from sweet to savory, from creamy to crunchy.

Viandas are one of the simplest ways to *daisify* a dinner or party. Once you get past the unusual shapes and names, they are about as difficult to prepare as a potato: Peel off the skin and boil them up. All you need is a little Garlic Dipping Sauce (page 114) for spooning, and you're in business. And just like a potato, there are a million things you can do with the members of this group. I've listed a few of them here, after a little introduction to each.

The following four *viandas* are tricky to find if you don't live near a market that carries Latin produce. If that's the case and you'd like to try these, check out Sources for mail-order options. I want to make you aware of them, in case you do spot them. Like yucca and plantains they are becoming more widely available each year. In the few recipes in this book that use them, I have offered substitutes, usually potato, squash, or sweet potato. If you run across them in your travels, pick them up and cook them however you would cook a potato.

TARO ROOT
(YAUTIA)

After yucca, taro is my favorite root vegetable. It is a brown-skinned root with pale yellow–white flesh that is creamy, buttery, and utterly delicious. If you ever see them in the stores, pick a few up and try them boiled and then drizzled with olive oil or Garlic Dipping Sauce (page 114). They are also delicious in stews, cooked escabeche style (see page 178), and in *pasteles* (see page 146).

ÑAME

There is no real translation, but please do not confuse what is often called a yam in the United States, which is really a sweet potato, with a *ñame*, which is a long, round tuber with off-white flesh and little darker squiggles running through it. The flesh is lightly starchy, like a cross between a russet and a waxy potato, and has a creamy texture and a mild potatoey flavor. Choose specimens that are firm and coated evenly with a fibrous "hair," and lack soft spots. Cut into large pieces, then peel them well and store in cold water until needed.

MALANGA

These are roughly the same size as taro root and oval, like a large potato. They are covered with striated, rough, almost barky dark brown skin. The flesh is off-white or pale lavender. They are usually boiled in a stew or served alongside baccala salad.

WHITE SWEET POTATO
(BATATA/BONIATO)

Anything you can do with an orange-fleshed American sweet potato you can do with *boniato*—roast them, mash them, simmer them, and so on.

Boniato is red-skinned, with either pearly white or golden yellow flesh. They are delicious roasted or fried. I even had them in a stew once, although this is not common. They are also known as Japanese sweet potatoes.

YUCCA
(CASSAVA)

Think of yucca as a potato with a pedigree—rich, almost creamy flesh and a wonderful flavor. It is the tuber of the yucca plant that has huge, gorgeous, serrated leaves. Yucca, also known as *cassava*, is irregularly shaped, sort of like a parsnip with a thick and thin end; it is covered with a scaly, mottled brown skin that must be peeled before cooking. It is not unusual to see yuccas in the market that have been covered with wax.

There is a hard woody core that runs more or less through the center of each yucca, but don't worry about removing it before cooking or serving. When you come across that hard core—and it's easy to spot—just pick it out and push it off to the side of the plate.

Once peeled, yucca is no more difficult to cook than a potato. The simplest way to enjoy yucca is to boil it in plenty of salted water until tender, about 45 minutes or so. (If your yucca breaks apart while it's cooking—which it often does, especially along the core—don't worry.) Drain them and eat them with a drizzling of olive oil or, better yet, spoonfuls of Garlic Dipping Sauce (page 114). It is often used in stews and in the making of empanadas, and, recently, yucca chips and yucca fries have found their way into Caribbean kitchens everywhere.

If you live near a supermarket with a decent selection of Latin American ingredients, look for frozen cleaned yucca (cassava) in bags. They've done all the work for you: Just open the bag and boil the contents. Even stores that do not stock fresh yucca are likely to keep some in the frozen food aisle.

YUCCA FRIES

YUCA FRITA

These are made like classic home-cooked french fries: fried once at a lower temperature to cook them through and get rid of excess water, cooled, and then refried at a higher temperature to turn them crispy and golden. A simple sprinkle of salt is fine. Garlic Dipping Sauce (page 114) is better.

1½ pounds uncooked yucca
Fine salt
Vegetable oil
Garlic Dipping Sauce (page 114)
  (optional)

MAKES 4 SIDE DISH SERVINGS

1. Peel the yucca. Cut the root into 4-inch pieces. If you don't plan to cook the fries right away, keep the yucca in a bowl covered with cold salted water.

2. Pour enough oil into a 3- or 4-quart heavy pot to fill 3 inches or so. Heat over medium-low heat until the tip of the handle of a wooden spoon gives off a faint but steady sizzle when immersed in the oil (about 300° F).

3. While the oil is heating, cut each piece of yucca into 4 wedges. Remove the light brown core from each wedge. Cut the pieces into matchstick pieces about ½ × ½ inch. Discard the trimmings; they would only burn during frying.

4. Slip the yucca pieces into the oil and cook, stirring very gently, until the bubbling subsides by about half and a piece of yucca is tender when poked with the tip of a knife, about 4 minutes. The yucca shouldn't brown this time; that will happen later. If they should start to color, lower the heat and remove the pan from the heat for a minute. Remove them with a slotted spoon or skimmer to a baking pan lined with paper towels. Drain and cool completely. Once they are fried for the first time, the yucca can be kept at room temperature for up to 4 hours.

5. Reheat the oil until the tip of the handle of a wooden spoon gives off a lively sizzle (about 350° F). Slip the yucca into the oil and cook, stirring gently, until crisp and deep golden brown, about 3 minutes. Remove with a slotted spoon to a baking sheet lined with paper towels. Serve hot and sprinkled with salt. If you like, pass the garlic sauce separately.

GREEN PLANTAINS
PLATANOS VERDES

Green—meaning both the color and degree of ripeness—plantains are eaten all over the Caribbean in various ways. The green plantain is eaten roasted, made into mofongo (another very typical dish; see page 115), or twice-fried to make delicious plantain chips known as tostones. It can be simmered in stews (like a potato) and is one of the ingredients in Root Vegetable and Meat Tamales, Puerto Rican Style (page 146).

TWICE-FRIED GREEN PLANTAIN CHIPS
TOSTONES

Here is the legal disclaimer I've been advised to attach to this recipe: You cannot eat one plantain chip. They are highly addictive and can result in a wonderful time being had by all, whether you're serving them with Guacamole (page 34), Garlic Dipping Sauce (page 114) or next to any stewy-saucy meat or chicken dish.

Serve with Garlic Dipping Sauce (page 114), Shrimp Creole style (page 182), or even in place of corn chips with guacamole.

EACH PLANTAIN YIELDS ABOUT 20 CHIPS

Green plantains
Salt
Canola oil

NOTES: *Before you can use a green plantain you have to peel it. And although it looks like a banana, it is a little trickier to peel. Just cut off the top of the stem to expose a little of the flesh. With a paring knife make a slit through the peel down to (but not into) the flesh. Starting at one end, peel back the skin; this will get easier as you go on. If you're not going to use plantains right after peeling them, soak them in a bowl of cold water so they don't turn dark.*

• *A tostonera is a little device made of two pieces of wood with handles that look like little bread boards. The two pieces are connected with a hinge on the ends without handles. Simply place a piece of fried plantain between the pieces and press the handles together to flatten it.*

1. Peel green plantains (see Notes), slice into ½-inch-thick rounds, and immediately soak in cold salted water. Pour enough canola oil into a skillet to fill about 1 inch. Heat until the tip of the handle of a wooden spoon dipped in the oil gives off a faint sizzle (about 325° F).
2. Drain the plantain rounds and dry them thoroughly. Slip as many of the plantain pieces into the oil as fit without touching. Fry, turning once or twice, until fork tender, but not browned. If the plantains start to brown before they are tender, remove the pan from the heat, lower the heat, and wait a minute or two before returning the pan to the heat. Remove and drain on paper towels. Let them cool 5 to 10 minutes or up to 2 hours.
3. Using a *tostonera* (see Notes), a kitchen mallet, or the broad side of a knife, whack the plantain slice so that it is smashed but still retains its shape. The chips can be prepared to this point up to a few hours before you serve them. Keep them covered at room temperature.
4. To serve the plantains, reheat the oil until the tip of the handle of a wooden spoon dipped in the oil gives off a lively sizzle (about 360°F). Slip a batch of plantains into the hot oil and fry, turning once, until golden brown, about 4 minutes. Drain on paper towels.

GARLIC DIPPING SAUCE

MOJITO

When you hear "mojito," you probably think of the Cuban cocktail made with rum, mint, and lime juice. That's half the story; this is the other half. Mojito is also a garlicky, oniony, citrusy sauce and/or dressing good for dipping and brushing onto all kinds of things. You can walk into any diner in the United States and see a bottle of ketchup on every table. In Latin America there is a bottle of mojito on every table. (After your first batch of homemade mojito, you'll be asking, "ketchup who?") How many recipes are there for mojito? As many as there are stars in the sky. Back in the day, when things were a little tight, my mother recalls many meatless meals when my grandmother boiled up viandas and served them with mojito. Mami says it was a poor meal, but everybody loved it because my grandmother's mojito was so delicious.

Because there are so many uses for mojito, I could have put it any-where in the book, but I chose to put it here, close to the tostones where it feels right at home.

MAKES ABOUT 1 CUP

Pound the garlic and salt to a paste using a mortar and pestle. (I tried making this in a food processor, but it simply is not the same; what you get is finely chopped garlic, not the lovely mush you get with a mortar and pestle.) Stir in the onions and then the remaining ingredients. Taste and add additional salt if you like. You can make this up to about 3 days in advance and keep it in the refrigerator. Bring it to room temperature about 1 hour before serving.

10 cloves garlic, peeled
1 teaspoon fine sea or kosher salt
1 medium Spanish onion, finely chopped
¾ cup gently warmed olive oil
¼ cup white vinegar
Juice of 1 each: lime, orange, and lemon
2 tablespoons cilantro (optional)

VARIATIONS: *You can add a smashed hot pepper of your choice or use flavored vinegar (homemade or store-bought) or add some chopped parsley or epazote (see Daisy's Pantry on page 170). In short, you can personalize your mojito with whatever you like or have on hand.*

• If you have a source for sour oranges (naranjas agrias; see Note on page 48), substitute two of them for the lemon and orange.

GREEN PLANTAIN AND SALT PORK MASH

MOFONGO

Mofongo, like time, waits for no one. Once finished, you should pull up a chair and eat. Traditionally, the plantains for this dish are boiled and then mashed along with garlic and pork cracklings. It is, to put it mildly, not a light dish. When I went to Puerto Rico recently, I stayed in a hotel in Arecibo that had its own restaurant, El Patio. Willy, the chef, is a native of Arecibo but was trained in cooking in Miami. He is one heck of a cook. I tried his mofongo, and one bite later I was flagging down a waiter asking to meet the chef. It turned out that Willy twice-fried the plantains, as you do for crispy plantain chips (page 113), and then blasted them in a food processor. What he ended up with is a lighter version with a fabulous texture. Even my mother, the mofongo queen of the Caribbean, says Willy's version is better than hers.

MAKES 12 SERVINGS (CAN BE EASILY HALVED)

1. Cut the salt pork through the skin into ½-inch slices. Turn the slices skin side down and cut through the fat down to, but not through, the skin at ½-inch intervals. Lay the slices on their sides in a cold skillet large enough to hold them all comfortably. Set the skillet over low heat. The salt pork will slowly render its own fat and then start to brown in the fat. Don't hurry the process; the idea is to draw as much fat from the salt pork as possible, leaving behind crispy cracklings (known as *chicharrones* in Spanish). Lift the cracklings out with a slotted spoon and drain them on paper towels. Chop the cracklings coarsely in a food processor. There should still be crispy-crunchy bits and more finely chopped bits. Discard the fat.

2. Peel the plantains (see Note on page 113), cut them into 1-inch lengths, and cook them according to the recipe for Twice-Fried Green Plantain Chips (page 113). Do not fry the plantains for the second time until just before you plan to serve the mofongo.

3. Using the vegetable oil, lightly grease twelve 4-ounce ramekins or custard cups. Working with half of the twice-fried plantains at a time, chop them coarsely in a food processor. Add half of the cracklings and garlic and enough olive oil to reach the correct consistency (something along the lines of chewy sushi rice with a bit of crunch from the cracklings). Pulse the processor once or twice to mix. Repeat with the second batch. Taste and add salt and pepper if you like. Pack the mofongo lightly into the prepared molds. Invert onto serving plates. Serve immediately.

1 pound salt pork
6 green plantains
6 garlic cloves, peeled
Vegetable oil
Olive oil
Salt and pepper to taste

VARIATIONS: *Stuffed Mofongo: You can "stuff" mofongo by filling a lightly greased 8-ounce ramekin or custard cup with mofongo and leaving a little "well" in the center. Fill the well with 2 tablespoons of your favorite filling. (Try the Pork Picadillo on page 60 or the Crab Filling for Yucca Fritters on page 59.) Cover the filling with more mofongo, pack it very lightly into the mold, and turn the stuffed mofongo out onto a flat surface. Pour enough vegetable oil into a deep, heavy skillet to fill about 1 inch. Heat until rippling and fry the mofongo, turning only once and handling gently, until golden brown and crispy.*

• Mofongo Ring: Pack the mofongo into a lightly greased ring mold as soon as it is made. Invert the ring mold onto a large serving platter and fill the center with something saucy, such as the Shrimp Creole style on page 182 or Shrimp in Garlic Sauce on page 184. Sprinkle fresh chopped cilantro over the top. This makes a delicious party dish.

BLACK (SWEET) PLANTAINS
MADUROS

Maduro means ripe. Sweet plantains are the ripe version of the green plantain. When plantains are fully ripe, the skin turns completely black and an indentation stays in when you press it with your finger. Everyone has a favorite way to eat sweet plantains. Mine is to fry them and serve them with chorizo and fried eggs for breakfast—as I did when my little Marky came home from college for the first time—although they are definitely not limited to breakfast. Black plantains, unlike green plantains, peel as easily as a banana.

SWEET PLANTAIN CANOES
CANOAS

Peel the sweet plantains. If they are much longer than 6 inches, cut them in half crosswise. Heat about ½ inch of vegetable oil in a large, heavy skillet over medium heat. Add the plantains and fry, turning once or twice, until softened, 4 minutes or so depending on how soft your plantains are to begin with. Remove and drain on paper towels. Hollow out the plantains, like a canoe, and fill the well with the filling of your choice. (The Pork Picadillo on page 60 and the Crab Filling for Yucca Fritters on page 59 work well.) Arrange the canoes, filling side up, in a baking dish in which they fit snugly. Bake at 375° F until the filling is heated through, 20 to 25 minutes.

STUFFED SWEET PLANTAIN FRITTERS
RELLENOS DE MADURO

Boil the sweet plantains until soft. Drain and mash. Using oiled hands, scoop up a ¼- to ½-cup ball of the mashed maduro and make a little well in it. Fill the well with your favorite filling (as mentioned in Sweet Plantain Canoes) and close the well with a little more mashed maduro, making a stuffed ball. Repeat with the remaining maduros and filling. Pour enough canola oil into a deep, heavy pan to fill 3 inches. Heat over medium heat until the handle of a wooden spoon dipped in the oil gives off a lively sizzle (about 350° F). Meanwhile, spread flour in a shallow bowl. Beat 2 to 3 eggs in a separate shallow bowl. Dredge the balls in flour, dip them in beaten egg, and then flour again. Fry in batches to avoid overcrowding until golden brown. Drain on paper towels and repeat with the remaining fritters. Adjust the heat as necessary during frying to keep an even oil temperature.

Depending on the size that you make your fritters, you can serve these as an hors d'oeuvre, an appetizer, or a light lunch dish.

GREEN BANANAS
GUINEITOS VERDES

In the Caribbean very green bananas that haven't developed any trace of sweetness are used as a savory side dish. They are often served boiled (in salt water) and served with fried pork or salt cod salad. Green bananas are also very popular eaten escabeche style—parboiled and then steeped in a vinegary marinade. They are also the main ingredient in the filling for *pasteles*, which along with rice and pigeon peas and roasted pork is the "national" Puerto Rican dish eaten on holidays and special occasions.

To make these and other savory green banana dishes you'll need super-green bananas that haven't even started to turn light green, let alone yellow. You may be able to find them at the supermarket, but the best place to look is a Latin market.

BREADFRUIT

PANAPÉN

Breadfruit is another starchy fruit, though we eat it as a vegetable. The taste is reminiscent of an artichoke but without the bitterness and has an underlying note of sweetness. Breadfruit is eaten boiled, dressed with just olive oil, fried (cooked twice like green plantain chips), or made into fritters (stuffed). My cousin Panchito in Puerto Rico even uses it in a flan for dessert!

Breadfruit are about 2 pounds each and about 4 inches across. No matter what you are making with breadfruit, they are prepared this way:

Have nearby a bowl of salted water large enough to hold the cut-up breadfruit. Cut the ends off the breadfruit and then cut the breadfruit into quarters through the core. Remove the core with a paring knife. Remove the green rind with a paring knife; this is easiest done by setting the piece, cut side down, on a cutting board, holding it firmly in place with one hand, and paring it with the other. Drop the peeled pieces into the salt water as you go to keep them from turning black. If they do darken a little, don't worry; they will still taste fine.

BREADFRUIT TOSTONES

Making *tostones*—twice-fried crispy chips—from breadfruit is as simple and straightforward as making *tostones* from plantains (page 113). The first frying, done to tenderize the breadfruit, can be done up to 2 hours before the second frying, which crisps them up.

1. Cut the breadfruit quarters (see opposite) into 1½-inch chunks. (Don't worry about making them perfect cubes; that won't happen because of the breadfruit's shape.) Pour enough vegetable oil into a deep, heavy skillet—cast iron is my weapon of choice—to fill about ½ inch. Heat over medium heat until the tip of the handle of a wooden spoon gives off a little sizzle when dipped in the oil.

2. Fry the breadfruit, turning frequently, until the pieces are tender when you poke them with the tip of a paring knife, about 12 minutes. If the breadfruit starts to brown before they are tender, lower the heat. They should be only very lightly browned (if at all) at the end of this first frying. Drain the breadfruit on a baking sheet lined with paper towels. Turn off the heat under the oil and let it cool off if you aren't serving the tostones right away.

3. As soon as they are cool enough to handle, pound the pieces of breadfruit lightly with a meat mallet until they are about ½ inch thick. You can fry and pound the breadfruit up to 2 hours in advance.

4. The second frying: Heat the oil over medium-high heat until the tip of the handle of a wooden spoon gives off a lively sizzle (about 360°F). Slip as many of the pounded breadfruit into the oil as will fit comfortably. Cook, turning once, until golden brown and crispy, about 6 minutes. Drain on paper towels and repeat with the remaining breadfruit.

PICKLED GREEN BANANAS

GUINEITOS VERDES EN ESCABECHE

8 very green bananas
Fine sea or kosher salt
Escabeche Sauce (below)

Green bananas in escabeche is the cole slaw of the Caribbean. It is served with everything from fried chicken or fish to pork chops. There is a little place in Naguabo, Puerto Rico, that serves fish right out of the water. They make this dish, and it is to die for.

Serve these anytime you'd serve potato salad—at a barbecue or on a picnic.

1. Peel the bananas as you would a plantain (see Note on page 113). Cut them into 1-inch lengths. Cook in a medium saucepan of boiling salted water until tender but not mushy, about 20 minutes. Drain thoroughly.

2. While the bananas are cooking, make the sauce.

3. Spoon the cooked bananas into a glass jar in which they fit comfortably (about 2 quarts) or divide them between two jars. Spoon the sauce into the jar, cover it tightly, and turn it over gently to mix all the ingredients. Cool to room temperature, shaking the jar gently from time to time. When cool, refrigerate for at least one day or up to one week before serving. Bring the bananas back to room temperature before serving and lift them from the marinade with a slotted spoon.

ESCABECHE SAUCE

SALSA DE ESCABECHE

1 cup olive oil
3 medium Spanish onions, sliced (about 6 cups)
1 cup alcaparrado or coarsely chopped pimiento-stuffed olives
¼ cup cider vinegar
¼ cup white vinegar
1 tablespoon black peppercorns
4 bay leaves
5 cloves garlic
½ teaspoon salt

In this book there are two dishes prepared *en escabeche*: the green bananas above and the seafood on page 178. You can prepare just about anything you like in this style: chicken or shrimp escabeche by coating and frying pieces of chicken or shrimp as you would the seafood, or boiled octopus escabeche, or even potato or breadfruit (see page 117) escabeche, following the same guidelines outlined above. Whatever you choose, you want the "host" to maintain its shape and absorb the delicious vinegary sauce.

MAKES 4 TO 5 CUPS

Heat the oil in a deep, heavy skillet. Add the onions and cook, stirring, until wilted and crisp-tender, about 6 minutes. Add the remaining ingredients and cook over medium heat for about 5 minutes. Pour into a large nonreactive container with a tight-fitting lid. Store in refrigerator for up to 2 weeks.

Recently, while talking to a friend about food (what else!), I was trying to explain how very closely food and love are tied together for me. In fact, for me food is an expression of love and nurturing, both in the giving as well as the receiving. It is why I run to a friend's house with a pot of soup or a cake or a tray of lasagna when I hear there is a crisis, loss, or even heartbreak. The fact that the food I bring is something I've made with my own hands makes the point further. And when it's me or mine that needs love or nurturing and someone brings a gift from the heart in a casserole dish or a pot, I am deeply moved by it.

There is no better example I can think of to illustrate this point than this story. The Martinez family suffered a terrible blow when my brother Joseph, a New York City police officer, was fatally wounded while on duty. In the days that followed, my family kept an around-the-clock vigil at the hospital, praying for a miracle. Friends and family came from all over the country to wait and pray with us as well as for us. My cousins from Massachusetts came down to support Mami. They are the very salt of the earth and very close to Mami because their mother, my mother's sister, died at a very young age. They've always looked to Mami as a maternal figure. Between the coming and the going of all the friends and family, I lost track of my cousins until they showed up again, this time with a large thermos, looking for Mami. "Well," they said, "we know Tia is very upset, and we figured she hasn't had anything to eat. So we bought her this." They handed me the thermos. "It's fresh chicken soup."

I couldn't believe it. "You brought this all the way from Massachusetts? How did you ever get it here, and how did you keep it hot?" I asked them. "Oh, no," my cousin Juan said. "We didn't bring it from home, we made it here." "Here? Here, *where?*" I asked, staring at him. "Here in the parking lot," he said. Juan went on to explain that they had kept all the things they needed for broth in a cooler on ice and packed a little one-burner stove. They had actually made the broth in the back of the van. "We figured Tia could use a little hot soup," Juan said. Even with the gravity of the situation at hand, I couldn't help but smile at the thought of my cousins, crouched in the back of their van in the parking lot, making chicken soup for their aunt who needed much love. They brought it to her, hot in a thermos.

VEGETABLES

VERDURAS/VEGETALES

My mother has a green thumb. *Her* mother had a green thumb. I, alas, do not. There is no amount of love and attention I can pay to a plant that will make it yield what Mami can draw from the same type of plant with no noticeable effort. And her garden? Gorgeous! When she lived in New York, she planted a vegetable garden every spring, and we ate from it all the way into the autumn. Lettuces, tomatoes, eggplants, peppers, *ajices dulces* (see *Daisy's Pantry,* page 6), and all kinds of beans flourished in Mami's garden. Her little patch of a garden in the backyard yielded so much that she'd feed all of us and send company home with bags of produce.

Now, in Florida, her herbs perfume the yard in the heat of summer. Basil, cilantro, thyme, marjoram, mint, sage, and even rue proliferate under her care. But if she gives me a little potted plant, it's brown before I get it home.

Mami doesn't lose faith, however, that one day she will make me as fine a gardener as she is. Even now when I visit her in Florida, she'll take me out to her penthouse patio that is brimming with potted plants. I'll spot the basil, lavender, mint, and culantro. She has little lettuces growing in pots, and little avocado trees. "Look, Daisy," she'll say. "These beans are from your aunt Gabriela's garden. She sent me some shelled beans from Puerto Rico, and one of them had a little sprout, so I planted it." The plants that came from that little sprout covered the wall of the patio! Tomatoes hang low and heavy from their stalks, so sweet that you can eat them like a peach.

I try to follow all the tips she gives me. For a while I added coffee grounds, then egg shells, and all kinds of plant food. Nothing. I turned the soil around the base of the plants. Nothing. I tried manure, top soil, peat. What did I get for my trouble? You guessed it: nothing!

So I made a deal with Mami. She'll grow it, and I'll be happy to find a new delicious way to cook it. And that is finally a compromise Mami can be happy with. Bring on the veggies, Mami. I'm ready!

POTATOES, CREOLE STYLE

PAPAS CRIOLLAS

Another case for keeping sofrito in your freezer. With that on your side, you can have these on the table in under half an hour. This is a very kid-friendly recipe; even the pickiest of yours will help to make these disappear.

You can make these several hours in advance, leave them on the stove with the heat off, and then reheat them gently just before serving.

MAKES 6 SERVINGS

2 pounds tiny white-skinned potatoes, the smaller the better
Fine sea or kosher salt
Olive oil
½ cup Sofrito (page 6)
One 8-ounce can Spanish-style tomato sauce
½ cup chopped fresh cilantro

1. Place the potatoes in a medium saucepan and pour in enough cold water to cover them completely. Throw in a small handful of salt and bring the water to a boil. Turn off the heat and scoop the potatoes with a slotted spoon onto a paper towel–lined baking sheet. Roll them around to dry the skins.

2. In a skillet or other pan that will hold the potatoes comfortably in a single layer (a paella pan works well), pour in enough oil to fill about ¼ inch. Heat the oil over medium heat until rippling. Add the potatoes and cook, shaking the pan so they cook evenly, until the potatoes just start to brown in spots. Don't worry about getting the potatoes crispy because they are going to simmer in sauce.

3. Add the sofrito, bring to a boil, and cook for 1 to 2 minutes. Stir in the tomato sauce and bring to a boil. Season lightly with salt. Adjust the heat so the sauce is simmering gently. Cover the pan and cook until the potatoes are tender but not mushy, about 15 minutes. Taste the sauce and add a little salt if necessary. Sprinkle the cilantro over the potatoes and serve.

MAMI'S POTATO SALAD

ENSALADA DE PAPAS DE MAMI

When my parents first got married, they moved into an apartment on Clymer Street in the Williamsburg section of Brooklyn. They lived down the hall from Don Santiago, who was a retired cruise ship chef. Don Santiago—we always referred to him as "Don"—showed Mami how to make his version of potato salad. Over the years, like most recipes, it evolved it into her own. My only change to Mami's recipe is to leave the skins on the potatoes. I like them that way and it makes the salad easier to prepare, too.

MAKES 8 TO 10 SERVINGS

1. Wash the potatoes well and cut them into quarters. Place them in a pot and add enough cold water to cover them by 2 to 3 inches. Add 2 tablespoons of salt and bring the water to a boil. Cook until the potatoes are tender, about 20 minutes.

2. Drain the potatoes and let them stand to air-dry and cool while you prepare the rest of the ingredients.

3. Heat a medium skillet over medium heat for 1 to 2 minutes. Add the chorizo and cook, tossing it around, until sizzling and shiny, just a minute or two.

4. Transfer the potatoes to a mixing bowl and sprinkle the onion powder over them. Stir the mayonnaise, sour cream, and 3 to 4 tablespoons of water together in a separate small bowl. Push the hard-boiled egg yolks through a sieve into the dressing, stir it well, and then pour it over the potatoes.

5. Chop the egg whites roughly and add them to the salad along with the red pepper and carrots. Stir well and gently until the vegetables are lightly coated with dressing. Add the vinegar, chorizo, and salt and pepper to taste, and stir again.

6. The potato salad will not be very creamy. To make it a little creamier, add warm water, a little at a time, and stir to mix. Scrape the potato salad into a serving bowl and sprinkle the cilantro over the top. You can let the potato salad sit at room temperature for up to 30 minutes before serving or chill it for up to a day. I like it best without refrigeration.

2 pounds small (about 2 inches) white-skinned new potatoes
Fine sea or kosher salt
2 chorizo, andouille, or any smoked garlicky sausages (6 to 8 ounces), casings removed if you like, and cut into ¼-inch dice
¼ teaspoon onion powder
1½ cups mayonnaise
½ cup sour cream
2 hard-boiled eggs (see Note), peeled and cut in half
1 large red bell pepper, cored, seeded, and finely diced
1 large carrot, peeled and coarsely shredded
½ teaspoon white wine or other vinegar
Freshly ground pepper
½ cup chopped fresh cilantro

NOTE: *To make hard-boiled eggs, bring eggs with enough water to cover to a boil. Adjust the heat so the liquid is simmering and cook 10 minutes. Drain and run under cool water.*

FRIED OKRA

GUINGAMBO FRITO

Not that my mother needs one, but these little gems are another reason for her to dig into a plate of okra, especially if there is a bowl of Garlic Dipping Sauce (page 114) nearby. A lot of people don't like okra because of the texture, which can be a little, well, slippery. When you cook okra like this, you put a little jacket on the okra slices so you get the sweet crunch of the cornmeal and the natural texture and green flavor of the okra. There is a whole range of flavors and textures in a single mouthful. Try this as a snack—it's kind of like Latin popcorn.

1 pound okra, trimmed of stems
1 cup all-purpose flour
1½ teaspoons fine sea or kosher salt
1 teaspoon ground cayenne pepper
Canola oil
2 eggs, well beaten
1 cup coarse cornmeal

MAKES 6 REGULAR OR 4 DAISY SERVINGS

1. Rinse the okra and shake it dry. Stir the flour, salt, and cayenne together in a shallow bowl. Dredge several pieces of okra at a time in the seasoned flour. Shake off the excess flour and lay the coated okra on a baking sheet.

2. Pour enough oil into a large, heavy skillet to fill about 1 inch. Heat over medium heat until the tip of the handle of a wooden spoon gives off a lively sizzle when dipped in the oil (about 375° F).

3. Meanwhile, dip the okra in the egg and let the excess egg drip back into the bowl. Roll in the cornmeal until thoroughly coated. When the oil is hot, add as much of the okra to the skillet as fits without touching. Fry, turning as necessary, until golden and crispy, about 5 minutes. Repeat with the remaining okra if necessary.

4. These are delicious on their own, but if you like, serve them with Garlic Dipping Sauce (page 114) or Ajilimojili (page 193).

ASPARAGUS WITH HAM AND SHALLOTS

ESPARRAGOS CON JAMÓN Y CEBOLLETA

Try this at least once with Serrano ham; it is a revelation. On the other hand, if you find yourself with some sliced deli ham, it is not at all bad—in fact it is a very nice side or brunch dish that you can put together in 15 minutes, less if you don't peel the asparagus

MAKES 6 SERVINGS

1 pound pencil-thin asparagus (see Note)
2 tablespoons olive oil
1 tablespoon water
3 shallots, finely chopped
¼ pound thinly sliced Serrano ham, prosciutto, or any ham you like

NOTE: *If your asparagus are thicker than a pencil, use more water, about ¼ inch, in the bottom of the pan.*

1. Cut off the thick ends of the asparagus spears. If they are truly pencil-thin, don't peel them. If they are thicker, and you like, peel the stalks from the tip to the ends.

2. Pour the oil and water into a large, heavy skillet. Add the asparagus and cook over medium heat just until the water has evaporated and the stalks are tender when poked with a knife, about 2 minutes for peeled asparagus, a minute longer for unpeeled. The water will evaporate quickly, leaving the asparagus to sizzle in the oil.

3. Add the shallots to the pan and toss with the asparagus. Lift the stalks onto a serving platter. Add the ham to the skillet and toss just until warmed through, about 1 minute for Serrano or prosciutto, a minute longer for deli or smoked ham. Scrape the ham mixture onto the asparagus. Serve hot or at room temperature.

ASPARAGUS WITH SOUR ORANGE VINAIGRETTE

ESPARRAGOS EN SALSA DE NARANJA AGRIA

In Spain mustard is not a condiment but a seasoning that adds a little something at the end. You can serve these hot or at room temperature, whichever you prefer. A bite of asparagus in sauce gives you the sweetness of the citrus, the spice of the mustard, and the grassy-fresh flavor of the asparagus.

MAKES 8 SERVINGS

1 tablespoon Dijon mustard

Juice of 2 sour oranges (*naranjas agrias;* see page 48) or 1 lemon and 1 orange

Juice of 1 orange (use only if using sour oranges)

Fine sea or kosher salt

1 cup olive oil

1½ pounds medium asparagus

1. Make the dressing: Whisk the mustard, citrus juices, and ½ teaspoon of salt together in a medium bowl. Dribble the oil very slowly into the mustard mix while whisking constantly. The dressing should be fairly smooth, but it's okay if some of the oil separates from the dressing. If that happens, whisk the dressing again just before serving. You can make the dressing up to 1 hour before serving.

2. Cut off the tough ends of the asparagus stalks. Peel as much or as little of the stalks as you like—even right up to the tip.

3. Heat about 1 inch of salted water in a wide, deep skillet to boiling. Add the asparagus, return quickly to a boil, and cook until the asparagus is crisp-tender, 2 to 3 minutes. Lift them with tongs to a bowl of cold water and let them stand until cold. Drain them completely. Pile the asparagus on a serving platter and pour the dressing over them.

SPANISH RATATOUILLE

PISTO MANCHEGO

Getting kids to eat vegetables in my house was never an issue. We got them started early on, and they've stayed with it. But even if your kids aren't vegetable savvy, they'll be all over this. Through slow cooking all the flavors come together to give you a flavor greater than the sum of the parts. Make this in the summer when the vegetables are at their best and cheapest. Prepare it ahead and serve it at room temperature with anything off the grill. This is also fabulous with fried eggs.

MAKES 6 TO 8 SERVINGS

1. Peel the potatoes and cut them into 1-inch cubes. Rinse in a colander under cold water and pat them dry thoroughly. Pour enough canola oil (about 2 inches) into a deep, heavy pot to cover the potatoes when they are added. Heat over medium heat until the tip of the handle of a wooden spoon gives off a lively sizzle when submerged in the oil (about 350 ° F). Slip the potatoes into the oil and cook, stirring gently from time to time, until golden brown and tender, about 5 minutes. Scoop them out with a slotted spoon and drain on a plate lined with paper towels.

2. Heat the olive oil over medium heat in a large skillet. Add the onion, peppers, and garlic, and cook until the onion and peppers are crisp-tender, about 4 minutes. Add the zucchini, thyme, and oregano, and season lightly with salt and pepper.

3. Raise the heat to high, add the cherry tomatoes, and toss just until the tomatoes are heated through. Taste and add more salt and pepper if you like. Sprinkle potatoes over the top.

2 medium Yukon Gold or Idaho potatoes
Canola oil
¼ cup olive oil
1 large Spanish onion, sliced
1 large red bell pepper, cored, seeded, and cut into 1-inch dice
1 large yellow bell pepper, cored, seeded, and cut into 1-inch dice
5 cloves garlic, sliced
1 medium zucchini, trimmed and cut into 1-inch pieces
1 teaspoon chopped fresh thyme
1 teaspoon chopped fresh oregano
Fine sea or kosher salt
Freshly ground black pepper
One 12-ounce bag cherry tomatoes on the stem, stemmed and quartered

POTATO AND GREEN BEAN SALAD

ENSALADA DE JUDIAS Y PAPAS

Waxy potatoes, such as red-skinned and new potatoes, are best for this because they hold together better than mealy potatoes such as Idahos or russets. Eat this hot, right out of the pan, or at room temperature. It makes an ideal dish for a picnic because there is no mayo involved. I have a friend, Richard, who has a German wife who likes things with a little vinegary kick. When he made this for her, she cleaned her plate. Who thought the Latins could give the Germans a run for their money when it comes to potato salad?

MAKES 6 SERVINGS

1. Fill a medium saucepan about two-thirds full with water. Add 3 tablespoons salt. Cut the potatoes into quarters and drop them into the water as you go.

2. Bring the water to a boil over high heat, boil for 1 minute, and then drain the potatoes and let them cool. Air-drying the potatoes helps them brown nicely and prevents splattering when you add them to the oil.

3. Pour the oil into a deep, large (12-inch or so) skillet. Heat over medium-high heat. Add the potatoes and cook, shaking the pan frequently, until they have a little color, about 10 minutes. Don't worry about crisping them.

4. Add the string beans to the skillet and season lightly with salt. Stir and cook for a minute or two. Pour in the vinegar, bring it to a boil, and cook until it has almost completely evaporated. Pour in the broth, bring it to a boil, and cover the pan. Cook the vegetables until tender but still firm, about 5 minutes. Uncover and cook until the liquid has evaporated and the vegetables are sizzling in the pan. Serve hot or at room temperature.

Fine sea or kosher salt

1½ pounds small (1½ to 2 inches) white new potatoes, cut into quarters

6 tablespoons olive oil

½ pound string beans, topped and tailed

2 to 3 tablespoons cider or sherry vinegar, or the vinegar of your choice

¼ cup Chicken Broth, homemade (page 155) or canned

ROASTED GARLIC

AJO ASADO

When you take a whole head of garlic and roast it slowly, you lose all the garlic's sharpness and gain a buttery texture and a mellow, sweet flavor. If you are going to roast a head of garlic, you may as well roast half a dozen. Squeeze the pulp out of whatever cloves you have left, beat in a little olive oil, and store it in the fridge. It is better than butter for bread and adds hugely to whatever dish you usually make with regular garlic. You can also serve the heads whole as a side dish for just about anything.

Heat the oven to 350° F. Peel extra paper off however many heads of garlic you'd like to roast. Cut off just enough of the top of the head to expose the tips of the garlic cloves. Make a double-layer square of aluminum foil large enough to hold all the garlic comfortably when sealed. Drizzle the garlic with a light coating of olive oil. Bring the sides of the foil to meet over the garlic and crimp the sides together to make a neat little package. Bake the garlic right on the oven rack until the cloves are very tender, about 1 hour. Serve warm or wait until cool enough to handle and squeeze the pulp out of the cloves.

STRING BEANS WITH ROASTED GARLIC

JUDIAS CON AJO ASADO

When I bring string beans home from the store, I "top and tail" them—cut off both ends—as soon as I get home. I wrap them in a damp paper towel and stick them in a plastic bag in the vegetable drawer. This recipe is the perfect excuse to keep extra roasted garlic on hand—as if you need one. With it, this dish is a ten-minute proposition. I like nice, crisp, bright green string beans. Combined with the smoky-sweet flavor of the roasted garlic, they're heaven.

MAKES 6 TO 8 SERVINGS

2 heads Roasted Garlic (see above)
1 cup Chicken Broth, homemade (page 155) or canned
2 tablespoons olive oil
1 pound string beans, topped and tailed
Fine sea or kosher salt to taste
Freshly ground pepper to taste

1. Squeeze the roasted garlic from the cloves. Combine the garlic pulp and broth in a blender, and blend at low speed until smooth.
2. Heat the oil in a large skillet over high heat. Add the string beans and season them with salt and pepper. Cook until there is a happy crackle going and the beans start to change color. Pour in the garlic-broth and bring to a boil. Cook until the sauce has thickened and the beans are crisp-tender and still bright green, about 5 minutes.

SPINACH WITH PINE NUTS AND RAISINS

ESPINACAS AL ESTILO DAISY

MAKES 4 SERVINGS

1. Pour enough hot water over the raisins in a small bowl to cover them. Let stand until plump, 20 minutes or so. Drain.

2. Heat the oil in a large skillet over medium heat. Add the garlic and pine nuts, and cook, stirring, just until the pine nuts start to color. Add as much of the spinach as fits and stir until it is wilted enough to make room for more spinach. Keep going until all the spinach has been added. Cook just until the spinach is wilted but still bright green. Add raisins, vinegar, salt, and pepper, and serve.

¼ cup raisins
3 tablespoons olive oil
4 cloves garlic, sliced
¼ cup pine nuts
4 bunches (about 2 pounds) or two 10-ounce bags spinach, washed and dried, preferably in a salad spinner
1 or 2 dashes of sherry vinegar
Fine sea or kosher salt to taste
Freshly ground pepper to taste

RED CABBAGE, CHRISTMAS STYLE

LOMBARDA NAVIDEÑA

Red cabbage cooked with raisins, brandy, and vinegar is as much a part of Christmas in Spain as rice with pigeon peas is in Puerto Rico. In honor of my Spanish and Puerto Rican heritage, both are on my table. Everybody has his or her own take on this dish that combines hearty red cabbage with the caramel kick of brandy and the sweetness of pears. Here's mine: It is just what we need around the holidays—a festive, beautiful side dish that is put together in no time at all.

MAKES 6 TO 8 SERVINGS

1. Pour the brandy over the raisins in a small bowl. Let stand until needed. Peel and core the pears. Cut them into quarters and then lengthwise into slices. Toss them together with the lemon juice in a small bowl. Set aside.

2. Mix the cabbage and ¼ cup of vinegar together with your hands in a large bowl. Let stand for 15 minutes. (Working the cabbage and vinegar together does two things: It fixes the color of the cabbage, and it gives it a silky texture.)

3. Meanwhile, bring a large pot of salted water to a boil. Fill a large bowl halfway with ice and water, and place it near the sink. Stir the cabbage into the boiling water, cook for 2 minutes, and drain. Plunge the cabbage into the ice water to stop the cooking. Drain in a colander, pressing to remove as much water as possible. Working in batches, remove as much water as possible by wrapping the cabbage in a clean kitchen towel and squeezing.

4. Put the chorizo, oil, and bay leaves in a large, heavy skillet with a cover. Place the skillet over low heat and cook until the chorizo begins to render its fat and starts to sizzle.

5. Add the raisins and any brandy left in the bowl to the pan. Cook until the brandy has evaporated. Add the pears and thyme, toss to coat with the fat, and then stir in the cabbage. Season lightly with salt and pepper, sprinkle the remaining ¼ cup of vinegar over the cabbage, and toss to mix. Cook, stirring occasionally, until the cabbage is wilted but still has a bite, about 15 minutes.

¼ cup brandy

1 cup raisins

2 ripe but firm pears, such as red Bartletts or Comice, cored, quartered, and cut into slices

Juice of 1 lemon

½ small head red cabbage (about 1½ pounds), cored and cut into ¼-inch strips (about 12 cups)

½ cup cider vinegar

2 chorizo, andouille, or any smoked garlicky sausages, thinly sliced

1 tablespoon olive oil

2 bay leaves

1 tablespoon chopped fresh thyme

Fine sea or kosher salt

Freshly ground pepper

CHICKPEAS AND SWISS CHARD

GARBANZOS CON ACELGAS

Italians combine all kinds of beans with all kinds of greens and cook them very simply. This is my variation on that theme. You can make it fairly dry, in which case it makes a good side dish, or leave it fairly brothy.

I like red chard in this dish, but you can use regular green if that's what you find in the market. You can make this several hours ahead and let it sit. In fact, it gets better. The smokiness of the bacon has a chance to permeate the buttery chickpeas, and the chard, with a slightly bitter edge, holds its own against both. This is another place where I'd pull canned beans off the shelf in a pinch.

MAKES 8 SERVINGS

1 pound dried chickpeas
One 6- to 8-ounce piece of slab bacon or 1 smoked ham hock
2 bay leaves
1 large bunch Swiss chard
½ cup Sofrito (page 6)
2 tomatoes, cored and coarsely chopped
1 cup (or as needed) Chicken Broth, homemade (page 155) or canned
3 sprigs of fresh thyme
Fine sea or kosher salt
Freshly ground black pepper

1. Soak the chickpeas in plenty of cold water to cover for at least 8 hours or overnight.

2. Drain the chickpeas and then put them, the bacon, and the bay leaves in a medium saucepan. Add enough water to cover them by 2 inches. Bring the water to a boil and then adjust the heat so it is boiling gently. Cook the chickpeas until near tender, about 2½ hours. Keep an eye on them; they should always be covered by liquid. When the liquid meets the level of the chickpeas, add cold water to cover by 1 inch or so.

3. While the chickpeas are cooking, clean the chard: Fill a clean sink with cool water. Trim any wilted or yellow leaves and remove and discard the stems. Cut the leaves into 1-inch pieces. Swish them around in the water and then drain them in a colander.

4. When the chickpeas are tender, remove the slab of bacon and let it cool. Cut it into about ½ inch pieces. Put the bacon in a deep medium skillet over medium-high heat until it starts to sizzle and brown, about 3 minutes. Stir in the sofrito and cook until the water has evaporated and the sofrito starts to sizzle. Add the tomatoes and stir until softened. Stir in the chard leaves and stir until wilted, then stir in the chickpeas. Pour in the broth, add the thyme, and bring to a gentle boil. Season to taste with salt and pepper. Cover and cook for 15 minutes to give the flavors a chance to blend.

5. Uncover the pan and check out the liquid. If you want to serve the beans and chard soupy, leave it as is. If you want to serve it a little drier, boil it until as much of the liquid as you like has evaporated. You can adjust the soupiness at the very end of cooking by adding additional broth.

STUFFED ARTICHOKES

ALCACHOFAS RELLENAS

If you ever looked at an artichoke in the supermarket and wondered what the heck to do with it, start here. Like everything else in the kitchen, you'll get the hang of it after one or two.

These make a great dish for family get-togethers or parties. Put them on plates and let people at them. If you're at a loss as to how to eat a whole artichoke, watch a kid eat one. It's really pretty instinctual—just use your teeth to scrape the meaty part from the leaf and discard the rest of the leaf. By the time you get to the bottom, with the choke already gone, there's nothing to do but enjoy. What more could you ask for than seeing a bunch of greasy smiles gathered around your table?

MAKES 6 SERVINGS

1. Cook the artichokes: Use kitchen shears to remove a row or two of the outermost (largest) leaves at their base. With a serrated knife, cut off about ½ inch from the top of the artichoke. Clip the pointed top from each remaining leaf. Rub the cut and peeled surfaces of the artichoke with a lemon half as you go in order to prevent them from darkening. Place the artichokes in a large pot of cold water acidulated with 1 tablespoon of vinegar or lemon juice. Weigh them down with a plate to keep them below water. Place over high heat, bring to a boil, and cook until the stems are very tender, about 45 minutes. Scoop them out with a slotted spoon into a bowl, reserving some of the cooking liquid if you're not using the chicken broth for baking. Let stand until cool enough to handle.

2. Make the stuffing: Heat ¼ cup oil in a large skillet. Add the onion, pine nuts, and garlic, and cook, stirring until the onion is softened, about 4 minutes. Add the bread crumbs and stir constantly until they turn an even golden brown. Make sure you scrape them up from the bottom so they don't burn. You'll notice that they'll start to turn color quickly at some point. When you see that happen, lower the heat right away, or they'll burn. Remove from the heat and stir in the cheese and parsley. After you take the pan from the heat, the delicate crumbs will keep cooking. Be sure to stir them often until they cool.

3. Cut off the stems flush with the bottom of the artichokes so they sit up without wobbling. Strip off the outer stringy layer from the stems and cut the soft insides into fine dice. Stir into the stuffing.

4. Preheat the oven to 350° F.

6 artichokes (about 6 ounces each, the size of your fist) (see Notes)
1 lemon, cut in half
¼ cup olive oil, plus more for baking
1 medium onion, diced
2 tablespoons pine nuts
4 cloves garlic, chopped
2 cups seasoned bread crumbs
¼ cup coarsely grated Zamorano or Parmesan cheese (about 1 ounce; see Daisy's Pantry)
1 tablespoon chopped fresh parsley
1 cup (or as needed) Chicken Broth, homemade (page 155) or canned, or reserved artichoke cooking liquid

5. Gently spread the artichoke leaves away from the center. Look into the center and, using a teaspoon, scrape out any purple-tipped leaves (which aren't edible) and the hairy choke that lies underneath them. Work carefully to avoid removing any of the edible leaves or solid artichoke heart underneath the choke. Spoon enough stuffing into the center of each artichoke to fill without packing down the filling. Gently spread out the outer leaves and spoon a little filling between those (a little bonus). Set the artichokes into a baking dish in which they fit comfortably. You can boil and stuff the artichokes up to a day in advance. Refrigerate them, covered, in their dish.

6. Pour in enough chicken broth or artichoke cooking liquid to fill the dish to 1 inch. Drizzle enough oil over the top to moisten the crumbs. It's fine if some of the oil ends up in the pan liquid. Cover the dish tightly with aluminum foil and bake until a leaf pulls very easily from the artichoke, about 30 minutes. Serve hot.

DAISY'S PANTRY *Zamorano cheese is a dry, nutty cheese made from sheep's milk. It is available in specialty cheese shops. I urge you to seek out Spanish cheeses, such as Zamorano. They don't have the popularity of Italian cheeses, but they are just as delicious, diverse, and versatile.*

NOTES: *Buy artichokes with the longest stems. You can use the stems in the filling or save them as a treat for the cook.*

• *Cutting off the largest leaves makes the artichoke look nice when you serve it, but the real reason I take them off is that they don't have a lot of tender pulp worth eating.*

• *Boiling the artichokes for 45 minutes is non-negotiable. Don't try to save time by cutting the boiling time. If they don't get tender enough before baking, they'll never do it in the oven.*

• *The secret to a light and fluffy stuffing for artichokes instead of one that is gooey and gluey is this: Toast the bread crumbs before making the stuffing.*

• *Use this stuffing to fill tomatoes, mushrooms, or whatever other vegetable you like. And if you have any left over, sprinkle over the next pasta dish you make. That's more Sicilian than it is Latin, but it sure is good.*

BAKED STUFFED EGGPLANT

BERENJENAS ASADAS Y RELLENAS

Spaniards wax poetic about their eggplant. If you're not Spanish, that may sound odd, but they have a way with eggplant, whether it's simmering the vegetable together with salt cod (page 189) or stuffing them, as here. I first tried this dish in Barcelona. We were there on New Year's Day, when everything was closed. As much as possible we avoided touristy restaurants (and we had eaten very well) by asking residents and looking in restaurant windows to see where locals ate. That's how we found Rincon de Estefan, which, fortunately, was open for the holiday. On the restaurant's wall hung a little article about how the Prince of Spain had eaten there not once but twice. Estefan was very proud of his wine list. I told him about my work on this book, and he said, "Put away your menus. Put away your wine lists. I am going to take care of you." This eggplant was part of that meal.

MAKES 6 SERVINGS

Fine sea or kosher salt
6 small eggplants (about 8 ounces each)
2 tablespoons olive oil, or as needed
1 medium Spanish onion, cut into ½-inch dice
3 cloves garlic, finely chopped
6 medium white mushrooms (about 2-inch caps), cut into quarters (about 2 cups)
½ red bell pepper, cored, seeded, and cut into ½-inch pieces
2 tablespoons chopped fresh parsley
3 to 4 ounces herbed or plain goat cheese, crumbled (⅔ to ¾ cup)
1 cup canned vegetable stock or chicken broth

1. Bring a large pot of salted water to a boil.

2. Meanwhile, prepare the eggplants: Cut off the stems. Slice about ½ inch from the top of each eggplant, starting at the wide end and working toward the stem, but stopping about 1 inch from the stem end. Scoop out the flesh from the eggplant, leaving about ½ inch attached to the skin on all sides. (A melon baller is the ideal tool to speed up the job of hollowing out the eggplants.) Again, don't scoop any from the stem end. The idea is to end up with a little eggplant "boat," perfect for stuffing. Chop the pulp coarsely if necessary and reserve. Slip the eggplants into the boiling water and cook for 3 minutes, poking them to keep them submerged. Scoop them out with a slotted spoon onto a baking sheet lined with a kitchen towel or paper towels. Let them cool while you make the stuffing.

3. Preheat the oven to 350° F. Heat the oil in a large skillet over medium heat until rippling. Add the onion and garlic, and cook, stirring, until the onion is softened, about 4 minutes. Stir in the mushrooms and cook until they give off their liquid, about 8 minutes.

4. Stir in the pepper and reserved eggplant pulp. Drizzle another tablespoon or so of oil over the vegetables and continue cooking, stirring often, until the eggplant is tender, about 10 minutes. Stir in the parsley. Remove the skillet from the heat. Stir the cheese into the filling, letting it melt and coat the vegetables.

5. Spoon the stuffing into the eggplants, mounding it slightly. Pour the stock into the pan and cover with aluminum foil. Bake until the eggplant shells are tender, about 30 minutes. Serve hot or warm.

TURNOVERS AND TAMALES

EMPANADAS Y TAMALES

"If you had to pick just one thing as the perfect food, what would it be?" I asked a friend during dinner one night. Without hesitation she said, "Pie." I don't think I quite understood exactly what she was driving at, but after some time, I had to admit she made a good point. What's better than your favorite ingredients wrapped snugly in dough?

Certainly pie fillings aren't limited to sweet ingredients—although those are delicious—but include all kinds of savory fillings as well. (Think chicken pot pie and shepherd's pie.) The only drawback with pie, as far as I can see, is that it doesn't travel very well. Pie has a first cousin that does travel well, however; the turnover—or, as we call them in Spanish, *empanada*. An empanada has a delicious flaky pastry crust that when broken into reveals a steamy, delicious, sweet or savory filling.

Tamales fall into the same category: savory fillings enclosed in a creamy cornmeal filling that is in turn wrapped in a leaf of some kind. Puerto Ricans use banana or plantain leaves, Mexicans use corn husks, and so on. The leaf wrapping protects the tender filling and adds flavor, too.

Both empanadas and tamales make terrific party foods because they can be made ahead and cooked (fried or baked in the case of empanadas; steamed in the case of tamales) just before you serve them. All your work is done ahead, and serving them is as easy as pie.

EMPANADA DOUGH

MASA PARA EMPANADA

If you live in an area with even a modest Latino population, you will most likely find empanada dough in the freezer section of your supermarket. If so, you can skip making the dough, but I believe there's nothing like homemade.

MAKES ENOUGH FOR TEN 6-INCH EMPANADAS OR THIRTY-SIX 3-INCH EMPANADAS

1. Stir the flour and salt together in a large bowl. Beat the water, egg, egg white, and vinegar together in a small bowl. Cut the shortening into the flour mixture with a pastry blender or two butter knives until it is broken up into small pieces. Make a small well in the center of the flour and pour the liquid ingredients into the center. Beat the flour into the wet ingredients with a fork until it's too stiff to mix easily.

2. Turn the dough out onto a lightly floured surface and knead the dough just until all the flour is incorporated and you have a nice, smooth dough. Wrap in plastic and refrigerate at least 1 hour or up to overnight. Any longer than that, freeze it.

3 cups all-purpose flour, plus more for kneading
1 teaspoon fine sea or kosher salt
½ cup cold water
1 egg plus 1 egg white
1 teaspoon sherry or cider vinegar
3 tablespoons vegetable shortening

VARIATION: *For a party you can dress up this dough with chopped fresh herbs: parsley goes with just about everything, cilantro if you want a kick. Just be sure the herbs are patted dry before chopping and are finely chopped.*

RED EMPANADA DOUGH

MASA COLORADA PARA EMPANADAS

Aside from the fact that achiote oil makes this look beautiful, it adds a nutty flavor that is delicate and delicious.

MAKES ENOUGH FOR TEN 6-INCH EMPANADAS OR THIRTY-SIX 3-INCH EMPANADAS

Place the flour, yucca, and salt in the work bowl of a food processor. Process until the mixture is crumbly. Add the oil and process until incorporated into the dough. With the motor running, add enough water (not more than a few tablespoons) to make a smooth, elastic ball. Cover with plastic wrap and refrigerate 1 hour to overnight. Any longer than that, freeze it.

2½ cups all-purpose flour
1½ cups boiled and mashed yucca (see page 110)
2 teaspoons salt
3 tablespoons Achiote Oil (page 9)
1 to 3 tablespoons water

EMPANADAS

6-INCH

Divide the dough of your choice in half. Roll each half out to about ⅛ inch thick on a floured board. Cut the dough into 6-inch circles. Brush the edge of the circle with beaten egg. Place about ⅓ cup of the filling slightly off center toward you. Fold the far edge of the pastry circle over the filling and press the edges firmly to seal. If you like, press the edges together with the tips of the tines of a fork, which makes it look nice.

3-INCH

Proceed as above, cutting 3-inch circles of dough. Fill each with about 1 tablespoon of filling.

TO FRY THE EMPANADAS

Pour enough vegetable oil into a large, heavy skillet to fill ½ inch. Heat over medium heat until the tip of the handle of a wooden spoon gives off a very lively sizzle when dipped into the oil (about 375°F). Slip as many empanadas into the oil as will fit without touching. Fry, turning once, until browned on both sides and the dough is cooked through, about 8 minutes for large empanadas or 6 minutes for smaller ones. Remove and drain on paper towels. Repeat with the remaining empanadas.

TO BAKE THE EMPANADAS

Brush the empanadas with beaten egg and bake in a 350° F oven until golden brown, 15 to 20 minutes for smaller empanadas or 20 to 35 minutes for the larger size.

NOTES: *Whichever size you're making, reroll the scraps of dough once to make as many more circles as you can. Rerolling the dough more than that will toughen it.*

• You can make either size empanada up to a few hours ahead and refrigerate them on a baking sheet. Or you can freeze them: Place them on a baking sheet, set it in the freezer until the empanadas are firm, then pile them into a sealable bag and store them in the freezer. Remove the empanadas from the bag (before they defrost, or they will stick together), place them on a baking sheet, and defrost them at room temperature before cooking.

CRAB FILLING FOR EMPANADAS

RELLENO DE CANGREJO PARA EMPANADAS

Traditionally, crab filling is made with a sofrito-seasoned tomato sauce, like the one used for Yucca Fritters on page 59. The crab is cooked in the sauce until it breaks up into little pieces. But here's the thing with lump crabmeat: I like to handle it as little as possible to keep the lumps from breaking up, so I season it lightly with lime, cilantro, tomato, and chili—the same seasonings you'd find in sofrito—and leave the lumps nice and big. I've found a great pasteurized lump crabmeat in one-pound cans at my local big-box store. I always keep a few on hand in the refrigerator, where they last several months.

1 pound lump crabmeat
1 small ripe tomato
3 or 4 thin stalks of cilantro, finely chopped
½ teaspoon salt
Grated zest of 1 lime
½ Scotch bonnet chili or any other chili you like (optional)

MAKES ABOUT 3 CUPS, ENOUGH TO FILL TEN 6-INCH EMPANADAS OR THIRTY-SIX 3-INCH EMPANADAS

1. Pick over the crabmeat, squeezing each piece gently to feel for bits of shell or cartilage. Work very carefully to keep the crab pieces as large as possible. Put the crab in a mixing bowl as you go.
2. Cut the tomato into slices, remove the seeds, and cut the slices into ¼-inch dice.
3. Add the tomato, cilantro, salt, lime zest, and chili, if using, to the mixing bowl. Toss all the ingredients together gently, to keep the crab from breaking up, until mixed.

SWEET PLANTAIN AND RAISIN FILLING FOR EMPANADAS

RELLENO DE MADUROS Y PASAS

The little bit of olive in the filling offsets the sweetness of the plantains and raisins. You'll find maduros—sweet or ripe plantains—with their black skins much easier to peel than their green unripe brothers. If you find yourself with a little leftover hot sausage, crumble it, add it to the filling, and enjoy.

MAKES 3 CUPS, ENOUGH TO FILL TEN 6-INCH EMPANADAS OR THIRTY-SIX 3-INCH EMPANADAS

3 ripe, very black plantains, peeled (see Note on page 113) and cut into 2-inch lengths
Fine sea or kosher salt
¼ cup plus 2 tablespoons raisins
1½ teaspoons dark rum
½ cup coarsely chopped alcaparrado (see Daisy's Pantry on page 13) or roughly chopped pimiento-stuffed olives
Freshly ground pepper to taste

1. Boil the plantains in a medium saucepan of lightly salted water until they are very tender, about 20 minutes. Drain thoroughly.
2. While the plantains are cooking, toss the raisins and rum together in a small bowl.
3. Mash the plantains until smooth. Stir in the raisins and rum and then the alcaparrado. Just before filling the empanadas, taste the filling and add salt and pepper if you think it needs it.

Making *pasteles*—one of Puerto Rico's national dishes—is a family memory that I cherish. Because there are so many steps and so many little "projects" involved in the composition of pasteles, it really is an "all hands on deck" type of endeavor. It's funny that whatever job we were first given, whether it was cutting the banana leaves, filling them, or tying up the bundles, it was ours to keep throughout our lives.

The whole process started out with Mami and me, or Mami and Papi, taking a trip to the Essex Street Market where she would buy 40 to 50 pounds of green bananas (no, you're not seeing things!) along with not-so-crazy amounts of green plantains, *yautia*, and *calabaza* (see pages 113, 110, and 78). And that's not mentioning the pork for the filling or the bones to make a broth. In addition to this, she would buy a few pounds of pasteles paper (parchment) and plantain leaves, which she used to wrap the pasteles before boiling them. We would stagger back to the car with our purchases and make our way home. On the following day (you cannot buy the green bananas too far in advance because they ripen) we would all assume our positions for our respective tasks.

Mami, of course, was always in charge of the bones and the meats. She set the bones to boiling with aromatic vegetables in a big stockpot. Soon the entire house was filled with the delicious aroma. She then cut the meat in little pieces, seasoned it, and set it to simmer, carefully skimming off the foam that rose to the top. My sister and I were always on grating detail; all those vegetables had to be peeled and grated to make a "batter." My brothers joined us once they were old enough. Mami did not like the way the filling (*masa*) came out in the food pro-

cessor, so we had to do our grating by hand— on the finest side of the grater, no less. We became very skilled and very fast so we did not skin our knuckles on the box graters. Once the batter and the meat were ready, we were all set to start building the pasteles. That's where Papi came in. He sat at the head of the table with the parchment paper, banana leaf, and a ball of string. Once he had everything just the way he wanted it, Mami set a square of banana leaf over a piece of the parchment and spooned batter and meat onto the center. Papi wrapped it and tied up the banana leaf bundle with string, stacking the pasteles in a large plastic tub. I still remember how quickly and precisely his hands worked, smoothing the paper and leaves out and deftly tying the string. We made 150 to 200 pasteles at a clip. (That explains the 50 pounds of green bananas!) Once Mami saw that we were almost finished, she set some pasteles in a pot of boiling water for our dinner. A reward for a job well done!

This year Mami and Papi came to my house to make pasteles with me for the graduation of our sons, Erik and Marc. Mami and I got up early to do our shopping and then came back to the house. I started peeling green bananas and the rest of the vegetables while Mami prepared the meat. We went through the entire process, and I was completely absorbed in my task. But at the end of the job I looked up and saw a flash from Papi's New York City Fire Department captain's ring as he tied up the last pastel. I got a lump in my throat. I remembered a quote from Gabriel Garcia Marquez's book *One Hundred Years of Solitude*. The maternal character Ursula says, "The more things change, the more they stay the same." I totally got it at that exact moment. I was happy I did.

ROOT VEGETABLE AND MEAT TAMALES, PUERTO RICAN STYLE

PASTELES PUERTORIQUEÑOS

Okay, here it is, possibly the most significant dish in all of the cooking of Puerto Rico. These are, no doubt about it, a production number—such an ordeal that when members of my family get together, we never make fewer than 100, pile them in the freezer, and enjoy them for months. Like money in the bank. Don't worry, I'm not going to ask you to make 125 as we usually do. This recipe makes about two dozen, but it is still an undertaking. You will not be sorry, however, when you unwrap your first pastel and breathe in the aroma. Take a crash course in the vegetables used in the batter by reading pages 110–113.

MAKES ABOUT 24

1. Make the pork stock: Preheat the oven to 400° F. Place the pork bones, onion, and bay leaf in a roasting pan large enough to hold them comfortably. Roast, stirring once or twice, until well browned, about 45 minutes.

2. Transfer the bones to a 5- or 6-quart pot. Pour in enough water to cover the bones. Add a big pinch of salt and a dozen or so peppercorns. Bring to a boil, then adjust the heat so the liquid is at a lively simmer. Cook for 1½ hours, skimming off any foam or fat that rises to the surface.

3. Make the pork filling: Put the pork in a 4-quart pot. Add the oil and bay leaf, and stir to coat. Pour in enough water to cover the pork. Bring to a boil. Cook for 45 minutes.

4. Stir in the sofrito, culantro, and salt, and continue simmering until the pork is tender, about 45 minutes.

5. When the pork stock and pork filling are ready, set them aside. Gather all the things listed under "You Will Also Need" on the opposite page together before making the root vegetable batter.

6. Make the root vegetable batter: Grate the green bananas, yautia, calabaza, green plantain, and potato by hand on the finest side of a box grater. Don't be tempted to do this in a food processor. Stir in the oil, pork stock, salt, milk, and broth from pork stew. The mixture should be the color of a sweet potato and the texture of a sticky batter.

7. Oil the center of a sheet of parchment paper with achiote oil and place a banana leaf over the oil. Oil the leaf lightly. Spoon about ¾ cup of the batter over the center of the leaf. Make a little well in the batter and spoon about ¼ cup pork filling and some juice into

FOR THE PORK STOCK

2 pounds pork bones
½ small onion, peeled
1 bay leaf
Fine sea or kosher salt
Black peppercorns

FOR THE PORK FILLING

2 pounds pork, preferably Boston butt, cut into ½-inch cubes
¼ cup Achiote Oil (page 9)
1 bay leaf
⅓ cup Sofrito (page 6)
1 tablespoon chopped fresh culantro (see Daisy's Pantry, page 6) or ½ bunch fresh cilantro tied with twine
Fine sea or kosher salt to taste

FOR THE ROOT VEGETABLE BATTER

8 pounds green bananas, peeled
¾ pound yautia, peeled
¾ pound calabaza, peeled
1 small green plantain, peeled
1 small (about 7 ounces) russet potato, peeled
⅓ cup Achiote Oil (page 9)
1 cup (or as needed) Pork Stock (see above)
2 teaspoons fine sea or kosher salt
¾ cup milk
¾ cup broth from the pork stew

the well. Top with an olive and piece of red pepper from the alca-parrado. Also a whole cayenne. Spoon the batter from the edges over the meat and vegetables. Fold the top and bottom sides of the leaf over the filling. Bring the long edges of the paper over the leaf so they meet at the top. Make 2 folds along the long edge so the pastel is wrapped nice and tight. Make a 1-inch fold along one of the short ends, then bring that end of the paper and banana leaf over the filling. Repeat with the other short side. You now have a pastel made up of the filling tightly wrapped in both banana leaf and paper. Set it aside, folded side down, on a baking sheet and repeat with the remaining filling, leaves, and paper.

Tie the pasteles: Fold one length of string in half and set it on your work surface with the loose ends closest to you. Center a pas-tel, folded side down, over the string about 4 inches from the folded end. Bring each loose end of the string outward slightly so each is sitting near the ends of the folds. Bring the loose ends of the string over the packet and then under the loop in the string. Keeping the string centered under the folds to hold them in place, pull the loose ends up and out. If this all sounds too complicated, simply tie the folds tightly with shorter lengths of string.

8. You can freeze some or all of the pasteles at this point. To cook freshly made or frozen pasteles: Put the number of pasteles you choose to serve in a pot large enough to hold them very comfort-ably. (Use 2 pots if necessary.) Pour in enough cold water to cover them by at least 3 inches. Toss in a handful of salt and bring to a boil. Adjust the heat so the water is boiling gently. Cook 1 hour.

9. Remove the pasteles and drain them thoroughly. Untie and serve in the leaf wrappers.

YOU WILL ALSO NEED

1 pound banana leaves (see page 94), cut into twenty-four 7-inch squares
24 pieces (12 × 18 inches) parchment paper
24 thirty-inch lengths kitchen twine
½ cup Achiote Oil (page 9) for assembling the pasteles
1 cup (or as needed) alcaparrado (see Daisy's Pantry on page 13)
24 whole small hot peppers, such as cayenne or bird peppers

TO FORM TAMALES AND HAYACAS

1. Prepare the tamale filling of your choice. Prepare the cornmeal batter.

2. While the cornmeal batter is cooling and becomes the right consistency, cut the banana leaves into rectangles approximately 10 × 15 inches. Don't worry if some are slightly larger or smaller. Save the trimmings; you may need some to patch up the tamales as you make them.

3. Set 1 piece of banana leaf in front of you with one of the long edges closest to you. Smear a rectangle 5 inches high by 3 inches wide with the oil on the center of the leaf. Spoon ¼ cup cornmeal batter over the oil and make an indentation in the center with the back of a spoon. Place ¼ cup of filling of your choice into the indentation. Lift up the short sides of the banana leaf to meet over the fillings. This will enclose the chicken or Venezuelan Christmas filling in cornmeal batter and center the filling over the leaf. Don't worry if the filling is not completely enclosed. Make 2 folds along the short edges so the fillings are tightly wrapped. Turn the tamale 90 degrees so one of the long edges is closest to you. Fold both sides toward the center to make a snug package. Tie with kitchen twine, following the directions for tying pasteles on page 146.

4. To cook the tamales: Set a steam rack or round cooling rack in the bottom of a shallow casserole or Dutch oven with a lid. You can even use a roasting pan with a raised rack. Pour enough water into the vessel so that it covers the bottom of the pan but is not high enough to reach the rack. Lightly salt the water.

5. Place the tamales on the rack. You can place them on top of each other if they don't all fit in 1 layer. Cover the pot (with aluminum foil if you don't have a lid) and bring to a boil over high heat. Lower the heat to a simmer.

6. Steam for 25 to 30 minutes, or until the tamales are slightly firm when poked.

Venezuelan Christmas Tamale Filling (page 150) or Chicken Filling for Tamales (page 149)

Cornmeal Batter for Tamales (page 149)

One 1-pound package banana or plantain leaves (see Daisy's Pantry, page 94)

⅓ cup Achiote Oil (page 9)

CORNMEAL BATTER for TAMALES

MASA PARA TAMALES Y HAYACA

You can certainly use canned broth for this, especially if you doctor it up by simmering some cilantro, onion, and whatever else you'd like in it for thirty minutes or so. But in cooking, as in life, you get as good as you give.

MAKES 6 CUPS, ENOUGH FOR ABOUT 15 TAMALES

Bring the broth to a boil in a 3-quart saucepan over medium heat. Gradually add the cornmeal, stirring constantly. Cook, whisking, until thickened enough for you to lift the spoon and write your initial with it on top of the filling. Stir in the cilantro, salt, and pepper. Let stand, whisking often to prevent lumps, until it is thick enough for a spoon to stand in.

6 cups Chicken Broth, homemade (page 155) or canned
1¼ cups yellow cornmeal (Quaker works well)
¼ cup chopped fresh cilantro
Fine sea or kosher salt to taste
Freshly ground black pepper to taste

CHICKEN FILLING for TAMALES

AJI DE POLLO

If you don't want to go the whole nine yards and make the tamales, this chicken filling is delicious served with rice. This is the old-school traditional.

MAKES 3½ CUPS FILLING, ENOUGH FOR ABOUT 15 TAMALES

1. Heat the oil in a medium skillet over medium heat. Add the sofrito and cumin, and cook until the liquid has evaporated and the sofrito begins to sizzle. Stir in the alcaparrado and bay leaf, cook 1 or 2 minutes, then stir in the chicken. Reduce the heat to low and cook until all the liquid has evaporated and the chicken is coated with the seasonings.
2. Blend the peanuts with the milk at low speed until smooth. Pour into the skillet and bring to a boil. Adjust the heat so the sauce is simmering, and cook until the sauce is reduced enough to cling to the chicken. Scrape into a bowl and let cool.

¼ cup Achiote Oil (page 9)
1½ cups Sofrito (page 6)
½ teaspoon ground cumin
⅓ cup alcaparrado or coarsely chopped pimiento-stuffed olives (see Daisy's Pantry on page 13)
1 bay leaf
3 cups shredded cooked chicken
⅓ cup peanuts
⅔ cup milk

VENEZUELAN CHRISTMAS TAMALE FILLING

HAYACAS NAVIDEÑAS VENEZOLANAS

This is the basic version of a Venezuelan holiday tradition. There are any number of variations, such as adding garbanzo beans, that crop up from town to town and family to family.

MAKES 3½ CUPS, ENOUGH FOR ABOUT 15 TAMALES

1. Heat the oil in a medium skillet over medium heat. Add the sofrito and alcaparrado, and cook until the liquid has evaporated and the sofrito begins to sizzle.

2. Cook the bacon until crisp and then drain. Stir in the chilies, bacon, and shrimp. Cook, stirring constantly, until the shrimp are cooked through, about 3 minutes. Scrape into a bowl and cool. Stir in the raisins

¼ cup Achiote Oil (page 9)

½ cup Sofrito (page 6)

¼ cup alcaparrado or coarsely chopped pimiento-stuffed olives (see Note on page 13)

¼ pound thickly sliced bacon, cut crosswise into ½-inch strips

½ teaspoon finely chopped hot chili pepper of your choice

1½ pounds small (40 to 50 per pound) shrimp, peeled and deveined

¼ cup raisins

CHICKEN, DUCK, AND TURKEY

POLLO, PATO, Y PAVO

The way I cook is the end product of many different influences, my mother and grandmother chief among them. The time I spent at the French Culinary Institute in New York helped open my eyes to a whole new world of cooking, too. I also read, ask a lot of questions, and never stop playing in the kitchen.

The way I evolved on my own as a cook is another story altogether. I mostly chalk it up to being a mom with a wildly chaotic schedule. I developed my own style of cooking by bringing all my influences to bear when I open the refrigerator door to see what's inside that can be turned into dinner. There is, without exception, Sofrito (page 6) in my freezer and either homemade or store-bought Dry Rub (page 19) on my pantry shelf. There are also usually a few potatoes in the house and a bottle of wine. So there you go: Chicken with Potatoes and Wine (page 154). What I love about the dish, besides its flavor, is that in a roundabout way it is a tribute to my grandmother. She loved to cook thick pork chops and chicken steamed in a skillet (*al vapor*, see page 23) and that's basically what's happening in that recipe—with a little dressing up à la Daisy, of course.

All of this improvising, respectful shortcuts, and play doesn't mean that I ever gave up on the classics. I just cut to the chase and get the most flavor I can with the least amount of fuss. Chicken with Figs (page 173), possibly my most requested dish, is a streamlined version of a Spanish classic, as is Chicken in Garlic Sauce (page 165).

Two notes: A 4-pound chicken as part of a meal that contains rice and/or beans and a vegetable will serve four people. All of these recipes can be doubled easily for a larger crowd. See individual recipes for tips. And if the Paella recipe on page 105 hasn't convinced you to buy a paellera—a wide, shallow pan with a tight-fitting lid—then these recipes should. You can brown, cook, and simmer the cut-up chicken in a single layer for more even cooking. Look for paella pans in big-box stores for about $20. Do yourself a favor and pick one up.

CHICKEN WITH POTATOES AND WINE

POLLO ASADO EN CAZUELA CON PAPAS

MAKES 4 DAISY SERVINGS OR 6 REGULAR SERVINGS

1. Place the potatoes in a large saucepan and add enough cold water to cover them. Add a small handful of salt. Bring to a boil over medium heat. As soon as they come to a boil, drain the potatoes and set them aside.

2. Wash the chicken pieces, pat them dry, and season generously with salt and pepper. Heat the oil in a paella pan or large, heavy skillet. Add as many of the chicken pieces, skin side down, as will fit without touching and cook, turning once or twice, until lightly browned, about 10 minutes. (Watch the heat under the pan, especially as you begin to remove chicken from the pan; the oil will taste unpleasant if allowed to get too hot.) Transfer the chicken pieces to a plate as they brown.

3. Preheat the oven to 375° F. Spoon all but 2 tablespoons of fat from the pan. Add the onions, garlic, and bay leaves. Cook, stirring, until the onions are softened, about 4 minutes. Pour in the wine, bring to a boil, and boil until reduced by about one-third.

4. Add the potatoes to the pan in an even layer and sprinkle them with the thyme, marjoram, and salt and pepper to taste. Top with the chicken, pour in the broth, and bring to a boil. Cover the pan and transfer it to the oven. Bake until the chicken is falling from the bone, about 1 hour and 15 minutes.

4 medium Yukon Gold potatoes (about 2 pounds), sliced on the bias into ½-inch rounds (no ends)

Fine sea or kosher salt

One 4-pound chicken, cut into 10 pieces (see page 164)

Freshly ground black pepper

¼ cup Achiote Oil (page 9)

2 medium Spanish onions (about 1 pound), halved and cut lengthwise into ½-inch slices

4 large cloves garlic, thinly sliced

2 bay leaves

1 cup dry white wine

1 teaspoon chopped fresh thyme

1 teaspoon chopped fresh marjoram or oregano

1 cup Chicken Broth, homemade (page 155) or canned

VARIATION: *This can also be finished on the stove top over a low flame. Stir gently from time to time and allow 1 hour for the chicken to become tender.*

CHICKEN BROTH

CALDO DE POLLO FRESCO

This is the way I make chicken broth—with a whole chicken cut into pieces. These pieces are plucked out and recycled into any number of chicken dishes, such as Grandma's Spaghetti with Chicken (page 156), Daisy's Chicken Diablo (page 161), and Braised Chicken with Little Potato Cubes (page 163). I end up with richly flavored chicken for whatever dish I've chosen to make, enough wonderful broth to use in that same dish, and a bonus of broth for the fridge or freezer for future use. If you're using the chicken from the broth to make any of the above-mentioned dishes, you can skip the step in that particular recipe where the chicken pieces are browned.

MAKES 3 TO 3½ QUARTS

1. Place the chicken, onions, and red pepper in a large stockpot. (Mine is 16 quarts.) Rinse the garlic head in cold water and then peel off the papery skin. Break up the garlic into individual cloves. Rinse and cut the roots off the cilantro. Cut a piece of cheesecloth the size of a kitchen towel. Put the garlic cloves, peppercorns, bay leaves, and cilantro on the cheesecloth, bring the ends together to make a little pouch, and tie the whole thing up loosely with kitchen twine. Give the pouch a few good whacks with a kitchen mallet and add it to the pot.

2. Add enough cold water to cover the chicken by at least 2 to 3 inches. Drop in the ham hock if using. Bring to a boil over medium-high heat, skimming foam off the top as it forms. When the water comes to a boil, adjust the heat so the broth cooks at a steady but not rolling boil. Cook for 30 minutes.

3. Check to make sure the breasts are cooked through and then remove them from the pot. Cook 15 minutes more, remove the legs and thighs, and set aside to make another chicken dish. If you're using backs, necks, wings, etc., you don't have to remove anything. Leave them in to further flavor the broth.

4. Cook for 1 hour. Set a strainer over a large bowl and line the strainer with a couple of layers of cheesecloth. Carefully strain the broth through the cheesecloth. (Ladling it is the easiest and safest way.) Add salt to taste.

One 5-pound chicken, cut into 10 pieces (see page 164), or 5 pounds chicken backs, wings, necks, and gizzards (without the liver; see Notes)
2 large Spanish onions (about 2 pounds), left whole and unpeeled
1 large red bell pepper, cored, seeded, and cut into quarters
1 large head of garlic
1 large bunch fresh cilantro
2 teaspoons black peppercorns
2 bay leaves
1 ham hock (optional)
Fine sea or kosher salt

NOTES: *You can add* ajices dulces *(see Note on page 6) and/or* culantro *(page 6) to this.*

- *If this broth is destined for a soup, like the Chicken Soup with Thin Egg Noodles on page 76, add a small pinch of saffron threads for a gorgeous golden color.*
- *Use the whole chicken if you'd like to end up with a chicken to use in another dish. If you're making broth to stockpile in the freezer, use the chicken backs, necks, and/or wings.*

GRANDMA'S SPAGHETTI WITH CHICKEN

POLLO CON ESPAGETI DE ABUELA

When I was a little girl, my family lived in my grandmother's two-family house in Brooklyn. I can tell you, those were very happy days—running downstairs to Abuela's house on Saturday mornings for breakfast and cartoons. She had one of those huge four-poster "grandma" beds that I would climb onto, and I can still remember the big cabbage roses on the wallpaper.

After breakfast Abuela would plan her shopping. If I promised to be very good (I always did), Abuela would let me take the bus with her to Thirteenth Avenue, where we would visit the live poultry store. There, Abuela would pick out the chickens she would be taking home for dinner that weekend. If we were lucky, sometimes our chicken would have little shell-less eggs inside, and we would save these for the broth that Abuela would make.

One of the special treats Abuela liked to make for my dad was spaghetti. Sometimes she made it with little pork ribs, but often she made the sauce with chicken, which she cooked until it was tender and almost falling off the bone. I'm sure she fancied her take on Italian cooking quite the thing, and looking back, I can remember the look of love and amusement on her face as she watched me messily and noisily slurping up spaghetti strands.

MAKES FOUR DAISY SERVINGS OR 6 REGULAR SERVINGS

1. Wash the chicken pieces and pat them dry with paper towels. Season generously with salt and pepper. Heat the oil in a large skillet—cast iron if you have one—over medium heat. Add as many of the chicken pieces, skin side down, as will fit without touching. Cook, turning once, until the chicken is golden brown on both sides, about 10 minutes. The chicken will be undercooked; it will finish cooking in the sauce. Remove and drain on paper towels and repeat with the remaining chicken if necessary.

2. Spoon off all but 3 tablespoons of fat from the skillet. Add the sofrito and cook until the water has evaporated and the sofrito starts to sizzle. Add the alcaparrado, white wine, cilantro, and cumin. Bring to a boil and cook until the wine has almost completely evaporated. Pour in the crushed tomatoes, add the bay leaves, and bring to a boil. Adjust the heat so the sauce is simmering.

3. Return the chicken to the skillet, cover, and cook until the chicken is very tender, 45 minutes to an hour.

4. When the chicken is almost ready, cook the spaghetti in a large pot of boiling salted water 1 to 2 minutes less than suggested on the package.

One 3- to 4-pound chicken, cut into 10 pieces (see page 164)
Fine sea or kosher salt
Freshly ground black pepper
3 tablespoons olive oil
1 cup Sofrito (page 6)
½ cup bottled alcaparrado (see Daisy's Pantry, page 13) or coarsely chopped pimiento-stuffed olives
½ cup dry white wine
3 tablespoons chopped fresh cilantro
1 tablespoon ground cumin
Two 28-ounce cans crushed tomatoes
2 bay leaves
1 pound spaghetti

NOTES: *This recipe works very well with an equal amount of chicken thighs. That is actually the way I prefer to make it.*

• If you can find them, a few finely chopped ajices dulces (see Note on page 6), would make a lovely addition. Use them along with or instead of the chopped cilantro.

5. While the spaghetti is cooking, transfer the chicken with a slotted spoon to one end of a large platter and cover it with aluminum foil to keep warm.

6. Drain the pasta and return it to the pot. Add the sauce and stir gently over low heat to finish cooking the pasta. Check the seasoning and then pile the spaghetti onto the other end of the platter. Serve with crusty garlic bread.

GARLIC BREAD

It may not be very Latin, but it sure is good, especially with Grandma's Spaghetti with Chicken (above).

Preheat the broiler. Chop 8 or more cloves of garlic in a food processor and add 4 tablespoons each of softened butter and olive oil. Process until the garlic is finely chopped. Add salt and pepper to taste. Take a short (about 16 inches) loaf of Italian bread and split it lengthwise. Spread the cut side of the bread with the garlic mixture. Broil about 4 inches from the heat until the edges of the bread start to color, about 2 minutes. Turn off the broiler and set the oven at 375°F. Bake the bread until crisp and the top is evenly brown, about 12 minutes. Serve hot.

CRISPY CHICKEN BITS

CHICHARRONES DE POLLO

The secret to making addictive, crispy *chicharrones* is frying them in really hot oil. I use thighs because they don't dry out when exposed to the intense heat of the hot oil the way chicken breasts might. I also like marinating the chicken in cider vinegar because it says enough without saying too much.

This is a snack dish and will disappear as quickly as you can make it. Or increase the amount and serve it as a main course or as part of a mixed fried dinner.

MAKES 6 SNACK-SIZE SERVINGS

1. Toss the chicken with the dry rub and the vinegar until coated. Marinate, covered, at room temperature up to 30 minutes or in the refrigerator up to 1 day. Drain the chicken thoroughly.
2. Pour enough oil into a deep, heavy pot to fill about 3 inches. Heat over medium-high heat until the tip of the handle of a wooden spoon dipped in the oil gives off a very lively sizzle (about 390° F).
3. While the oil is heating, dredge the chicken in flour until coated. Tap off any excess flour. Once the oil is hot enough, carefully slip as many of the floured chicken pieces into the oil as will fit comfortably. Let them bob around, turning them with a spoon once or twice, until deep golden brown and cooked through, about 4 minutes. Remove and drain on paper towels and then repeat with the remaining chicken. Serve hot.

1½ pounds boneless, skinless chicken thighs, cut into pinky-size strips
2 teaspoons Dry Rub, homemade (page 19) or store-bought
1½ tablespoons cider or your favorite vinegar
Vegetable or canola oil
All-purpose flour

VARIATION: *As delicious as these are plain, they are even better with Spicy Pineapple Vinegar (page 218) or Garlic Dipping Sauce (page 114).*

BUTTERFLIED CHICKEN COOKED UNDER a BRICK

POLLO A LA PLANCHA AL LADRILLO

I keep a few bricks around just for this use. A brick just seems to be the right size and weight to cover the chicken and also a lot of fun. I usually send my daughter Angela, a budding archeologist and a great collector of rocks, to find the perfect brick and to wrap it in foil for me. This dish is best eaten right away, while the chicken is still nice and moist.

MAKES 6 SERVINGS

Two 3-pound chickens
2 tablespoons Dry Rub, homemade (page 19) or store-bought
3 cups cider vinegar
1 cup water
3 cloves garlic, smashed
Juice of 1 lemon
4 bay leaves
Vegetable oil

1. Cut the tips off the chicken wings. Remove the backbones from the chickens by cutting along both sides with a heavy kitchen knife or a pair of kitchen shears. Using a paring knife or the tip of a boning knife, cut out the wishbones. Remove the keel-shaped breastbones: Free the wide part of the bone (closer to the neck) from the meat by cutting around the sides of it with a paring or boning knife. Once the wide part of the breastbone is free, it will be easy to pull the bone from the chicken. Spread the chicken out, skin side down, on a board and cover it with a sheet of plastic wrap. Pound the chicken lightly with a meat mallet until it is more or less of even thickness. Repeat with the second chicken. Rub all sides of both chickens with the dry rub. Put each chicken in a sealable 1-gallon plastic bag.

2. In a large measuring cup, mix the vinegar, water, garlic, and lemon juice. Pour half of the mixture into each bag, drop 2 bay leaves into each bag, and refrigerate for at least 2 hours or up to overnight. Turn the bags occasionally.

3. Heat a gas grill on high for 10 minutes, then lower the heat to medium. Or light a charcoal fire and wait for the coals to be covered with white ash. (See "A Word About Grills", on page 193.) Using a pair of tongs, dip a paper towel in the oil and rub the grill with it. Place the chickens skin side down and side by side. Place a baking sheet over the chickens and weigh it down with a foil-covered brick. Close the grill cover and cook until the skin is crispy and browned, about 15 minutes. Flip the chicken and cook until the juices run clear, not pink, when you poke the thickest part of the thigh with the tip of a paring knife, about 30 minutes. Serve immediately.

FRIED CHICKEN

POLLO FRITO

Eat this hot or cold, as we did when we brought it to the beach. Since we kids would always fight over the legs, Mami would sometimes make a batch of this with just legs and thighs. We kids would eat all the legs we wanted, and Mami and Papi ate the thighs! That works for me now, too. If I get home close to dinner time, I throw a batch of this together and we eat it hot. More often, in a house with six people with six different schedules, I'll set out a big platter of this in the late afternoon and let people take what they want when they want it. My kids love this with rice and corn (page 92), which I put up while the chicken is frying. That's good hot or cold, too.

MAKES 6 DAISY SERVINGS OR 8 TO 10 REGULAR SERVINGS

1. Lay out the chicken pieces in a baking pan large enough to hold them comfortably. (An 11 × 13-inch pan works well.) Scatter the onion, garlic, and oregano over the chicken. Stir the vinegar and both juices together in a small bowl and pour them over the chicken. Cover tightly and refrigerate at least 2 hours or up to 1 day. Turn the chicken pieces 2 or 3 times as they marinate.

2. To cook: Pour 4 inches of oil into a 4- to 5-quart heavy pot. Heat over medium heat until the tip of the handle of a wooden spoon gives off a lively sizzle when dipped in the oil (about 375° F). While the oil is heating, drain the chicken thoroughly on paper towels.

3. Carefully—the oil will foam up dramatically—slip into the pan as many pieces of chicken as will fit without touching. Fry, turning once, until the juices run clear, not pink, when poked down to the bone, about 15 minutes. The breast pieces will be cooked before the legs, thighs, and wings. Drain the chicken on paper towels and serve hot or cold.

Two 3-pound chickens, cut into 10 pieces each (see page 164), or 6 pounds of chicken parts of your choice
1 large Spanish onion, diced
3 to 4 cloves garlic, smashed
1 tablespoon dried oregano
1 cup cider or other vinegar
Juice of 3 oranges
Juice of 1 lemon
Vegetable or canola oil

NOTES: *If you plan to serve the chicken hot and your pan isn't large enough to fry the chicken in one batch, keep the first batch hot on a baking sheet in a 250° F oven while frying the second.*

• If they are available, sour oranges (naranjas agrias; see note on page 48) make a nice addition to the marinade. Use two in place of the lemon and one of the oranges.

DAISY'S CHICKEN DIABLO

POLLO AL DIABLO A LA DAISY

My friend Susan has told me more than once that learning to make Sofrito (page 6) changed her life. She swears there is always some on hand in her freezer. (See, it's not just me!) She and her husband, Alan, have a beautiful house in Montauk, Long Island, with a fabulous view of the beach. Alan, a gifted drummer who has played with Tito Puente and accompanied Barbra Streisand, among others, loves to cook. He was supposed to man the grill for dinner during one of our visits to their house, but he got held up (on the golf course with my husband), and I stepped in. Susan and I rustled around her kitchen and dug up canned tomatoes, cilantro, hot peppers, pasta, and, true to Susan's word, some sofrito in her freezer. That's how this dish, which is also delicious with yucca, was born.

MAKES 4 DAISY-SIZE SERVINGS

1. Wash the chicken pieces and pat them dry with paper towels. Season all sides generously with salt and pepper. Heat the oil in a Dutch oven over medium-high heat until rippling. Add as many of the chicken pieces, skin side down, as fit without touching. Cook, turning once, until the chicken is golden brown on both sides, about 10 minutes. Remove and drain on paper towels and repeat with the remaining chicken if necessary.

2. Spoon off all but 2 tablespoons of fat from the pan. Add the red pepper flakes and cook until sizzling, just a few seconds. Add the chorizo, stirring quickly so it releases its color and aroma. Stir in the sofrito and cook, scraping all the browned bits from the bottom of the pan, until the water has evaporated and the sofrito is sizzling. Stir in the alcaparrado and bay leaves. Pour in the white wine, bring to a boil, and cook until the wine has almost completely evaporated. Stir in the tomatoes and marjoram, and tuck the chicken into the sauce in a single layer. Turn the chicken to coat with the sauce. Bring to a boil, then adjust the heat so that the sauce is simmering. Add the chicken broth, cover, and cook until the chicken is tender, about 30 minutes.

3. Remove the cover and cook until the sauce is slightly reduced, about 10 minutes more. Check the seasoning, adding salt and red pepper flakes if you think it needs it. Serve the chicken right from the pot or transfer it to a deep platter. Either way, scatter the chopped cilantro over the chicken just before serving.

One 4-pound chicken, cut into 10 pieces (see page 164)
Fine sea or kosher salt
Freshly ground pepper
¼ cup canola oil
1 tablespoon hot red pepper flakes
2 chorizo, andouille, or any smoked garlicky sausages (about 6 ounces), diced
½ cup Sofrito (page 6)
½ cup alcaparrado or coarsely chopped pimiento-stuffed olives with brine (see Daisy's Pantry on page 13)
2 bay leaves
½ cup dry white wine
Two 28-ounce cans crushed tomatoes
1 teaspoon chopped fresh marjoram
1 cup Chicken Broth, homemade (page 155) or canned
¼ cup chopped fresh cilantro

While I was in high school, Mami decided it had been too long since we had spent a Christmas in Puerto Rico, so she packed us all up and away we went. I had been dying to experience the island at Christmastime because as a teenager my cousins had gotten me psyched for the whole *paranda*, or caroling, phenomenon. *Parandas* involve groups of carolers, sometimes in caravans of cars, going from house to house with guitars, maracas, and *guiros,* instruments made from notched dried gourds; the notches are "strummed" (with something that looks like a fork made in a garage!) to make a cool, rasping sound. They sing holiday songs in exchange for Christmas foods and drinks of Puerto Rican Egg Nog (page 273). From what I'd heard, the whole deal usually lasts into the morning hours, and much fun is had by all. I couldn't wait!

The pace for Christmas was set by the pig roast at Tia Gabriela's house, but my other aunts and uncles had festivities of their own planned. And Mama Clotilde (my mother's mother) was not to be left behind. Tio Hector, the youngest of Mami's siblings and my favorite uncle, lived around the corner from Mama Clotilde, and we could always count on him to come over and have everyone in stitches within minutes with his stories and jokes.

With the air redolent with the smell of rice with pigeon peas and roasting pork, my grandmother called for Mami to get the turkey she had been fattening up in the yard. I figured this was a sight I would not soon have a chance to see again, so, siblings in tow, we followed Mami into the large yard to get the turkey. Now I had seen Mami make short order of chickens with no problem at all, but this turkey was having none of it. The minute Mami opened the pen door, the turkey rushed her, got by her, and took off, with Mami in hot pursuit and me, my sister, and my brothers on the floor laughing.

It took some doing, but Mami finally cornered that turkey (with absolutely no help from us) and maybe even took a little extra satisfaction in getting him ready to go to that great turkey farm in the sky. Mama Clotilde dressed him with Wet Rub (19), and we thoroughly enjoyed him on Christmas Day. To this day I can never eat turkey without remembering Mami chasing that bird all around Mama's yard.

BRAISED CHICKEN WITH LITTLE POTATO CUBES

POLLO GUISADO CON PAPITAS

The potatoes will be very tender, especially if you cook the chicken for the longer amount suggested. That's how my kids like this dish—with potatoes soft enough to mash into the sauce.

MAKES 6 SERVINGS

1. Wash the chicken pieces and pat them dry with paper towels. Season all sides lightly with salt and pepper. Heat the oil in a paella pan (see page 105) or wide, heavy skillet over medium-high heat until rippling. Add as many of the chicken pieces, skin side down, as will fit without touching. Cook, turning once, until the chicken is golden brown on both sides, about 10 minutes. Remove and drain on paper towels and repeat with the remaining chicken if necessary.
2. Add the sofrito to the pan and cook until the water has evaporated and the sofrito starts to sizzle. Stir in the alcaparrado, cumin, sugar, bay leaf, marjoram, and cinnamon. Pour in the tomato sauce and broth, and bring to a boil. Return the chicken to the pan and turn to coat with the sauce. Cover and cook over low heat for 15 minutes. Add the potato cubes, cover the pan, and cook for 15 to 30 minutes, depending on how you like your chicken done; 15 minutes will give you tender chicken, 30 minutes will give you chicken that is falling off the bone.
3. Pile the chicken, potatoes, and sauce onto a platter or serve right from the pot. Sprinkle fresh chopped cilantro over the dish before serving.

One 5-pound roasting chicken, cut into 10 pieces (see page 164)
Fine sea or kosher salt
Freshly ground black pepper
1 tablespoon Achiote Oil (page 9)
½ cup Sofrito (page 6)
½ cup alcaparrado (see Note on page 13) or coarsely chopped pimiento-stuffed olives
1 teaspoooon ground cumin
1 teaspoon brown sugar
1 bay leaf
Leaves from 1 sprig of fresh marjoram or oregano, chopped
Pinch of ground cinnamon
One 8-ounce can Spanish-style tomato sauce
1 cup Chicken Broth, homemade (page 155) or canned
2 medium russet potatoes (about 1¼ pounds), peeled and cut into 1-inch cubes
Chopped fresh cilantro

> **VARIATION:** *Piloncillo (see Note on page 43) or molasses would make a nice substitute for the brown sugar.*

HOW TO CUT A CHICKEN INTO TEN PIECES

The simplest way to cut a chicken into ten pieces is to buy a chicken already "cut in eighths" from the supermarket. Cut off the wing tips if necessary and trim any overhanging skin and excess fat. Lay the breasts, skin side up, on the cutting board and cut them in half crosswise with one firm stroke.

If you are starting from scratch with a whole chicken, first make sure you have a sharp, sturdy knife and a pair of kitchen shears. With the shears cut along the backbone on both sides to remove it. Lay the chicken flat, skin side down, on the cutting board and cut in half right through the middle of the breastbone. Cut off the legs and then cut them in half at the knee joint. Cut off the wings where they meet the breast. The easiest way to cut the leg in half and separate the wing from the breast is to cut through the meat down to the bone. Take a peek to find the joint and cut through the middle of the joint—it's easier than trying to cut through bones. Cut off the wing tips, cut the breast in half as described above, and trim any overhanging skin and excess fat.

You can also cut a duck into serving pieces in the same way. Go slowly; the joints in a duck aren't as easy to cut through as those of a chicken.

CHICKEN IN GARLIC SAUCE

POLLO AL AJILLO

This is a relative of Shrimp in Garlic Sauce (page 184), but it takes longer to cook. That is why I like to use chicken thighs here—they won't dry out during cooking. If you like white meat, go ahead and use it; just cook it a little less.

MAKES 6 SERVINGS

1. Wash the chicken thighs and pat them dry with paper towels. Season the chicken generously with salt and pepper. Heat the oil in a large, heavy skillet over medium-high heat. Add as many of the chicken thighs, skin side down, as will fit without touching. Cook until the skin is golden brown, about 10 minutes. Flip the chicken pieces and cook until the second side is golden brown, about 5 minutes more.

2. Remove the pan from the heat and spoon off all but about 2 tablespoons of the fat, leaving all the lovely brown bits behind. Return the pan to low heat, stir in the garlic and thyme, and cook until the garlic starts to turn golden, a minute or two.

3. Pour in the sherry, increase the heat to medium, and bring to a boil. Let it boil a minute or two, then return the chicken to the pan, skin side up. Reduce the heat to low, pour in the chicken broth, and bring to a simmer. Cover the pan tightly and cook for 20 minutes. Flip the chicken pieces (or rotate them from top to bottom if using a smaller pan) and cook until the chicken is very tender, about 20 minutes. Serve hot.

12 large chicken thighs (about 4 pounds)
Fine sea or kosher salt
Freshly ground black pepper
¼ cup canola oil
10 cloves garlic, sliced
2 teaspoons chopped fresh thyme
½ cup dry sherry
½ cup Chicken Broth, homemade (page 155) or canned

VARIATION: *If you like a mix of white and dark meat, substitute a 4-pound chicken cut into 10 pieces (see opposite page). Let the thighs, drumsticks, and wings cook in the sauce for 15 minutes before adding the browned breast pieces. If you want to use all white meat, cut the breasts in half crosswise, brown them as described above, but let the sauce cook down for 10 to 15 minutes after adding the broth before adding the chicken breasts.*

NOTE: *This is another place a paella pan (see page 105) comes in handy. If you have a smaller Dutch oven, brown the chicken in batches and rotate the pieces from top to bottom as they simmer in the sauce so the pieces cook evenly.*

CRACKER JACK CHICKEN

POLLO VILLAROY

This is my version of the classic chicken Villaroy, which traditionally is not stuffed but is coated with béchamel sauce and then a coating of crispy crumbs. Since I'm always playing around in the kitchen, I decided to borrow a little from another classic chicken dish—chicken cordon bleu—and filled the chicken breasts with ham and cheese.

Stuffing, browning, and coating the chicken—the most time-consuming part of this dish—can be done well in advance. For best results, though, bread and fry the chicken immediately before serving.

My kids call this "Cracker Jack" chicken because there is a surprise inside. You'll call it out of this world.

MAKES 6 SERVINGS

1. Butterfly the chicken breasts: Lay one flat on the cutting board and, holding the knife parallel to the board, cut along the long, thick side of the breast until almost but not quite cut in half horizontally. Open up the chicken breast like a book and with a meat mallet pound it out to a little less than ½ inch thick. Repeat with the remaining chicken breasts.

2. Season both sides of the butterflied chicken breasts with salt and pepper. Cover the top of the chicken breasts with ham, leaving a ½- to 1-inch border around the edges and tearing the ham slices as necessary. Place a finger of cheese on the edge of the ham closest to you. Fold the chicken over the cheese and then roll up the breast to make a compact bundle. Tie the chicken rolls securely at 1-inch intervals with kitchen twine.

3. Spread the flour on a plate. Roll the chicken bundles in the flour until coated on all sides. Tap off the excess flour. Heat ¼ inch of oil in a large, heavy skillet over medium-low heat. Add as many of the floured chicken rolls as will fit without touching. Cook, turning often, until golden brown on all sides and the chicken is cooked through, about 10 minutes. The key is to keep the heat slow and steady and turn the chicken pieces often so they don't turn too brown before they are cooked through. Remove and cool.

4. While the chicken is cooling, make the béchamel sauce. (Working with the béchamel sauce hot from the stove will make it easier to coat the chicken evenly.)

5. Line a baking sheet with waxed paper, shiny side up. Using a fork, turn one of the chicken rolls in the béchamel sauce until coated on all sides. Lift it out of the sauce, let the excess sauce drip back into the pot, and then set the chicken roll on a paper-lined tray. Repeat

FOR THE CHICKEN

6 large boneless, skinless chicken breasts (about 3 pounds)
Fine sea or kosher salt
Freshly ground black pepper
6 thin slices Serrano ham, prosciutto, or deli ham
6 pinky-size pieces of Monterey Jack, Havarti, or tetilla cheese (see Daisy's Pantry)
¼ cup all-purpose flour
Canola oil

Béchamel Sauce (page 167)

FOR COATING AND FRYING

3 large eggs
1 cup Italian-style bread crumbs
Canola oil

DAISY'S PANTRY *Tetilla is a semisoft cheese with a natural rind that is made in Spain. If you have a cheese or specialty store near you that carries tetilla, you might want to try it. See Sources for ordering information.*

with the remaining chicken rolls. Refrigerate uncovered until the sauce is set, at least 45 minutes or up to 4 hours. Bring to room temperature 30 minutes before frying.

6. Coat the chicken: Beat the eggs in a shallow bowl until foamy. Spread the bread crumbs in a separate shallow bowl. Stick a fork into one end of a chicken roll, and turn it in the beaten eggs until coated. Lift the chicken out and let it drain a few seconds over the dish. Roll the chicken in the bread crumbs until coated, then set on a baking sheet. Repeat with the remaining chicken rolls.

7. Pour 4 inches of oil into a large, heavy pot. The oil will foam up after adding the chicken so be sure there is at least 4 inches of headroom. Heat over medium heat until the tip of a wooden spoon dipped in the oil gives off a very lively sizzle immediately (about 360°F). Carefully slip 3 of the breaded chicken rolls into the oil. The oil will foam. Cook until the foaming dies down and the chicken is a gorgeous uniform golden brown, about 2½ minutes. Remove with a skimmer or slotted spoon to paper towels to drain. Repeat with the remaining chicken. Serve right away.

BÉCHAMEL SAUCE

SALSA BÉCHAMEL

1. Melt the butter in a small saucepan over medium-low heat. When it is foaming, stir in the flour. Cook, whisking, for 4 minutes.

2. Slowly pour in the milk, whisking constantly. (When whisking a flour-thickened sauce like béchamel, pay attention to the corners. It's there that the sauce is most likely to stick and burn.) Add the thyme and bay leaf. Bring to a boil, whisking constantly. Adjust the heat so the sauce is simmering and cook, whisking occasionally, until thickened and smooth, about 15 minutes. Stir in the salt and nutmeg.

4 tablespoons butter
¼ cup all-purpose flour
2 cups hot milk
3 sprigs of fresh thyme
1 bay leaf
Fine sea or kosher salt to taste
Small pinch of nutmeg

CHICKEN AND CRISPY TORTILLA CASSEROLE WITH TOMATILLO SAUCE

CHILAQUILES

Chilaquiles, a casserole of crispy corn tortillas layered with sauce, cheese, and poultry or meat, originated as a way to use day-old corn tortillas in Mexican households. In Brooklyn there are a million places to buy freshly made tortillas, so I hardly ever have leftovers, but I do buy them fresh and leave them out for a day just to make this dish.

The sauce for chilaquiles can be green or red. This is a green version, made with tomatillo sauce that keeps its remarkable fresh flavor even after it is simmered and baked. To make the red version, prepare an enchilada sauce similar to the one for the pork on page 206. If you make that pork and have any left over, shred the pork back into the sauce and use that mix in place of the chicken in green sauce here to make the chilaquiles. You will be so happy, you'll want to send me flowers!

MAKES 6 SERVINGS

FOR THE SAUCE

1½ pounds tomatillos (see Daisy's Pantry)

1 medium Spanish onion, cut into 1-inch chunks

⅓ cup (loosely packed) mint leaves (see Daisy's Pantry)

1 bunch cilantro, stems and all, very roughly chopped (about 1 cup)

1 jalapeño, cored and seeded

4 cloves garlic

3 cups shredded cooked chicken, turkey, pork, beef, or other meat you prefer

2 teaspoons, or as needed, fine sea or kosher salt

Vegetable oil

Ten 6-inch corn tortillas, cut into 2-inch-wide strips

1 cup grated Monterey Jack cheese

1 cup grated Parmesan, Manchego, or Cotijo cheese (see Daisy's Pantry)

1. Remove the papery covering from the tomatillos. Wash and core them. Cut the tomatillos into 2-inch chunks.

2. Blend the tomatillos at low speed until liquidy. Add the onion and blend until smooth. Add the mint and cilantro, and blend until the herbs are finely chopped. Add the jalapeño and garlic, and blend until smooth. Pour the liquid into a medium, heavy saucepan. Bring to a boil over high heat, then adjust the heat so that the sauce is simmering. Cook until the sauce has thickened slightly, about 20 minutes. Set aside ½ cup of sauce.

3. Stir the shredded chicken into the remaining sauce. Stir in the salt.

4. Heat the oven to 350° F. Pour about ¼ inch of oil into a large, heavy skillet over medium heat. Dip a corner of one of the tortilla strips into the oil; when it gives off a lively sizzle, the oil is ready. Add to the pan as many tortilla strips as will fit without overlapping. Fry the tortillas, turning once, until golden brown on both sides, about 4 minutes. Remove and drain on paper towels. Repeat with the remaining tortilla strips.

5. Butter a 9 × 11-inch casserole or baking dish that is at least 2½ inches deep. Place a layer of the fried tortilla strips on the bottom. (It doesn't matter if the layer is perfectly even or not, just be sure to cover the bottom.) Spoon half of the sauce and chicken over the tortillas. Top with ⅓ cup each of the Monterey Jack and Manchego or

VARIATIONS: *Although I haven't tried it, I bet these would be good made in individual portions.*

• *If you'd like to make this and have no leftovers, cook 1 pound of boneless and skinless chicken thighs or breasts any way you like—grilled, baked, poached, or broiled—and shred them coarsely.*

• *The tomatillo sauce on its own is delicious with grilled chicken or fish.*

Parmesan cheese. Make another layer of the tortillas, sauce, and cheeses. Top with another layer of tortillas and spread with the remaining sauce. Top with remaining cheeses.

6. Bake until the edges of the casserole are bubbling and the top layer of cheese is golden brown, about 35 minutes. Let stand 5 to 10 minutes before serving.

DAISY'S PANTRY *Tomatillos are related to tomatoes but are quite different; they have a firm texture and a tart flavor. Tomatillos look like firm green tomatoes and range in size from a golf ball to a tennis ball. They are coated with a papery husk that should be peeled before washing. You will find tomatillos in Latin markets, specialty produce stores, and an increasing number of supermarkets.*

• You can use epazote in place of the mint. Epazote is an aromatic herb with a unique flavor and fragrance. It can be found in Latin markets and growing wild over much of the Americas, including the streets of New York City!

• Cotijo is a hard, dry cheese with a Parmesan-like flavor; it is used for grating over and into dishes like this.

• See Sources for tomatillos, epazote, and Cotijo cheese.

RICH BROWN SAUCE, DAISY STYLE

SALSA ESPAGNOLE ESTILO DAISY

This quick take on a classic sauce has many uses. Stir some into a panful of sautéed chicken or pork chops toward the end of cooking. Use it as the start of a great beef stew. Hell, it's even good on turkey.

1. Remove the skin from the slab bacon and cut the bacon into ½-inch slices. Cut the slices crosswise into ½-inch strips. Toss the bacon pieces into a 4- to 5-quart skillet and place the pan over medium heat. Cook the bacon, stirring it once or twice, until it starts to give up its fat. Cook, stirring often, until it is well browned, about 10 minutes.

2. Scoop the bacon onto paper towels with a slotted spoon (reserve it for the Chicken with Figs recipe or another use) and then pour off almost all the fat from the pan. Add the celery, carrots, onion, and thyme, and cook, still over medium heat, until lightly browned, about 10 minutes. Sprinkle the flour over the vegetables and stir everything together until the flour coats the vegetables and picks up all the fat. Adjust the heat to low and keep stirring until there are no traces of the flour sticking to the vegetables, which would give an unpleasant taste to the finished sauce. Stir in the tomato paste and cook for 1 to 2 minutes.

3. Remove the pan from the heat and pour in the cognac. Return the pan to the heat and boil until the cognac has almost evaporated. Stand back from the pan once you add the cognac; there is a chance it could burst into flames.

4. Pour the broth into the pan and stir to dissolve the flour. Add the bay leaves and cloves, and bring to a boil. Adjust the heat so the sauce is at a gentle boil and cook, stirring occasionally, until the sauce is lightly thickened, about 30 minutes. Skim off the foam and fat that rises to the surface as the sauce cooks. Strain the sauce.

1 pound slab bacon (see Notes)
3 celery stalks, trimmed and cut into 2-inch pieces
2 carrots, peeled, trimmed, and cut into 2-inch lengths
1 large Spanish onion, cut into 2-inch chunks
2 big sprigs of fresh thyme or ½ teaspoon dried thyme
3 tablespoons all-purpose flour
2 tablespoons tomato paste
⅓ cup cognac
One 48-ounce can chicken broth
2 bay leaves
5 cloves

NOTES: *I love slab bacon for this sauce because you can cut it into big pieces that taste great. But if you can't find it, buy the thickest sliced bacon in your supermarket and cut it crosswise into ½-inch strips.*

• To remove the skin from the bacon, start by using a paring knife to separate the skin from the fat at one corner, then lift the skin up as you continue cutting, making it easier to see what you're doing.

CHICKEN WITH FIGS

POLLO CON HIGOS

Chicken with figs is a classic Spanish dish traditionally made with Sauce Espagnol, a rich brown sauce that starts with diced celery, onion, and carrot, and is hours in the making. My version (see page 171) makes short work of the sauce and is no less delicious. I use big chunks of the vegetables instead of taking the time to dice them, and then I strain them out of the finished sauce.

This is a great party dish, so I'm giving you a recipe using two chickens. Even if you're not feeding a crowd, you'll thank me for the leftovers after you've tasted this.

This dish is wonderful made with fresh figs; the figs melt into the sauce and thicken and sweeten it. If you see beautiful ripe figs in the market, pick them up and make this dish with them. But since fresh figs are in season only part of the year and this is one of my favorite party dishes, I started making it with dried figs. Recently I discovered dried "figlets," small figs sold in resealable bags in the supermarket. They are perfect for this dish, so that's how I make it now.

MAKES 6 TO 8 SERVINGS

1. Make the brown sauce and reserve the bacon as directed.

2. While the sauce is simmering, brown the chicken: Season all the pieces generously with salt and pepper. Pour enough oil into a large, deep skillet to lightly coat the bottom. Heat over medium-high heat until the oil is rippling. Add to the pan as many pieces of chicken, skin side down, as will fit without crowding. Cook, turning once, until dark golden brown on both sides, about 10 minutes. The chicken doesn't have to be cooked through; it will finish cooking in the sauce. Transfer the browned pieces to a large *paellera* (see page 105) or Dutch oven and brown the rest of the chicken, in batches if necessary.

3. Meanwhile, pour enough boiling water over the dried figs in a heat-proof bowl to cover them completely. Let stand until the figs are softened, about 20 minutes depending on the figs. You don't need to do this if you are using fresh figs. Drain the figs and discard the liquid.

4. Return all chicken to the pan if necessary. Ladle the sauce through a fine strainer over the chicken. Scatter the reserved bacon and figs over the chicken, breaking up some of the figs as you go to help the sauce thicken. Bring the sauce to a boil, cover the pan, and cook until the chicken is tender and the figs are very soft and have started to dissolve into the sauce, about 1 hour (see Notes). Serve on warm plates, spooning some of the chicken, bacon, and figs for each serving.

Rich Brown Sauce, Daisy Style (page 171)
Two 4-pound chickens, cut into 10 pieces each (see page 164)
Fine sea or kosher salt
Freshly ground black pepper
Vegetable or canola oil
Two 1-pound bags dried "figlets" or 2 pounds dried figs, cut in half, or 1 pint fresh figs (see Notes)

NOTES: *If your stove top is occupied, you can finish cooking this dish in an oven preheated to 350° F. It will take about the same amount of time as the stove top version. Handle the wide, heavy pan carefully when moving it into and out of the oven.*

• If using fresh figs, wash them gently and cut them into quarters before adding them.

PUERTO RICAN ROAST TURKEY

PAVOCHON

Pavo is Spanish for turkey and *lechón* is Spanish for a whole roast suckling pig. Recently I visited the town of Lajas in Puerto Rico, famous for the best *lechón* on the island—*supposedly!* Apparently they've never been to my aunt Gabriela's house in Arecibo!—and saw a sign for *pavochon*. Intrigued, I walked into the *fonda* to see what this mysterious new dish was and was very amused to find that it was turkey seasoned in the style of a suckling pig.

MAKES 12 SERVINGS WITH LEFTOVERS (EXCEPT IN MY HOUSE)

1 small (12- to 14-pound) turkey
¾ cup Wet Rub (page 19)
1 large Spanish onion
1 large carrot, peeled, trimmed, and
  cut into 1-inch pieces
3 celery stalks, trimmed and cut into
  1-inch pieces
2 bay leaves
2 teaspoons arrowroot or 4 teaspoons
  cornstarch
Fine sea or kosher salt
Freshly ground black pepper

1. Remove the bag of giblets and neck from the turkey. Discard the liver and cut the remaining giblets and neck into large pieces with a cleaver or heavy knife.

2. Wash the turkey, pulling out and discarding any large pockets of fat from the body cavity as you do. Pat the turkey dry and set it on paper towels on your cutting board. Work your fingers between the skin and flesh of the turkey; do this carefully and slowly to prevent tearing the skin. Once you have separated the skin from the breast, thigh, and as much of the leg meat as you can, press the wet rub into the flesh and inside the turkey. Truss the turkey with kitchen twine. (See instructions for trussing a chicken on page 18.) Refrigerate for at least 2 hours or up to overnight.

3. Preheat the oven to 400° F. Scatter the onion, carrot, celery, bay leaves, and reserved neck and giblet pieces in a roasting pan. Pour in 2 cups of water. Place the turkey, breast side down, on a roasting rack (preferably a V-shaped one). Roast the turkey 13–15 minutes a pound, until the juices run clear, not pink, from the thickest part of the thigh. Check this by poking down to the bone with a paring knife. About 30 minutes before the turkey is cooked, turn it breast side up to give it a lovely color. (Wear washable oven mitts when turning the turkey and removing it from the pan. It may not look pretty, but it works.)

4. Remove the turkey from the rack and let it rest on a cutting board. Add water if necessary to make about 2 cups of liquid in the pan. Skim the fat from the liquid and place the pan over high heat. Cook, stirring up the bits from the bottom, and bring to a boil. Strain through a fine sieve. Discard the solids and return the liquid to the pan. Stir the arrowroot and 2 tablespoons of water together in a small bowl until the arrowroot is dissolved. Add to the liquid in the pan and stir over medium-high heat until the gravy is slightly thickened and glossy. Check for seasoning, adding salt and pepper if necessary.

DUCK IN RED WINE

PATO EN VINO TINTO

This is a European dish with a Venezuelan accent. Both Venezuelan and Argentinean cooking borrow heavily from classical European cooking, thanks to the tremendous number of Germans and Italians who have made those countries their home. This is not medium-rare French-style duck breast but falling-apart tender duck. It is marvelous food for company, especially when you serve it with little roasted potatoes

MAKES 4 TO 6 SERVINGS

1. Make the stock: Preheat the oven to 425° F. Place the duck backbone, wing tips, neck, and gizzards—but not the liver—and the celery, carrots, and onion in a flame-proof roasting pan large enough to hold the ingredients comfortably. Drizzle enough oil over the bones and vegetables to coat lightly, and toss. Roast, stirring the bones and vegetables every 15 minutes or so, until well browned, about 1 hour.
2. Lift the roasting pan onto the stove top and place over medium heat. Pour in enough water to cover the bones and vegetables, and bring the liquid to a boil. Stir to scrape the brown bits that cling to the pan. Adjust the heat so the liquid is simmering and cook, stirring occasionally, for 30 minutes. Strain through a fine sieve, using a ladle if you like. Discard the solids and set the broth aside.
3. Lay the duck, skin side down, in a large, cold nonstick pan. Set the pan over medium heat and cook until the duck begins to sizzle and render its fat. Continue cooking, adjusting the heat so there is a nice lively sizzle, until well browned, about 8 minutes. Flip the pieces and brown the other side. Remove the duck pieces to a bowl as they brown.
4. Spoon off all but about 1 tablespoon of fat from the pan. Pour in the Grand Marnier and let it bubble up. Pour in the wine, add the cloves, bring to a boil, and cook until reduced by about half.
5. Add the duck broth to the reduced wine and return the duck pieces to the skillet. Bring the liquid to a boil, adjust the heat so the sauce is simmering, and cover the pan. Cook, turning the pieces occasionally so they turn a rich purple on all sides, until the meat is falling from the leg bones, about 1¼ hours. Check the pot from time to time; there should be enough liquid to moisten the duck. If not, add water as necessary.
6. Stir the arrowroot into 2 tablespoons of water in a small bowl until dissolved. Pour into the duck sauce and cook just until thickened, about 1 minute. Serve the duck hot, spooning some of the sauce over each piece.

One 5-pound duck, cut into 10 pieces
(see page 164)
3 celery stalks, trimmed and cut into
2-inch lengths
2 carrots, peeled and cut into 2-inch
lengths
1 small Spanish onion, cut into 2-inch
chunks
Splash of olive oil
2 tablespoons Grand Marnier or other
orange liqueur
2 cups dry red wine
5 whole cloves
2 teaspoons arrowroot or 4 teaspoons
cornstarch

FISH AND SHELLFISH

PESCADO Y MARISCOS

One of the drawbacks of knowing how to cook (the only one, now that I think about it) is that people are hesitant to invite you over for dinner. Because I tend to go all out when guests come by, people feel that they must do the same. It's true that I've been known to put out ten dishes for a buffet and serve five or six courses for a sit-down dinner because I love to cook and share my food with people. Still, I think that a couple of shrimp on the grill, a nice salad, and good friends are all it takes to make a pleasant evening.

Most people love seafood, but many people are afraid to cook it at home. I believe that is the reason people ask me for shrimp and seafood dishes all the time. My family is very big on seafood, so I make it once or twice a week for my friends as well as my family. What I love to hear is that people have incorporated something of mine into their repertoire. That is truly the best compliment you can give a chef.

Second only to the Yellow Rice recipe on page 13 when it comes to recipes requested of me is my Shrimp in Garlic Sauce (page 184), followed closely by Shrimp and String Beans (page 183). Each takes 15 to 20 minutes to make (if you have got sofrito in the freezer). Both are delicious, simple, and very company worthy.

Another step up the ladder for those of you who love to cook and love good seafood is a grilled whole fish such as the Grilled Red Snapper on page 192. It's super simple to prepare but for most people a little tricky to eat—that is, of course, until you follow the steps I give on page 192. Serve it with a bowlful of Garlic Dipping Sauce (page 114), and you will find yourself licking your fingers. Easy, delicious, and gorgeous to look at—what is wrong with that? These are the dishes that I am most proud of—probably because they've helped people overcome their fear of cooking fish at home. After you try them once, they'll be among your favorites, too.

SEAFOOD IN ESCABECHE SAUCE

PESCADO EN ESCABECHE

You will find escabeche in one form or another throughout South America and the Caribbean. I think cooking seafood and then pickling it, which essentially is what this is, probably started as a way of preserving very perishable seafood. But today you will find all kinds of things done in that style, from green bananas (see page 118) to chicken wings, which make a fabulous appetizer at a party.

MAKES 6 SERVINGS

1. Toss the flour, salt, red pepper flakes, and paprika together in a medium bowl. Add the shrimp, toss them until coated with flour, and then shake them in a sieve to get rid of the excess flour.

2. Heat the oil in a large, deep skillet until the end of a coated shrimp dipped in the oil gives off a lively sizzle. Add the shrimp and cook, turning once, until golden and crisped, about 4 minutes.

3. While the shrimp are frying, flour and sift the tilapia ribbons as you did the shrimp. When the shrimp are done, fry the tilapia in batches. Drain the shrimp and fish on paper towels as each batch is done.

4. Place the fried fish in a nonreactive receptacle (a large glass jar works well). Pour the escabeche sauce over the fish. Refrigerate overnight or up to 3 days. Turn the jar every once in a while. Serve the escabeche right out of the refrigerator or at room temperature.

1 cup all-purpose flour
2 teaspoons fine sea or kosher salt
1 teaspoon hot red pepper flakes
1 teaspoon paprika
1 pound extra-large (about 15 to a pound) shrimp, peeled and deveined
1 cup canola oil
2 tilapia fillets, cut in half and then cut on the bias into 1-inch-wide "ribbons"
Escabeche Sauce (page 118)

NOTES: *Escabeche makes a delicious meal when teamed with boiled Yucca (page 110) or Twice-Fried Green Plantain Chips (page 113) and a green salad.*

• Smoked paprika (see Sources), now widely available, will give this escabeche a nice twist.

DAISY'S CLAM "ZUPPA"

ALMEJAS MARINERA

I'm married to an Italian man and I love Italian food, but I can never get away from my roots. So when I set out to recreate a deliciously spicy dish of zuppa di clams that we had eaten at a local Italian restaurant, I ended up with achiote oil and sofrito in the mix. I think you will like these as much as I do.

MAKES 4 SERVINGS

1. Heat the oil in a wide, deep skillet or Dutch oven over medium-low heat until rippling. Add the peppers and stir until fragrant, about 2 minutes.

2. Add the sofrito and wine, and cook, stirring, until most of the liquid has evaporated, about 5 minutes.

3. Add the clams to the pan in an even layer. Pour in the tomatoes, raise the heat to medium-high, and bring to a boil. Season with salt and pepper. Cover the pan and bring to a boil. Cook until the clams are open, about 10 minutes. Shake the pan once in a while so the clams cook evenly.

4. Place two slices of Italian bread in each of 4 bowls. Ladle out the clams and tomato broth on the bread, discarding any clams that do not open. Sprinkle the chopped parsley over the clams and serve immediately.

3 tablespoons Achiote Oil (page 9)
3 finger or cayenne chili peppers or the hot chilies of your choice, stemmed and chopped (see Note)
1 cup Sofrito (page 6)
½ cup dry white wine
4 dozen littleneck clams, scrubbed and soaked in a cornmeal bath (see below)
One 28-ounce can crushed tomatoes
Fine sea or kosher salt to taste
Freshly ground pepper to taste
Eight 1-inch slices of Italian bread, toasted
Chopped fresh flat-leaf parsley

NOTE: *Adjust the heat level in this dish by the type and amount of chilies you choose. In a pinch you can always use dried red pepper flakes.*

CORNMEAL BATH FOR CLAMS

To rid clams of sand and grit (both inside and out), first scrub the clams with a stiff brush under cold running water. Then place the clams in a bowl large enough to hold them comfortably. Pour in enough cold salted water to cover. Add a tablespoon or two of cornmeal for each dozen clams. Swish the clams around and refrigerate them for 1 to 3 hours, swishing occasionally. The clams will eat the cornmeal and rid themselves of sand in the process. Drain and rinse the clams thoroughly before cooking.

GRILLED SWORDFISH with WARM EGGPLANT RELISH

PES ESPADA A LA PLANCHA CON SALSITA DE BERENJENA

The Moors brought eggplant to Spain, but the Spaniards took over from there. Eggplant and swordfish may seem an odd couple, but the combination will blow you away. I made up this eggplant relish to go with one of my favorite fish—swordfish on the grill. This recipe is delish with white rice.

MAKES 4 DAISY SERVINGS OR 6 REGULAR SERVINGS

1. Marinate the fish: Stir the rub, citrus juices, and vinegar together in a rectangular baking dish. Place the swordfish steaks in the marinade and refrigerate for 2 hours, turning a few times.

2. Make the relish while the fish is marinating: Heat the olive oil in a large skillet over medium heat. Add the chorizo and cook, stirring, until it starts to give up some color. Add the onion and garlic, and cook, stirring, until the onion is soft, about 5 minutes. Stir in the eggplant, turning to coat the cubes with the chorizo mixture. Pour in the tomato sauce and clam juice and bring to a boil. Adjust the heat to simmering, cover, and let cook until the vegetables are very soft, 30 to 45 minutes. Stir in the zucchini and olives, cook for 5 minutes, and then remove the relish from the heat and keep warm.

3. Heat a gas grill to high or build a charcoal fire. Lower the heat to medium. Grab a wadded paper towel with tongs, dip it in vegetable oil, and oil the grill.

4. Lay the steaks on the grill, cover the grill, and cook for 4 to 5 minutes. Turn the steaks and cook until the meat is firm, 4 to 5 minutes. To serve, cut the steaks as you would a London broil, diagonally in ¼-inch slices. Spoon the warm or room-temperature relish over the fish and sprinkle with parsley.

FOR THE SWORDFISH

2 tablespoons Dry Rub, homemade (page 19) or store-bought
Juice of 2 oranges
Juice of 1 lemon
1 cup white wine vinegar
2 swordfish steaks, each about 1¼ pounds and at least 1 inch thick

FOR THE RELISH

½ cup olive oil
2 chorizo, andouille, or any smoked garlicky sausage links (about ½ pound), skinned and cut into small dice
1 medium Spanish onion, chopped
4 cloves garlic, minced
1 medium eggplant (about ¾ pound), peeled and cut into 1-inch cubes
½ cup canned Spanish-style tomato sauce
½ cup bottled clam juice or water
1 small zucchini, quartered lengthwise and cut into ⅛-inch slices (about 1¼ cups)
½ cup chopped pitted black olives (brined or oil-cured)

Vegetable oil
Chopped fresh flat-leaf parsley

VARIATIONS: *If you have a source for sour oranges (naranjas agrias; see Note on page 48), substitute 2 of them for the lemon and 1 of the oranges.*

• Leftover eggplant relish (if there is any) is delicious on pasta, served alongside grilled chicken, or spread on a fresh mozzarella sandwich.

• A simpler relish could be made by tossing orange segments and grapefruit segments together with chopped fresh cilantro and finely diced red onion.

• Vary the liquid you use to make the relish depending on what the relish will accompany—chicken broth for chicken, and so on.

SEA BASS CREOLE

CORVINA CRIOLLA

On a recent trip with my family to Peru, we all enjoyed this dish in the city of Lima. Even though we were there for only a short while, half a day, we managed to make time to share a meal. Lima is known for its wonderful beaches and delicious seafood, and sea bass is prominently featured on its menus. Here is my interpretation of our seaside dinner in Lima.

MAKES 6 SERVINGS

1. To prepare the bass: Heat the oven to its lowest setting or "warm." Stir the flour, cayenne, salt, and oregano together in a shallow bowl. Dredge the sea bass in the seasoned flour and shake off the excess.

2. Pour enough oil into a large, heavy skillet to coat the bottom generously. Heat over medium-high heat until a corner of a fillet gives off a very lively sizzle when dipped in the oil. Lay the fillets in the pan, lower the heat to medium, and cook, turning once or twice, until the fillets are golden brown on all sides and barely opaque in the center, about 10 minutes. Transfer the fish to a paper towel–lined baking sheet and keep them warm in the oven.

3. To make the sauce: Wipe out the skillet with a wad of paper towels. Add 2 tablespoons of oil and place over medium-low heat. Stir in the tomatoes and cook until the water has evaporated and they start to sizzle. Pour in the clam juice and cook until evaporated, breaking up the bits of tomato as you go. Lower the heat to a simmer.

4. Heat 2 more tablespoons of oil in a separate skillet over medium heat. Add the onion, cubanelle pepper, and garlic, and stir until soft and fragrant, about 4 minutes. Add the tomatoes and salt and pepper to taste. Cover the pan and keep the sauce warm off the heat.

5. To serve, spoon some of the sauce on the bottom of each plate. Set a bass fillet in the puddle of sauce. Sprinkle with chopped cilantro and serve immediately.

FOR THE BASS

1 cup all-purpose flour
1 teaspoon ground cayenne or piquin chili powder
2 teaspoons fine sea or kosher salt
½ teaspoon dried oregano
Six 6-ounce sea bass fillets, each about 1 inch thick
Canola oil

FOR THE SAUCE

Olive oil
4 large ripe tomatoes, peeled, seeded, and chopped (see page 56)
One 8-ounce bottle clam juice
1 small Spanish onion, halved and then slivered lengthwise
1 cubanelle pepper or Italian frying pepper, seeded and slivered
3 cloves garlic, thinly sliced
Fine sea or kosher salt
Freshly ground pepper

Chopped fresh cilantro

SHRIMP WITH SWEET RED PEPPERS

CAMARONES CON PIMIENTOS DULCES

Shrimp can give off an odd sort of white goop when you cook them. That's why I take a couple of seconds to wipe out the pan before the rest of the ingredients are added. It makes a nicer looking dish and beats using two pans.

MAKES 4 SERVINGS

1. Toss the shrimp, achiote oil, and garlic together in a medium bowl. You can keep this in the refrigerator up to a few hours until you're ready to make the shrimp.

2. Heat 1 tablespoon of olive oil in a large skillet over medium-high heat. Add the shrimp and toss until pink and almost cooked through, about 3 minutes. Scrape the shrimp onto a dish and set aside. Carefully wipe out the pan with a wad of paper towels.

3. Pour the remaining 2 tablespoons of oil into the skillet and set over high heat. Add the onion and peppers, season with salt, and cook, tossing and stirring, until crisp-tender and aromatic, about 4 minutes.

4. Return the shrimp to the pan, pour in the sherry, and cook until it has evaporated. Sprinkle the oregano over the shrimp and peppers. Taste and add salt if you think it needs it.

1½ pounds large shrimp (about 20 per pound), cleaned and deveined
3 tablespoons Achiote Oil (page 9)
1 clove garlic, sliced
3 tablespoons olive oil
1 large Spanish onion (about 1¼ pounds), halved and then cut into thin slices
3 large red bell peppers (about 1¼ pounds), cored, seeded, and cut into ¼-inch strips
Fine sea or kosher salt to taste
Splash of dry fino sherry
1 teaspoon chopped fresh oregano

VARIATIONS: *Traditionally this dish is served with rice, but I love to fill warmed flour tortillas with it instead.*

• To make Shrimp Creole style: Omit the sherry and add ½ cup each canned Spanish-style tomato sauce and bottled clam juice. Substitute ¼ cup chopped fresh cilantro for the oregano. Proceed as above.

SHRIMP AND STRING BEANS

CAMARONES CON JUDIAS

There was practically nothing *Mama*, my maternal grandmother, couldn't cure with things she pulled, picked, or dug out of the garden. One sure cure for an upset stomach was one of her teas made with fresh ginger that she had growing in the backyard. It still does the trick for me. You might find ginger in some Latino desserts, but it is much less prevalent in savory things. Let's just say that it has found its way into Daisy's kitchen, where I often officiate over marriages of the "old" to the "new."

MAKES 6 SERVINGS

1. Bring a pot of salted water to a boil. Fill a large bowl halfway with ice water. Cook the string beans in boiling water for 3 minutes, drain, and plunge into the ice water. Let stand for 1 to 2 minutes, then drain and set aside.

2. Heat the oil in a large skillet over medium heat. Add the sofrito, alcaparrado, oregano, cumin, and ginger. Season lightly with salt and pepper. Cook until most of the liquid has evaporated. Add the wine and cook until that has evaporated, 1 or 2 minutes. Pour in the tomato sauce and bring to a boil. Raise the heat to high and stir in the shrimp. As soon as the shrimp start to turn pink, stir in the string beans and clam juice. Lower the heat to medium, cover, and cook just until the shrimp are cooked through, 2 to 3 minutes. Taste and season with salt and pepper if necessary. Sprinkle with the cilantro before serving.

Fine sea or kosher salt
1 pound string beans, topped and tailed
2 tablespoons olive oil
½ cup Sofrito (page 6)
⅓ cup alcaparrado (see Daisy's Pantry on page 13) or coarsely chopped pimiento-stuffed olives
1 tablespoon chopped fresh oregano
1 teaspoon ground cumin
½ teaspoon grated fresh ginger
Freshly ground black pepper
1 tablespoon dry white wine
One 8-ounce can Spanish-style tomato sauce
1 pound large (about 20 per pound) shrimp, peeled and deveined
½ cup bottled clam juice
Chopped fresh cilantro

SHRIMP IN GARLIC SAUCE

CAMARONES AJILLO

This is so straightforward that there's no place for mediocre ingredients to hide. You cannot compromise on the quality of the olive oil for this recipe. If you have a secret stash of the good stuff, now is the time to use it.

MAKES 6 SERVINGS

1. Heat the oil and red pepper flakes in a large, heavy skillet over medium-low heat just until the oil starts to color. Don't heat the red pepper flakes over high heat or they will discolor and turn the oil bitter. Stir in the garlic and cook, shaking the pan, just until it begins to color, about 2 minutes.

2. Increase the heat to high, add the shrimp, and season them with 1 teaspoon of salt. Stir the shrimp so they cook evenly until they turn pink. Keep an eye on the garlic. It will continue to brown, but don't let it burn. If it starts to darken, lower the heat and remove the pan from the heat for a few seconds.

3. When the shrimp are pink all over, pour in the sherry and bring it to a boil. Cook, stirring, until the shrimp are cooked through and the liquid has been reduced by about half and lightly thickened, about 3 minutes. Stir in the parsley. Scrape the shrimp and the sauce into a serving bowl and serve hot.

⅓ cup extra-virgin olive oil
1 tablespoon hot red pepper flakes
12 garlic cloves, sliced
2 pounds jumbo (about 10 per pound) shrimp, peeled and deveined
Fine sea or kosher salt
½ cup dry sherry
¼ cup chopped flat-leaf parsley

NAVY BEAN AND SHRIMP CAKES

ACARAJE

This dish comes from Brazil via Daisy's kitchen. Traditionally prepared with beans and shrimp ground to a paste, I prefer my shrimp and bean cakes with more texture, which I get by mashing the beans coarsely and dicing the shrimp. Another break with tradition: Instead of frying these bean cakes in dende oil (a type of palm oil popular in Brazil that has a very high level of saturated fat) I use vegetable oil. Even though this dish is loaded with shrimp, it doesn't have to set you back a lot of cash. Use smaller (cheaper!) shrimp because you'll be chopping them up anyway.

MAKES 6 APPETIZER SERVINGS OR A LIGHT SUPPER WITH A SALAD

1 pound navy beans or black-eyed peas, cooked and drained (see page 96)
2 pounds small shrimp, peeled, deveined, and diced
½ small Spanish onion, very finely diced (about ½ cup)
2 tablespoons chopped fresh cilantro
2 teaspoons fine sea or kosher salt
½ Scotch bonnet chili pepper or chili pepper of your choice, finely chopped
½ teaspoon freshly ground black pepper
¼ teaspoon ground cumin
Vegetable oil
All-purpose flour

1. Mash about two-thirds of the beans to a paste in a large bowl. Stir in the remaining beans and then the shrimp, onion, cilantro, salt, chili, black pepper, and cumin. Form the mixture into six 3½-inch patties, lining them up on a baking sheet as you go. Refrigerate at least 30 minutes or up to 8 hours. Refrigerating the cakes will firm them up and make them easier to handle.

2. Pour enough oil into a 12-inch skillet to fill ½-inch, about 1 cup. Heat the oil over medium-high heat until rippling.

3. Meanwhile, spread a thick layer of flour on a plate. Coat both sides of the patties, handling them gently. Slip the patties into the oil and cook, turning once, until golden brown on both sides and cooked through, about 8 minutes. Drain on paper towels and serve hot.

SEARED SCALLOPS WITH BLACK-EYED PEAS

VIERAS CON FRIJOLES CARITA

This dish is a great excuse for me to visit Spain again. The sweetness of the scallops paired with the richness of the peas and the brine of the anchovies is enough to make one fall in love!

MAKES 6 SERVINGS

1. Place the pork in a cold medium skillet over medium heat and cook until it begins to render its fat. Continue cooking, turning as necessary, until browned on all sides, about 12 minutes.

2. Meanwhile, place the clam juice, peas, and bay leaves in a medium saucepan. Set over medium heat and bring to a boil. Adjust the heat so the liquid is at a simmer. Skim off any foam that rises to the surface.

3. When it is brown, transfer the pork to the saucepan. Add the salt and continue cooking, skimming as necessary, until the peas are tender but still whole, about 35 minutes from the time the water came to a boil. Add water as necessary to keep the peas submerged.

4. While the peas are cooking, make the dressing: Heat the oil in a small skillet over medium heat. Add the shallots, garlic, and 6 anchovy fillets. Cook, stirring, until the shallots start to brown and the fillets melt. Add the capers, let them sizzle for a minute, and then remove from the heat.

5. When the peas and dressing are ready, cook the scallops: Pat them dry with paper towels and season lightly with salt and pepper. Paint the bottom of a large, heavy, nonstick pan with the oil and set over high heat. When hot, add the scallops in 1 layer. Cook until golden on the bottom, about 4 minutes. Turn over and cook the other side.

6. Drain the peas and return them to the pot. Add the parsley and dressing, and toss the peas to mix well. Check for seasoning. Spoon the peas onto serving plates and set the seared scallops on top. Arrange anchovy fillets randomly over the scallops.

FOR THE BEANS

1 pound salt pork or slab bacon with rind removed (see Notes on page 171)
Four 8-ounce bottles clam juice
1 pound black-eyed peas
2 bay leaves
1 tablespoon salt

FOR THE DRESSING

3 tablespoons olive oil
4 shallots, finely chopped
2 cloves garlic
One 2-ounce can plus 6 anchovy fillets, drained
2 teaspoons capers

2 pounds sea scallops, preferably dry scallops or diver scallops (see Note on page 14)
Fine sea or kosher salt
Freshly ground pepper
Canola oil
¼ cup finely chopped fresh flat-leaf parsley

TO PREPARE AND COOK SALT COD

Salt cod (*bacalao*) is an ancient dish. It seems that every culture with access to cod and salt was on to it. Salt cod is whole cleaned cod or cod fillets that have been heavily salted to draw out the moisture, to preserve it, and then air-dried. It needs lots of water and a fair amount of time to reconstitute it. After salt cod has been soaked and cooked, it should taste pleasantly salty and just slightly more intense than fresh fish. It should never taste overly salty, unpleasant, or funky. Look for real cod that has been salted, not hake or pollock. Not only is the flavor more subtle, but I find that the texture of cod is much silkier. And, when possible, buy salt cod on the bone. It's a little more effort to work with because of the bones, but the flavor is truly worth it.

ONE POUND OF BONE-IN SALT COD THAT HAS BEEN COOKED AND FLAKED YIELDS ABOUT 2 CUPS OF SHREDDED COD.

1. Place the salt cod in a bowl or pot large enough to hold it comfortably. Pour in cold water to cover the cod completely and soak it, changing the water several times, until it is just pleasantly salted. This can take anywhere from overnight to a full twenty-four hours or even a little more. Tear off a little piece to taste it from time to time. Knowing when it has soaked long enough is very subjective; some people like it fairly salty while others like it fairly mild. Drain it when it tastes right to you. The thickness and cure of each piece also determines the soaking time.

2. To cook: Put the salt cod in a pot large enough to hold it comfortably. Fill with cold water and bring to a boil. Adjust the heat so the water is simmering and cook until the fish flakes easily, about 20 minutes. Drain carefully.

TIP: *If you forget to soak the salt cod the night before, here's a quick fix: Put it in a large pot and cover it with cold water. Bring to a boil and boil gently for 5 minutes. Drain, replace the water, and repeat anywhere from two to four times, depending on your cod, until the cod tastes nice to you. This method both desalts and cooks the cod.*

SALT COD SALAD

ENSALADA DE BACALAO

MAKES 8 TO 10 SERVINGS

1. Flake the cod with your hands into a serving bowl. Add the onion, oil, and parsley, and toss together. The oil should coat the cod generously. (I always add a little extra so I have some oil to mop up with bread.)

2. Cut the eggs in half and place them around the edge of the bowl. Serve immediately or chill first.

4 pounds bone-in salt cod or 2½ pounds salt cod fillet, soaked and cooked according to the instructions on page 188
1 small Spanish onion, cut into thin strips
½ cup olive oil, or to taste
1 bunch flat-leaf parsley, leaves only, finely chopped
4 hard-boiled eggs (see Note on page 123)

SALT COD WITH EGGPLANT

BACALAO CON BERENJENA

This dish will inspire you, if not to poetry, at least to a second helping. Every Caribbean country has its version and this version is one I remember eating as a child. You would never forgive yourself if you did not try this dish.

MAKES 8 SERVINGS

1. Heat the oil in a heavy 5- or 6-quart pot over medium heat. Add the sofrito and cumin, and cook until most of the liquid has evaporated.

2. Add the tomato sauce and bay leaves, and bring to a boil. Stir in the eggplant until coated with sauce, then stir in the salt cod. Add the culantro and water. Bring to a boil, adjust the heat so the sauce is simmering, and cover the pot.

3. Cook until the eggplant is very tender, about 45 minutes. It is easy to scorch this dish if you let the liquid evaporate. It is easy to prevent, too. Just cook over low heat and check the pot every once in a while, adding a little water if it starts to look dry.

4. Serve with white rice or plantain chips or crusty bread as a light supper.

¼ cup Achiote Oil (page 9)
½ cup Sofrito (page 6)
1 teaspoon ground cumin
Two 8-ounce cans Spanish-style tomato sauce
2 bay leaves
1 large eggplant (about 20 ounces), stemmed, peeled, and cut into 1½-inch chunks
3 pounds bone-in salt cod or 1¾ to 2 pounds salt cod fillets, soaked, cooked, and flaked (see page 188)
3 leaves culantro, torn into rough pieces, or ½ cup chopped fresh cilantro
1 cup water, or as needed

SALT COD SYMPHONY

BACALAO IN SAMFAINA

Samfaina is a Catalan term that, loosely translated, means a stir-fry or vegetable hash. I think this looks and tastes like a well-orchestrated symphony of vegetables.

MAKES 6 TO 8 SERVINGS

1. Place the potatoes in a medium saucepan and pour in enough cold water to cover. Add a small handful of salt and bring to a boil over medium-high heat. Cook until tender, about 12 minutes. Drain and let air-dry until cool.

2. Pour enough oil into a large, heavy skillet to film the bottom generously. Let it heat 1–2 minutes until rippling. Add the potatoes and cook, occasionally stirring gently, until they begin to brown. Add the onion and garlic, and cook until the onion is wilted, about 4 minutes. Stir in the tomatoes and zucchini, and cook, stirring gently from top to bottom, just until the zucchini is softened, about 3 minutes. Add the cod and stir gently until warmed through.

3. Scrape into a serving bowl and sprinkle the chopped parsley on top. Serve hot or at room temperature.

2 large waxy red potatoes (about 8 ounces), scrubbed and cut into 1-inch pieces
Olive oil
1 large Spanish onion, cut into ½-inch wedges
3 cloves garlic, chopped
4 plum tomatoes, peeled, seeded, and chopped (see page 56)
1 large zucchini (about 10 ounces), cut into quarters lengthwise and then crosswise into ½-inch pieces
2 pounds salt cod on the bone, soaked, cooked, and shredded (see page 188)
Chopped fresh Italian parsley

NOTE: *Save yourself a pot: You can use the same pot of boiling water to cook the potatoes and blanch the tomatoes before peeling them.*

Papi is fond of saying that salt cod, which was once considered a poor man's meal, is now as expensive as steak! That's probably because word has gotten around as to how delicious it is, coupled with the fact that we've depleted some of the largest cod fishing grounds. The funny thing is, you can find salt cod in one form or another in almost every culture and as far back as recorded history. I've even seen Asian recipes for salt cod!

When I was growing up, we ate a lot of salt cod—in salad, fritters, with eggplant, in "soupy rice" (page 85), and stirred into yellow rice. There really are not many places salt cod can't go. Papi says he will walk right past a lobster dinner to have a plate of salt cod. While I know this is true of my father, it is definitely not true of my mother. Mami—although she has a special place in her heart (and her palate) for *bacalao*—is very much a fresh lobster and shrimp girl, and let's not even talk about fresh crabmeat!

In fact, there is no one in my family who doesn't like bacalao, although when my kids were small, it took a bit of encouragement for them to try it. Salt cod, to lay it on the line for you, does not look very appetizing. Actually, when you first start to cook it, you may find the initial smell a bit strong. But with a little coaxing and love, bacalao will release its magic and reward you with pearly white flakes of delicious, mildly flavored fish with just a hint of salt and a lovely satiny texture with a bit of a bite. In fact, many people prefer the taste of salt cod to that of fresh cod, which can be rather bland. Adding the fact that salt cod is an excellent source of protein, I'm left with the thought: "What could be bad?"

GRILLED RED SNAPPER

CHILLO ALLA PARILLA

I use a gas grill at home, one that gets very hot. I don't want to char the skin of the fish because we love to eat it. So I set the dial to about medium-high and let it heat up for 10 minutes or so before cooking. If you don't have a gas grill, see the box on page 193 for more information on how to control the heat of your charcoal grill.

MAKES 4 SERVINGS

1. Sprinkle the fish inside and out very liberally with the dry rub. Place them side by side in a baking dish large enough to hold them comfortably. Squeeze the lemons and sour orange, if using, over the inside and outside. Cover and refrigerate the fish for up to 1 hour (any longer and the lemon juice may start to cure the fish).

2. Heat a gas grill to medium-high or build a banked coal fire (see opposite). Grill the fish, turning once, until the meat along the backbone close to the head is opaque and firm, 15 to 20 minutes. If you are working over coals, start the snapper on the hotter side of the grill and then gently move it, after about 5 minutes, to the middle zone. The skin should be golden and crispy in spots. Serve whole.

3. To serve the fish: Make a cut along the backbone. Insert the knife and, working gently, separate the fillet from the bones, starting at the head and working toward the tail. Take it slowly and you will see that the fillets separate easily from the bone. Don't worry about making perfect fillets the first time out; you'll get better with more practice. Each diner can finish removing bones from the fish as they work their way through the fillet. That's part of the fun of eating a whole fish.

Two 1½-pound cleaned red snappers, left whole
Dry Rub, homemade (page 19) or store-bought
2 lemons, cut in half
Juice of 1 sour orange (*naranja agria*; see Note on page 48) or juice orange (optional)
Ajilimojili (page 193) or Garlic Dipping Sauce (page 114)

NOTE: *I cook the fish separately in very handy nonstick fish-shaped grill baskets, made specifically for this purpose. If you don't have fish baskets, oil the fish and then the grill with a thick wad of paper towels dipped in oil before grilling. Use two long kitchen forks to turn and remove the fish.*

A WORD ABOUT GRILLS

I use a gas grill at home for convenience and easy control of heat. Mine is fairly large and has three burners and therefore three heat zones. Sometimes they are all running at the same temperature; sometimes each one is set to a separate temperature so I can move things from zone to zone to control the cooking.

To get the same effect with a charcoal grill, light the coals as you normally do. After that you have three options: (1) Spread the coals in an even layer in the center for a steady, hot fire. (2) Spread the coals around the exterior of the grill to create a center zone with gentle heat. (3) "Bank" the coals. Rake the coals so they are thicker on one end of the grill than the other. That will give you a hot zone for searing or marking foods and a less intense zone for finishing thick cuts, such as pork chops or filet mignon. It's also good for the preceding snapper recipe.

Whichever type of grill you use, individual recipes will guide you in terms of heat.

AJILIMOJILI

Pronounced ah-HEE-lee-moh-HEE-lee, this is delicious with grilled chicken, meat, or fish. You can also use this as a condiment for any of the root vegetables on pages 110 through 117.

MAKES ABOUT 1½ CUPS

Shake all ingredients in a glass jar with a tight-fitting lid. Place in the refrigerator at least overnight for the flavors to blend. Lasts about 1 week in the refrigerator.

1 red bell pepper, cored, seeded, and diced fine
6 ajices dulces (see Daisy's Pantry on page 6), cored, seeded, and finely diced, or ½ cubanelle pepper, cut into small dice
1 jalapeño, cored, seeded (or leave the seeds in if you like heat), and finely diced
1 clove garlic, minced
½ cup chopped fresh cilantro
Fine sea or kosher salt
Freshly ground pepper
¾ cup olive oil
¼ cup white wine vinegar
2 tablespoons lemon juice

SEAFOOD SKEWERS

PINCHO DE MARISCO

In Spain there is almost nothing that can't end up on a *pincho* (skewer)—vegetables, chicken, pork, fruits, just name it. I chose these ingredients because I love them together, but you can pick what appeals to you. Make these on shorter skewers, and you have yourself a great cocktail party dish.

MAKES 6 SERVINGS

1. Cut the crown off the pineapple and then cut a thin slice off the bottom so it doesn't wiggle as you work with it. Working from top to bottom, cut the peel off the pineapple, removing as many of the eyes under the peel as you can without wasting any pineapple. (Save the peelings for Spicy Pineapple Vinegar [page 218].) Cut the pineapple in quarters through the core from top to bottom. Lay the quarters flat and remove the cores. Cut the quarters into about 1½-inch pieces.

2. Divide your ingredients into two groups: pineapple, scallops, and chorizos; and bell peppers, shrimp, mango, and jalapeño (see Notes). You will be using two skewers for each serving; that will help the ingredients stay in place while you cook and turn them. Alternate ingredients from each group on each double skewer, arranging them in whatever order you like.

3. Heat a gas grill to medium-high or build a charcoal fire. Grill the skewers, turning them often, until the shrimp and scallops are cooked through and the vegetables are softened, about 15 minutes. Serve hot.

1 ripe pineapple (see Notes)
1 pound large sea scallops (about 20), preferably dry (see page 14)
4 links chorizo, andouille, or any smoked garlicky sausage (about 1 pound), cut into 1-inch slices
2 red bell peppers, cored, seeded, and cut into 1½-inch pieces
1¼ pounds very large (about 15 per pound) shrimp, peeled and deveined
1 ripe but firm mango, peeled and cut into 1-inch cubes
3 jalapeño peppers, stemmed, seeded, and cut into 1-inch pieces

NOTES: *A ripe pineapple has a nice, flowery aroma and gives a little when you press it. Pineapple cores make great drink stirrers.*

• If you like, marinate any or all of the ingredients in pineapple juice, Spicy Pineapple Vinegar (page 218), or Sour Orange Marinade (page 47).

• Don't worry if the amounts of ingredients don't work out exactly. You will definitely have more pineapple than you'll need for the skewers. Save some for a snack and distribute the rest along with whatever else you have with your skewers and enjoy.

• I grouped the ingredients on the skewers because I think they taste wonderful this way. There is nothing to stop you from making your own matches or even alternating all the ingredients on a single skewer.

HOW TO HANDLE A MANGO

Ripe mangoes, ready for eating, have a little give when pressed and a wonderful perfume. Grandma's house in Puerto Rico, where my aunt Emerita now lives, has a huge mango tree in the backyard. In addition to being a great place to climb into during hide-and-seek, that tree was the source of football-size fruit. You could hear the ripe mangoes plunk as they fell from the trees onto the ground or onto the roof (which always made us kids jump). To eat them, we'd simply cut off one end, peel back the skin, and gobble them up right out of hand. They were messy, juicy, and delicious.

To eat mangoes with a little more decorum, peel off the skin with a paring knife and cut the two "fillets" from either side of the large center pit. They're neater to eat that way, but you miss the best part—sucking the ripe mango off the pit. That is summer to me.

For things like *pinchos* (skewers), choose firmer mangoes that can be cut into cubes and hold their shape. Peel off the skin, cut the two fillets from either side of the pit, and cut into whatever shape you like.

FRESH COD WITH CLAM BROTH

BACALAO FRESCO CON ALMEJAS

Mild cod is the ideal fish to serve in a briny clam broth bath, especially when it is given a blast of freshness at the end with cilantro and cherry tomatoes. All that and good looks, too!

MAKES 4 SERVINGS

1. Drain the clams in a colander and rinse them under cold water to remove any cornmeal.

2. Heat enough oil to coat the bottom of a heavy 4- to 5-quart pot over medium-low heat. Add the garlic and cook, shaking the pan once or twice, just until the garlic starts to take on color, about 3 minutes. Don't let it get too dark.

3. Slip the clams into the pan with the garlic, pour in the wine, and bring it to a boil. Cover the pot and cook just until the clams open, about 5 minutes.

4. Heat enough oil in a wide, heavy skillet over medium heat until rippling. While the oil is heating, season the cod fillets generously with salt and pepper and roll them in the flour to coat on all sides. Tap off any excess flour and lay the cod in the oil. Cook, turning the fillets once, until they are golden brown and barely opaque in the center. The clams will open while the cod is cooking; turn off the heat and let them stand until you need them. Discard any clams that don't open.

5. Scatter the cherry tomatoes over the clams and shake the pot a little so they settle in. Scatter the cilantro over the clams. Let the mixture stand just a minute or two to warm the tomatoes through.

6. Drain the fish fillets on paper towels and transfer them to shallow bowls. (Warming the bowls first is a nice touch.) Spoon some of the clams, tomatoes, and broth around each fillet and serve hot.

18 littleneck or other hard-shell clams, soaked with cornmeal (see page 179)
Olive oil
4 to 5 cloves garlic, thinly sliced
½ cup (approximately) dry white wine
Four thick 8-ounce fresh cod or halibut fillets
Fine sea or kosher salt
Freshly ground pepper
All-purpose flour
8 cherry tomatoes, halved
¼ cup chopped fresh cilantro

SOLE BAKED IN A BANANA LEAF

LENGUADO EN HOJA DE GUINEO

By taking the ingredients for Sofrito (page 6) and cutting them into chunks instead of pureeing them, you get the lovely flavor of sofrito and a built-in side dish. This is a nice dish for company: It's pretty, quick to make, and delicious. You can also make the packets hours ahead and put them into the oven or on the grill when ready. Break out the good olive oil for this one; cooking in a banana leaf will preserve the delicate flavor of even the best oil.

MAKES 6 SERVINGS

1. Toss the tomatoes, onion, yellow pepper, cilantro, oil, and garlic together in a large bowl. Season with salt and pepper to taste. Let the vegetables sit while you prepare the rest of the ingredients.

2. Cut six 18-inch lengths of banana leaves. Wash them well under cold running water and let them drain. Season the fish fillets generously with salt and pepper. Center a seasoned fillet on one of the banana leaf pieces. Top with about ⅔ cup of the onion-tomato mixture. Fold the sides of the leaf one at a time over the fish and vegetables to enclose them loosely. Fold the ends in and tie them like tamales (see page 146). If you're cooking the fish on a grill, simply wrap the banana leaf loosely in heavy-duty aluminum foil. The ends will unfold, but that's okay. If you're cooking the fish in the oven, wrap the packets in foil or parchment paper and place them, fold side down, on a baking sheet.

To grill the packets: Set your gas grill to low or build a banked-coal fire (see page 193). Grill (over the cooler part of the grill if using charcoal) until the fish is cooked through and the vegetables are soft, about 15 minutes.

To bake the packets: Preheat the oven to 375° F. Line up the packets on a baking sheet. Bake until the fish is cooked through and the vegetables are soft, about 20 minutes.

To serve: Carefully remove the aluminum foil and string, leaving the sole and vegetables wrapped in banana leaf. Serve each leaf, seam side up, on a plate large enough to hold it comfortably. Let each person unfold the leaf and eat the fish and vegetables right off the banana leaf.

3 ripe medium tomatoes, cored and cut into chunks (about 2½ cups)
1 large Spanish onion, cut into large dice (about 1½ cups)
1 yellow bell pepper, cored, seeded, and cut into ½-inch dice (about 1 cup)
⅓ cup chopped fresh cilantro
2 tablespoons olive oil
4 cloves garlic, finely chopped
Fine sea or kosher salt
Freshly ground pepper
Banana leaves (see Daisy's Pantry on page 94)
Six 6- to 7-ounce sole fillets, each about ¾ inch thick

NOTES: *The grilled version will give the sole a smokier flavor because the banana leaf will dry out and perfume the fish. The oven version has a subtler, fresher flavor. Both are delicious.*

• *Save odds and ends of banana leaves to cover Yellow Rice (page 13) as it cooks.*

• *Timing the fillets is the best way to judge if they're done. A 1-inch-thick fillet will cook in about 20 minutes. Because the fish is tightly wrapped with lots of juicy vegetables, you can overcook by a few minutes without the fillets drying out.*

CRAB CAKES

TORTAS DE CANGREJO

I came up with these crab cakes for a birthday dinner I made for Mami. She loves seafood, and when I serve these crab cakes, I give her another reason to love crab, not to mention me!

MAKES 6 SERVINGS

1. Place the crabmeat in a medium bowl. Pick over the crabmeat gently, removing all the cartilage and bones but leaving the pieces as large as possible. Add the red pepper, cilantro, and chili to the bowl. Sprinkle on the flour and pour the egg over the ingredients. Mix together gently until well blended. Refrigerate for at least 1 hour.

2. Using a scant ½ cup of crab mix for each, form 3-inch cakes. Spread the cornmeal out on a plate and coat the cakes with it, tapping off any excess. Place the coated cakes on a baking sheet.

3. Pour about ½ inch of oil into a large, heavy skillet. Heat over medium heat until rippling. Add as many of the cakes to the pan as will fit without touching. Cook, turning once, until golden brown on both sides, about 5 minutes. Serve hot.

1 pound lump crabmeat
2 tablespoons very finely diced red bell pepper
1 tablespoon chopped fresh cilantro
½ habanero chili pepper or the chili pepper of your choice, minced
2 tablespoons all-purpose flour
1 egg, beaten
Fine cornmeal
Canola oil

SHELLFISH MEDLEY

SALPICON DE MARISCOS

No, you're not seeing double. This recipe is very different from the *mariscada* recipe (Twenty-Minute Shellfish Sauté, page 14) in the Top Ten chapter. This is not as "brothy" as that recipe, and the sauce has a very different slant. It's more intense and direct, while the mariscada is smooth and seductive. This can be served with Yellow Rice (page 13), Twice-Fried Green Plantain Chips (page 113), or Mofongo (page 115).

MAKES 4 SERVINGS

1. Heat the oil in a wide, deep skillet over medium heat. Add the garlic, chili, and thyme. Cook 1 to 2 minutes, until fragrant. Pour in the brandy and boil until it has evaporated. Stand back from the pan in case it bursts into flames.

2. Add the wine, raise the heat to high, and bring the wine to a boil. Add the monkfish, clams, and mussels. Cover the pan, lower the heat to medium, and cook until the monkfish is opaque, about 15 minutes. Taste the sauce and add salt and pepper to taste.

⅓ cup olive oil
4 cloves garlic, sliced
1 hot chili pepper of your choice
1 sprig of thyme
3 tablespoons Spanish brandy
½ cup dry white wine
1 pound monkfish fillets, cleaned (see page 83) and cut into 1-inch slices
8 littleneck clams, soaked with cornmeal and water (see page 179)
10 to 12 mussels, scrubbed and debearded
Fine sea or kosher salt
Freshly ground pepper

VARIATION: *If you are feeling flush, order a steamed lobster from the supermarket or fish store. Remove the meat from the shell, cut it into 1-inch pieces, and stir it into the dish 1 minute before serving. I have started to see cooked pasteurized lobster packed in cans in my bulk foods store. It is excellent, handy to have on hand, and a breeze to work with.*

SEAFOOD PIE WITH CORN BREAD CRUST

PASTEL DE CHOCLO CON MARISCOS

Versions of a meat pie, made with one version of picadillo (page 60) or another and topped with a corn bread crust, abound in South America. In Chile, which has a spectacular coastline and a wonderful assortment of fish and shellfish, you'll find a version made with seafood. Have you ever had a really delicious fish chowder with rings of corn on the cob? Do you remember how delicious the corn you cooked at your last clambake tasted? Well, that magic flavor combination comes alive in this dish. You savor the sweetness of the corn with the salt and brine of the ocean. This is my take on the Chilean classic, made with readily found ingredients. It makes a great party dish.

MAKES 8 REGULAR OR 6 DAISY SERVINGS

1. Prepare the crust ingredients: Stir the cornmeal, flour, sugar, baking powder, and salt together in a medium bowl. In a separate bowl, beat the milk, egg, and melted butter together until well blended. Set both bowls aside.

2. Plunge the lobster into a large pot of boiling water. Cook for 8 minutes, then drain. When the lobster is cool enough to handle, remove the meat from the shell.

3. Heat the oil in a large skillet over high heat. Add the onion and garlic, and cook just until the onions start to wilt (you don't want them to color at all), about 2 minutes. Add the scallops and shrimp, and cook, stirring, until the shrimp turn pink, about 2 minutes. Add the cilantro and tomato paste, and stir until the seafood is coated. Do the same with the flour. Cook for 1 minute, then pour in the clam juice. Reduce the heat to low and cook, stirring constantly, for 1 minute. Stir in the lobster and then scrape the mixture into an 11 x 11-inch baking dish.

4. Preheat the oven to 400° F. Pour the milk mixture into the bowl of dry ingredients. Add the corn, if using, and stir just until blended. If the batter is a little lumpy, that's okay. Spread the batter in an even layer over the seafood. It doesn't matter if the seafood pokes through in a few places. Bake until the edges are bubbling and the topping is golden brown in places, about 25 minutes. Let stand for 5 minutes before serving.

FOR THE CRUST

1 cup fine yellow cornmeal
1 cup all-purpose flour
⅓ cup sugar
4 teaspoons baking powder
2 teaspoons fine sea or kosher salt
1 cup milk
1 egg
4 tablespoons butter, melted
1 cup frozen or canned corn kernels, drained (optional)

FOR THE FILLING

One 1½-pound live lobster
2 tablespoons olive oil
1 medium Spanish onion, diced
3 cloves garlic, finely chopped
1 pound sea scallops
1 pound large (about 20 per pound) shrimp
½ cup chopped fresh cilantro
2 tablespoons tomato paste
2 tablespoons all-purpose flour
½ cup bottled clam juice

NOTES: *Set up your wet and dry ingredients for the batter before you cook the shellfish, but don't mix them until the last second. Once baking powder gets wet, it starts to lose its oomph.*

• Some people make this with fresh corn kernels, some with frozen corn, and some with no corn at all. Because this is home cooking, and my home in particular, there is no exact science. Use what you like.

VARIATION: *You can brush the corn bread batter with melted butter or olive oil before baking if you like. It will give a nice glossy finish.*

NOODLE PAELLA

FIDEUA

I enjoyed a beautiful version of this dish on a gorgeous balmy after-noon at the piers of Barcelona, within view of the statue of Christo-pher Columbus pointing west. I swore to try to duplicate it the minute I got home. It is now one of the most requested recipes in my house, and it seems that no matter how much I make, it is never enough! I never have leftovers! In the short time it takes to put this together, it's remarkable how the noodles take on the flavor of the seafood.

MAKES 8 SERVINGS

1. Heat the oil in a wide, shallow skillet or paella pan over medium-low heat. Add the garlic and cook, shaking the pan, just until fra-grant. Break the noodles into 4-inch lengths. Stir them into the oil and stir constantly until the noodles are lightly toasted, about 3 min-utes.

2. Stir the shrimp and scallops into the pan and cook until the shrimp turn pink, about 2 minutes. Add the mussels. Pour in enough hot clam juice to barely cover the noodles. Adjust the heat so the liquid is at a happy bubble. Continue cooking, making sure there is enough liquid to cover the pasta. Add a little at a time if necessary. Keep tamping the noodles down under the broth to keep them sub-merged.

3. When the pasta is tender and the seafood is cooked, about 5 minutes, lower the flame and continue cooking until all the liquid has evaporated and the noodles start to crisp up. Discard any mus-sels that haven't opened. Taste and add salt and pepper if you like. Spoon onto a serving platter, scatter the parsley over the top, and serve hot.

¼ cup Achiote Oil (page 9)
4 cloves garlic, thinly sliced
¾ pound angel-hair pasta or two 6-ounce packages thin egg noodles
1 pound medium (about 30 per pound) shrimp, peeled and deveined
1 pound sea scallops
1 pound mussels
2½ cups (or as needed) bottled clam juice, hot
Fine sea or kosher salt to taste
Freshly ground pepper to taste
Chopped fresh flat-leaf parsley

PORK

CERDO

I never met a piece of pork I didn't like. Whether I'm having it as chops, roasted, or slow-cooked and braised, pork is delicious. One of my earliest memories is of my grandmother turning the corner to the entrance of our apartment (we lived on the top floor of a two-family house), carrying what appeared to my three-year-old self as the biggest serving platter of her famous fried pork chops. It must have been summer because she had on a pretty sleeveless dress. The vision is so clear to me that if I close my eyes, I can smell the delicious aroma of the salty vinegar-marinated pork chops, and I can see her grinning from ear to ear as she watched us savor the succulent meat.

It was the first time I remember her making them, but it certainly was not the last. My husband accuses me of inviting him to dinner at Abuela's house to ensnare him with her delicious cooking! She would always say that the way to a man's heart was through his stomach, and she would set plate after plate of delicious beans, aromatic stuffed peppers, rice, and garlicky roast chicken in front of him. I can't understand how he put so much food away in one sitting; it's not like I forced him to eat anything. Can you imagine the nerve of that man making an accusation like that? Besides, it wasn't her pork chops that did the trick—it most certainly had to be her pork roast!

PORK BRAISED IN GUAJILLO CHILE SAUCE

PUERCO EN CHILE GUAJILLO

Most pork is very lean, so I try to find cuts of pork with a little fat in them; they braise better and stay moister that way. You might have better luck finding marbled pork if you buy a whole shoulder or butt and cut it into pieces yourself. (Don't worry if the pieces come out uneven.) But whether or not you're cutting the meat yourself, do search for the pieces of "silver skin" and remove them by cutting beneath them with the tip of a sharp knife.

Toasting the chilies brings out their flavor, and blackening the onions and tomatoes brings out their natural sweetness—a little work up front that pays off big-time down the line. Serve hot with some kind of rice, white, yellow, or, best of all, Yellow Rice with Corn (page 92).

MAKES 8 SERVINGS

1. Put the pork in a heavy Dutch oven large enough to fit it comfortably. Pour in enough cold water to cover the meat by 2 inches. Add the salt and bay leaf. Bring the liquid to a boil and simmer for 1 hour. Skim off the foam from the surface as necessary.

2. Meanwhile, remove the stems from the chilies and tap out the seeds. Heat the olive oil in a medium skillet over medium heat. Add half of the chilies and toast them, turning with tongs until they start to change color and crisp up a bit, about 4 minutes. Heat them gently so they don't burn. Lift them out and place in a bowl. Repeat with the remaining chilies. Pour enough boiling water over the toasted chilies to cover them. Soak until completely softened, about 20 minutes. Drain well.

3. While the chilies are soaking, wipe out the skillet with paper towels. Place the onion and tomatoes, cut sides down, in the skillet. Cook, turning the vegetables as often as necessary, until the tomatoes are blackened on all sides and the onions are blackened on both flat sides.

4. After the pork has been cooking for 1 hour, remove 2 cups of the cooking liquid and pour it into a blender jar. Add the onions and tomatoes, and puree until smooth. Add the chilies and blend until smooth. Remove another 2 cups of the cooking liquid and set aside. Drain the pork, discarding the remaining liquid, and wipe out the pot.

5. Set the pot over medium-low heat and add the canola oil. Stir in the flour and cook, stirring, for 3 to 4 minutes. Pour the chili sauce into the pot slowly. As it comes to a boil, it will thicken. Stir well,

4 pounds boneless pork shoulder or butt, cut into 2-inch cubes
2 tablespoons fine sea or kosher salt
1 bay leaf
10 guajillo chilies (see Daisy's Pantry)
2 tablespoons olive oil
1 large Spanish onion, peeled and cut in half through the middle
3 fresh plum tomatoes, cut in half lengthwise through the core
¼ cup canola oil or lard
2 tablespoons all-purpose flour

DAISY'S PANTRY *Guajillo chilies are the dried version of fresh mirasol chilies. They are long, tapered, and wrinkled, have a reddish brown color, and are fairly spicy. They are available in specialty stores or by mail (see Sources).*

VARIATION: *Shred leftover pork and stir it back into the sauce. Use that to make a delicious version of chilaquiles (page 168).*

especially in the corners, to prevent the sauce from sticking and scorching as it thickens.

6. Add the pork and return the liquid to a simmer, cover the pot, and cook until tender, about 1 hour. While the pork is cooking, there should be enough sauce to keep it moistened. If not, add the reserved pork cooking liquid as needed.

SAUSAGE, ONION, PEPPER, AND POTATO ROAST

ASADO DE LONGANIZA, CEBOLLA, PIMIENTOS, Y PAPAS

This is another of those "Daisy" dishes. After tasting *linguica*, Portuguese sausage, while on vacation with my family in Cape Cod, I decided to try this combination at home. The results were better than I could ever have hoped for. The potatoes drink up the aroma of the onions and peppers, and the sausage perfumes everything with paprika and garlic. Be still my beating heart!

MAKES 6 SERVINGS

2 pounds of garlicky sausage such as linguica, andouille, or Italian sausages seasoned with garlic
1 pound white potatoes, scrubbed and cut into ½-inch rounds on the bias
Fine sea or kosher salt
1 teaspoon dried oregano
Olive oil
1 each red, yellow, and orange bell peppers, cored, seeded, and cut lengthwise into ¼-inch strips
1 large Spanish onion, halved and then cut into thin slivers
2 sprigs of fresh thyme
Freshly ground pepper
Chopped fresh cilantro

1. Place the sausages in a skillet with ½ cup of water. Cook over high heat, turning the sausages until the water has evaporated and the sausages start to sizzle in their fat, about 6 minutes. The sausage centers will be pink. Cut the sausages into 1-inch slices on the bias. Set aside.

2. Place the potatoes in a medium saucepan and add enough cold water to cover them. Add a small handful of salt and bring the water to a boil over high heat. As soon as the water comes to a boil, drain and set aside.

3. Preheat the oven to 425° F. Toss the sausages, potatoes, and oregano together in a roasting pan with enough oil to coat them lightly. Cover with aluminum foil and roast for 30 minutes, shaking the pan every once in a while.

4. Toss the peppers, onions, and thyme with the sausages and potatoes. Season lightly with salt and pepper and return to the oven. Roast, uncovered, until the onions and peppers are tender but not melted, about 20 minutes. Check the seasonings. Scatter the cilantro over the top and serve hot.

STUFFED CHICKEN, SALVADORIAN STYLE

POLLO ASADO SALVADORENO

What's a chicken recipe doing in the pork chapter? Every culture across Latin America has its own version of roast pork (*pernil*). The people of El Salvador make one that is very similar to the recipe on page 212, and when there are leftovers, they chop them up and use them to stuff a seasoned chicken. The results are wonderful and, like the Cuban Sandwich on page 215 that follows, reason enough to cook a *pernil*.

MAKES 4 TO 6 SERVINGS

One 3½-pound chicken
Dry Rub, homemade (page 19) or store-bought
3 tablespoons olive oil
1 medium Spanish onion, diced
1 cup coarsely chopped leftover Puerto Rican Roast Pork Shoulder (page 212)
1½ cups day-old bread, cut into cubes
Chicken Broth, homemade (page 155) or canned

1. Preheat the oven to 400°F.

2. Work your hand under the chicken skin to loosen it. Season the meat under the skin liberally with dry rub. (See page 17 for detailed instructions.)

3. Heat the oil in a large skillet over medium heat. Add the onion and cook, stirring, until softened, about 4 minutes. Stir in the leftover pork and then the bread. Pour the broth into the pan and cook until the bread is evenly moistened.

4. Fill the chicken with the pork stuffing and then truss the chicken according to the instructions on page 18. Smear the chicken skin liberally with dry rub. Place the chicken, breast side down, on a rack in a roasting pan. Roast for 45 minutes.

5. Turn the chicken right side up and continue roasting until one of the legs moves very easily when you wiggle it and the juices run clear, not pink, from the thickest part of the thigh when poked, about 45 minutes. Let the chicken rest about 10 minutes and then scoop the stuffing into a bowl and carve or cut up the chicken.

One of my fondest Martinez family memories is the Christmas that Papi decided to roast an entire pig in our yard. We had often observed this ritual in my aunt Gabriela's house. Her husband, Luis Mario, was famous for his pig roasts during the Christmas holidays and for any other special occasion. There was one huge difference: Luis Mario had ample land to have a pig roast, and everyone was involved in the process from the slaughter of the animal to breaking down the animal, and the sausage making—everything. There was no way we could do anything that involved in our little New York yard, so we had to make some modifications.

First, Mami paid a visit to the Spanish butcher on Smith Street in Brooklyn. She ordered a pig, about 50 pounds, that we could roast in our yard. Papi, always the fireman and conscious of all safety codes, built a contraption out of a steel drum, complete with hand-operated rotisserie, and found the perfect spot in our yard to roast the pig. Everybody wanted to be involved in some way or other so we could say we had been part of the big Martinez Family Pig Roast of '78!

The day was finally here, Christmas Eve, and Mami had had the *lechon* marinating in wet rub (page 19) for two days. Papi got up at the crack of dawn to start the coals that would roast our pig, managed to secure the pig on the rotisserie pole, and even had his morning coffee out there while he turned the pig for a while. Then he turned to look for all the volunteers who had pledged to sit and turn the spit, but to no avail. Of course, we all had good intentions of helping out with the pig; hadn't we all done it at Tia Gabby's with no problem? Yup! We sure had, but there was one huge difference: When we roasted the pig in Puerto Rico, it had been a delightful 80 degrees, and here in New York it was about 26 degrees—a small factor we had forgotten to take into account!

In the end Papi pulled rank. We bundled up and in no time, wrapped in scarves and hats, and with mugs of hot chocolate to keep us warm, we managed to make it one of the most memorable family Christmas Eves ever.

CRISPY PORK BITES

MASITAS

If you've tried the roast pork on page 212 and have become as big a fan of crispy pork skin as I am, then look for boneless pork butt with the skin left on to make this recipe. If you're not so sure, start with skinless pork butt—it's easier to find anyway.

When you order this at any of Puerto Rico's many mom-and-pop, casual restaurants that dot the island, you get a big piece of steamed yucca dressed with olive oil, Twice-Fried Green Plaintain Chips (page 113), and a lettuce, tomato, and avocado salad. Pack my bags, I'm outta here.

MAKES 6 TO 8 SERVINGS

1. Toss the pork and enough dry rub together in a bowl to coat it generously. Add the paprika and oregano, toss again, then pour in the vinegar. Marinate the pork (in the bowl or a sealable plastic bag) at room temperature for 30 minutes or in the refrigerator for up to 1 day.

2. Drain the pork and pat the pieces dry with paper towels. Pour enough oil into a heavy 4- or 5-quart pot to fill about 3 inches. Heat over medium-high heat until the tip of the handle of a wooden spoon gives off a very lively sizzle when dipped into the oil (about 390° F). Slip as many pieces of the pork—one at a time and very carefully—as fit without touching. (Because the oil is so hot, it will foam up when the pork is added. Be sure the oil comes no more than halfway up the side of the pot before heating it so that the oil doesn't boil over when the pork is added.) Occasionally stir the pieces gently with a long-handled spoon until they are mahogany brown and just a trace of pink remains in the center, about 5 minutes. Remove them and let stand just a minute or two. Eat them as hot as you can stand. Repeat with the remaining pork, adjusting the heat under the oil to keep it at a constant temperature.

3 pounds boneless pork butt, skin on or not as you prefer, cut into large (about 2 inches) pieces; don't worry if they're irregular (see Notes)
Dry Rub, homemade (page 19) or store-bought
1 tablespoon paprika (see Notes)
1 tablespoon dried oregano
1½ cups white vinegar
Vegetable oil

NOTES: *I like to make these with fairly fatty pork; much of it melts away as the pork cooks. Even if you're watching your fat, this is one place to cheat a little.*

• If you'd like to play a little, there are all kinds of paprikas out there. Try Hungarian hot or sweet paprika or, for a real kick, smoked paprika, which is just that— paprika made from smoked dried peppers.

PUERTO RICAN ROAST
PORK SHOULDER

PERNIL

If you were to ask me, "What does Christmas smell like?" I wouldn't say "pine" or "fresh snow," I would say, "Pernil." By the time my kids finish their cereal on Christmas Eve morning, the house is filled with the wonderful aroma of roast pork.

You want the shoulder, not the butt, for this, and you definitely want the skin on. If you have the opportunity to marinate the roast for three days, two days, or even overnight, you'll be rewarded with a roast that has juicy, fragrant, tender meat and crispy, salty, mahogany-colored skin. It's so good, I'm almost afraid I have to bring it up in confession!

MAKES 8 LARGE SERVINGS PLUS LEFTOVERS

One 4½-pound skin-on pork shoulder roast
Wet Rub (page 19)

> **NOTE**: A good rule of thumb for roasting pork is to cook the roast half an hour for every pound.

1. Up to 3 days before you serve the roast, set it in a bowl, skin side up. With a paring or boning knife, make several slits about 1½ inches apart through the skin of the roast and into the meat. Make the slits as deep as you can. Wiggle a finger in the slits to open them up a bit and then fill each one with wet rub using a teaspoon. (A pair of latex gloves comes in handy when it comes time to rub the wet rub into the pork.) Do the same on all sides. If you have rub left over, smear it all over the outside of the roast. Refrigerate, covered, at least 1 day or up to 3 days.

2. Preheat the oven to 450° F.

3. Set the roast, skin side up, on a rack in a roasting pan. Roast for 1 hour, turn the heat down to 400° F, and roast until the skin is a deep golden brown and crackly and with no trace of pink near the bone, about 1½ hours or until an instant reading thermometer inserted near the bone registers 160° F. Let the roast rest at least 15 minutes before carving.

4. To serve, remove the crispy skin. It will pull right off in big pieces. Cut them into smaller pieces—kitchen shears work well for this—and pile them in the center of the platter. Carve the meat parallel to the bones all the way down to the bone. (It will get trickier to carve neat slices as you get near the bone; don't let that bother you.)

CUBAN SANDWICH

CUBANOS

If you have a panini maker or grilled sandwich maker, this is a good place to use it. Be generous with the meat—make it as if it's for someone you really love.

MAKES 4 SERVINGS

1. Preheat the oven to 350° F. Split the bread lengthwise and spread the bottom of the loaf with mayo. Make an even layer of the pork, then add the ham, pickles, and cheese. Top with the other piece of bread and press lightly but firmly.

2. Wrap the sandwich(es) securely in foil and lay between 2 baking sheets. Set on the oven rack and weight the top sheet with a heavy ovenproof skillet. Bake until warmed through and the cheese has softened, about 30 minutes. Serve warm, cut into manageable pieces.

1 loaf Italian bread (about 24 inches long) or 4 hero rolls
Mayonnaise
Sliced leftover Roast Puerto Rican Pork Shoulder (page 212)
3 fairly thick slices boiled ham
Sliced "bread and butter" pickles or any other type of pickle you like
½ pound fairly thickly sliced Swiss cheese

BRAZIL'S NATIONAL DISH: BLACK BEANS AND PORK

FEIJOIDA

In this country we are not used to heavy lunches, but this dish is a Saturday afternoon tradition all across Brazil. To me it's more suited to a big gathering, especially because it gets better as it sits. I'll put it together, let it bubble away on the stove all afternoon, and then let it sit for a few hours before reheating for company.

One of my favorite things to put in my feijoida are trotters, or pig's feet. Now before you turn your nose up, hear me out: Aside from making the sauce silky and unctuous, the trotters offer something else: You can suck the meat off all the little bones. I haven't steered you wrong yet, so take one little leap of faith.

Traditionally, feijoida is made with all different cuts of pork, such as the hocks, belly, and bacon featured here. But it is not unusual to see versions containing beef and even chicken on menus nowadays.

MAKES 8 SERVINGS

2 trotters (pig's feet), split
1 cup white vinegar
1½ one-pound bags black beans
1 smoked ham hock
3 bay leaves
3 leaves culantro or ¼ cup chopped fresh cilantro
1¼ pounds slab bacon, rind removed (see Note on page 171) and cut into 8 pieces
1½ pounds pork belly, cut into about 4 pieces
Fine sea or kosher salt
Freshly ground pepper
1¼ pounds andouille, chorizo, or any other pork sausage (spicy is good)

1. Place the trotters in a bowl large enough to hold them comfortably. Pour in enough cold water to cover them completely. Add the vinegar. Let stand for 30 minutes or so, then drain and rinse thoroughly under cold water.

2. Put the trotters, beans, ham hock, bay leaves, and culantro in a large (at least 12 quarts), heavy pot. Pour in enough cold water to cover the beans by 2 inches. Bring to a boil, then adjust the heat to simmering. Skim off any foam that rises to the top as the beans cook. Cook for 1 hour.

3. Pour ½ cup water over the bacon in a medium saucepan. Bring to a boil over medium-high heat and cook until the water has evaporated and the bacon begins to cook in its fat. Lower the heat slightly and cook, turning, until the bacon is browned. Set the bacon aside, but leave the fat in the pan.

4. While the bacon is cooking, season the pork belly with salt and pepper. Once the bacon has been removed, add the pork belly pieces to the bacon fat and cook, turning often, until well browned on all sides, about 15 minutes.

5. Place the bacon, pork belly, and andouille in the pot after the beans have been cooking for 1 hour. Continue cooking until the beans and meats are tender, about 1 hour.

6. Transfer the meats to a carving board, cut them into slices, and arrange them on a platter. Spoon the beans into a serving bowl. White rice is a must with this dish.

DAISY'S PANTRY *Pork belly is just what it sounds like. Think bacon without the curing and smoking. It used to be hard to find, but with restaurant chefs featuring it on their menus, it has made something of a comeback.*

NOTES: *I know that pig's feet aren't everybody's cup of tea, but I love them in hearty dishes like feijoida and even in spaghetti sauce. The gelatin from the pig's feet makes a rich, silky gravy. If you don't want to use them, try country-style spareribs or pork riblets.*

• This is a splurge dish, not in terms of money, because the ingredients are cheap, but in terms of fat and calories. I don't eat like this every day, so when I make feijoida, I tend to go all out. You can, however, make a delicious version featuring leaner meats such as smoked pork chops and Canadian bacon.

BREADED PORK CHOPS WITH SPICY PINEAPPLE VINEGAR

CHULETAS CON VINAGRE

My father-in-law is Sicilian and makes a traditional dish for me that I love—pork chops with pickled hot cherry peppers. This is my Latin riff on that dish; it features breaded pork chops browned in a pan and finished in the oven topped with Spicy Pineapple Vinegar (see page 218) and some of the peppers from the jar. I love the chops that come from the loin end, the ones that look like little T-bone steaks, but you can use whatever type of chop appeals to you. This is not a dish for the faint of heart: If you like spice, you'll love these. Angela, my only daughter and the youngest of my kids, likes to keep up with her older brothers, all of whom love these spicy chops. She's working on it—taking one bite more each time I serve them.

MAKES 4 DAISY SERVINGS

1. Preheat the oven to 400° F.

2. Pat the pork chops dry with paper towels. Season both sides generously with salt and pepper. Beat the eggs in a shallow bowl until foamy. Spread out the bread crumbs and flour in separate shallow bowls. Dredge a chop in the flour until coated, then tap off the excess. Turn the coated chop in the eggs until coated and then let it drain a second or two over the bowl. Lay it in the bread crumbs and turn a few times, patting the crumbs onto the chop so they stick better. Set the chop on a baking sheet and repeat with the remaining chops.

3. Pour ½ inch of oil into a large, heavy skillet. Heat over medium heat until the tip of the handle of a wooden spoon gives off a lively sizzle (about 375° F). Add half of the pork chops to the oil and cook, turning once, until golden brown on both sides, about 4 minutes. Transfer to an 11 × 15-inch baking dish or any baking dish that holds all the chops snugly and will allow them to overlap along one side of the pan. Repeat with the remaining chops.

4. Spoon over the chops as much as you like of the onions and peppers from the pineapple vinegar (about ½ cup works for me). Drizzle a healthy amount of vinegar over the chops and bake until no trace of pink remains near the bone, about 25 minutes. Serve immediately.

Eight 1-inch-thick loin pork chops
  (about 4½ pounds)
Fine sea or kosher salt
Freshly ground black pepper
4 eggs
Seasoned bread crumbs
All-purpose flour
Canola or vegetable oil
Spicy Pineapple Vinegar (page 218)

VARIATION: *If you have some dry adobo on hand, use it in place of the salt and pepper.*

SPICY PINEAPPLE VINEGAR

VINAGRE

References are made to *vinagre*—a condiment that gives sparkle, a citrus-fruity tinge, heat, and aroma—throughout this book. It takes just about any dish to places it has never been before. If you don't know about vinagre, you could probably live a full and happy life, but once you taste it, you'll be lost without it. My mother used to place the jar of vinagre in the sun, but I just pour the pineapple liquid over the vegetables while it's still hot, which achieves the same thing—getting the vinagre off to a head start.

It is probably easier to list the things you *can't* use vinagre for. Try it over any rice dish, drizzled into soups and stews at the very end of cooking (pass some at the table, too), and anything grilled.

MAKES ABOUT 1 QUART

2 ripe pineapples
½ large Spanish onion, thinly sliced
1 tablespoon smashed fresh oregano leaves
1 teaspoon black peppercorns
20 garlic cloves, crushed
6 habanero or chili peppers of your choice, stems removed and coarsely chopped
1 tablespoon cider vinegar, or as needed
½ teaspoon fine sea or kosher salt, or as needed

1. Cut the tops off the pineapples and discard them. With a big knife, cut off the rind from the pineapples with as little pineapple attached as possible. Put the rinds in a pot large enough to hold them comfortably and pour in enough water to cover them. Bring to a boil and boil until the pineapple peel is very tender, about 30 minutes. Add water if necessary to keep the rinds submerged.

2. Meanwhile, put the onion, oregano, peppercorns, garlic, peppers, vinegar, and salt in a large jar with a tight-fitting lid.

3. Strain the pineapple liquid over the seasonings. If there is not enough liquid to cover the ingredients, cover the pineapple with water again and boil for 20 minutes. Taste and add salt and vinegar if you think it needs it. You can use it as soon as it cools, but it will get better as it sits. Keep at room temperature 1 day, then refrigerate.

STUFFED PORK ROAST

CUBA LIBRE

To most people *cuba libre* means a rum and coke cocktail. To many Latinos it means a dramatic and delicious party dish. Slices of the glossy mahogany roast reveal whole hard-boiled eggs and soaked prunes. This is one of those dishes that you make when there is an extra pair of friendly hands in the kitchen to help with the rolling. You can always lure a friend or two with the promise of the wonderfulness to come!

MAKES 12 GENEROUS SERVINGS

1. Prepare the pork: Before seasoning and stuffing the roast it is necessary to butterfly it—in other words, to open it up to a large, thinner piece of meat. Make a cut along one long side of the roast about one-third of the way from the top that goes almost but not completely through the roast. Peel that top layer away from you. Cut the bottom, thicker portion of the roast toward you in the same way so you have in front of you a large, fairly even, flat piece of pork. Pound the pork with a heavy kitchen mallet to an even thickness.

2. Season both sides of the pork generously with dry rub. Roll up the pork and place it in a large, heavy plastic bag. Place the bag in a large bowl or roasting pan and pour the vinegar into the bag. Add the onion, garlic, and bay leaves, and squish the ingredients to distribute them around the roast. Refrigerate overnight, turning the pork in the bag from time to time.

3. Chop the carrots, onions, and celery coarsely one at a time in a food processor. (Alternately, you can chop the vegetables by hand.) Heat the olive oil in a large skillet over medium heat until rippling. Add the vegetables and chopped garlic, and cook, stirring occasionally, just until softened and without coloring them, about 4 minutes. Set aside.

4. Make the glaze: Bring the malta to a boil in a small saucepan over medium heat. Add the sugar and cook, stirring to dissolve the sugar, until the glaze is syrupy and has been reduced by about two-thirds. Set aside.

5. Preheat the oven to 400° F. Remove the pork from the marinade and drain it well. Pat it dry on both sides with paper towels. Lay the roast out on your work surface. Cut twelve 2-feet lengths of kitchen twine and keep them handy.

6. Cover the top of the roast with the sliced ham, leaving a border of about 1 inch around the edges.Cut a slit along one side of each pepper. Lay them out flat to cover the ham. It doesn't matter if they overlap a little or if there is a bare spot or two.

FOR THE MARINADE

One 7-pound boneless pork loin
Dry Rub, homemade (page 19) or store-bought
3 cups white vinegar
1 medium Spanish onion, sliced
6 cloves garlic, smashed
2 bay leaves

FOR THE VEGETABLES

1 pound carrots, peeled, trimmed, and cut into 3-inch lengths
2 medium Spanish onions, cut into 2-inch chunks
4 stalks celery, trimmed and cut into 3-inch lengths
¼ cup olive oil
6 large cloves garlic, chopped

FOR THE GLAZE

One 12-ounce bottle malta (see Daisy's Pantry) or one 12-ounce bottle of beer plus 1 tablespoon molasses
2 tablespoons dark brown sugar

½ pound thinly sliced ham
One 24-ounce jar fire-roasted peppers, drained
3 links (about 10 ounces) chorizo, andouille, or any smoked garlicky sausage, cut into ½-inch dice
One 12-ounce box pitted prunes, coarsely chopped
4 large hard-boiled eggs (see page 123), peeled and cut in half
Salt

7. Stir the chorizo and prunes into the cooked vegetable mix, then spread them over the half of the peppers closest to you. Arrange the eggs, cut side down, along the edge of the vegetable mix closest to you.

8. Bring the edge of the pork closest to you up and over the eggs. Continue rolling up the roast, keeping the roll tight as you go. Set the rolled roast seam side down. Use the lengths of twine to tie the roast tightly at 2-inch intervals. (To keep the roast in a tight roll, wiggle the lengths of twine one at a time under the roast and bring the 2 ends together over the roast before tying.)

9. Gently transfer the roast to a roasting pan large enough to hold it comfortably. If you don't own such a pan, cut the roast in half crosswise and roast the halves side by side in a large pan or in 2 separate pans. Roast, basting with the malta glaze every 15 minutes or so, until a meat thermometer inserted in the thickest part of the roast registers 150° F, about 2 hours. Check for doneness after 1½ hours.

10. Remove from the oven and let rest for 10 to 15 minutes. Cut into 1-inch-thick slices using a serrated knife and a gentle sawing motion.

DAISY'S PANTRY *Malta is a nonalcoholic malt beverage popular throughout the islands where athletes in training claim it is a boost to energy and performance. If you can find it, use that instead of the beer and molasses.*

NOTES: *Pork is lean these days, so I leave whatever fat there is on the loin. It will melt during roasting and help keep the pork moist.*

• Because there is so much filling, which is what makes this such a festive dish, an extra set of hands comes in handy when it's time to roll up the roast. Two people can stand side by side and each one work on an end of the roast.

STUFFED POBLANO PEPPERS

CHILES RELLENOS

If you have access to epazote (see Daisy's Pantry on page 170), chop 2 leaves and add to the picadillo.

MAKES 6 SERVINGS

Pork Picadillo (page 60)
6 large fresh poblano peppers
Beer Batter (page 223)
Enchilada Sauce (page 223)
Canola oil for frying (about 4 cups)
1½ cups shredded Monterey Jack cheese

1. Prepare the picadillo. Set aside to cool.

2. Roast the poblanos (see To Roast Peppers on page 67), turning until charred on most sides. It isn't necessary to char the skins completely. Set aside to cool.

3. Meanwhile, make the beer batter and enchilada sauce.

4. Using the edge of your knife, scrape off the charred skin from the poblano. If you have some patches of skin that you cannot remove from your pepper, it's not a big deal.

5. Make a slit along the length of each pepper starting and ending about 1 inch from each end of the pepper. Working with a small knife, cut out the core and seeds, being careful not to cut through the pepper. Keep the stem attached.

6. Using a tablespoon, fill the peppers through the slit with the pork mixture. Do not overstuff the peppers—you should be able to press the edges of the slit together to completely enclose the filling.

7. Pour enough canola oil into a large saucepan or fryer to fill 3 to 4 inches. Heat over medium heat until the tip of the handle of a wooden spoon gives off a lively sizzle (about 360° F). Hold each pepper by the stem and dip in the batter, turning to coat evenly. Let excess batter drip back into the bowl. Slip 2 to 3 of the peppers into the oil gently. Fry, turning the peppers with a slotted spoon if necessary to cook them evenly, until peppers are golden brown. Remove with the slotted spoon and drain on paper towels. Repeat with the remaining peppers and batter.

8. Preheat oven to 350° F.

9. Pour the enchilda sauce into a baking dish into which the peppers fit comfortably. Turn the peppers in the sauce to coat. Sprinkle generously with shredded cheese. Bake for about 20 minutes, or until the cheese is bubbly and golden.

BEER BATTER

Put flour in a medium mixing bowl. Pour the beer in slowly, whisking gently and constantly until the batter is thick enough to generously coat a spoon when dipped in the batter. Add salt and pepper. Set aside to rest at least 5 minutes.

2 cups all-purpose flour
One 12-ounce can or bottle of beer (or as needed)
1 teaspoon fine sea or kosher salt
Freshly ground pepper to taste

ENCHILADA SAUCE
SALSA ENCHILADA

Stir together all ingredients in a mixing bowl. The sauce may be refrigerated up to 1 day.

One 8-ounce can Spanish-style tomato sauce
¾ cup chicken stock or broth
1 teaspoon chili powder (or ground chile of your choice)
2 epazote leaves, chopped
Fine sea salt or kosher salt to taste
Freshly ground pepper to taste

BEEF, LAMB, AND GAME

RES, CORDERO, Y CAZA

There is no getting around it: I come from a long line of carnivores, and now my family shares this trait as well. That shouldn't come as a surprise: My father was a member of New York City's Fire Department for thirty-one years. Meat played a big role in firehouse dinners, and my mother helped her mother and sisters butcher livestock for food. We are very familiar with meat, and happy to be so. This is true of much of Latin America, and although meat was once thought of as food for the affluent set, we "commoners" often found ways to use the less choice parts and come up with delicious dishes that found their way into our history and our cookbooks—or, at the very least, our grandmothers' cookbooks.

I remember riding to the Essex Street Market on Saturday with my mom to do her shopping when I was a little girl. We had this little routine: Mami drove to Abuela's and dropped off the little ones; then she and I drove to La Marketa to buy all the things she needed for her kitchen during the week. We'd get the cilantro, *achiote*, pigeon peas (fresh when they had them), and then move on to the butcher for skirt steak, pork chops, cooking ham, and stewing lamb. Sometimes we'd have to make more than one trip to the car to carry all our packages.

When we got back to Abuela's, she'd have a terrific lunch waiting for us, and I'm not talking about sandwiches here. She'd have skirt steak with fried yucca or peppers stuffed with picadillo (page 222), Puerto Rican pot roast with white rice (p. 232) or stewed beef with potatoes (p. 234). Whatever it was, there was always something delicious.

Today I enjoy making many of those same dishes for my family and friends. They taste as delicious today as they did back then, and I have the added bonus of having learned recipes from other Latinos that I have since made my own. Whether it's pot roast from Puerto Rico, *ropa vieja* from Cuba, or stuffed flank steak from Colombia, it sounds to me like it's time for a culinary road trip. Join me!

CREOLE-STYLE STEAK

BISTEC CRIOLLO

The term *Creole* pops up whenever the cultures of the Spanish conquistadors, indigenous populations, and Africans come together, as they did in the Caribbean and all over Latin America. Creole cooking is a mixture of Old World and New World ingredients, featuring tomatoes, onions, sweet peppers, okra, peanuts, and a few ingredients specific to the region.

Traditionally, steak Creole is made with top round steak that is pounded thin and cooked in a sauce made up of the ingredients in this recipe, with the addition of cilantro. Given my penchant for playing in the kitchen, I set out to "daisify" this dish and came up with this version, which uses the same ingredients as the classic, but they are cut into pieces and left uncooked, more or less like a salsa. On a hot day this proved to be exactly what the doctor ordered.

MAKES 6 LARGE SERVINGS OR 8 REGULAR SERVINGS

1. Marinate the steaks: Mix the vinegar, olive oil, onion, garlic, and oregano together in a 1-gallon sealable plastic bag or roasting pan. Add the steaks and refrigerate for about 2 hours, turning once or twice.

2. Prepare the sauce: In a serving bowl toss together the tomatoes, onion, pepper, cilantro, oil, lime juice, garlic, and salt and pepper to taste. Set aside. You cannot cut the avocado until you are ready to serve the steaks, because it will turn black.

3. Heat the grill to high or light a charcoal fire and rake the coals into an even layer (see page 193). Using tongs, dip a wadded paper towel in vegetable oil and oil the grill. Grill the steaks to your liking—about 6 minutes on the first side and 4 minutes on the second side will give you medium-rare. Let the steaks rest for 5 to 10 minutes or so.

4. While the steaks are resting, prepare the avocado and toss gently with the other sauce ingredients. Check the seasoning and serve on top of the steak. Sprinkle a little Spicy Pineapple Vinegar, if you like, over the steak and vegetables.

FOR THE STEAK

1¼ cups cider vinegar

¼ cup olive oil

1 large Spanish onion, sliced

4 cloves garlic, smashed

2 teaspoons dried oregano

6 New York strip steaks, each about 1 inch thick (about 4 pounds)

FOR THE SAUCE

2 medium tomatoes, seeded and cut into large dice

1 medium-large Spanish onion, cut into large dice

1 cubanelle or Italian frying pepper, stemmed, seeded, and cut into large dice

1 cup (loosely packed) chopped fresh cilantro

½ cup olive oil

Juice of 2 limes

3 cloves garlic, minced

Fine sea or kosher salt

Freshly ground black pepper

1 medium Florida avocado, pit removed and peeled (see page 34), cut into large dice (just before serving)

Vegetable oil

Splash of Spicy Pineapple Vinegar (page 218) (optional)

NOTES: *Feel free to make this sauce the traditional way, with the sauce ingredients (except the avocado) cooked in the pan after the steaks are removed. Stir in the avocado just before serving.*

• A sturdy grill pan set on the stove top over medium-high heat is a good alternative to outdoor grilling.

GRILLED SKIRT STEAK WITH GARLIC-PARSLEY SAUCE

CHURRASCO

Skirt steaks can vary in size. Plan on 8 ounces a person, and you'll be safe. Some people like to pound their steaks before cooking to tenderize them. You can do that if you like, but I don't—I like a little bite to my steak. Skirt steak has a richer, "beefier" flavor than a lot of meat, and dressed with the saltiness of the dry rub, the sparkle of the citrus, and the fragrance of the onions and garlic, your mouth will think it's the Fourth of July (or at least *Cinco de Mayo!*).

Skirt steak is always served with Garlic-Parsley Sauce (chimichurri), but that's not the limit of chimichurri. Spoon it over Twice-Fried Green Plantain Chips (page 113), any of the *viandas* on pages 110 to 117, or grilled chicken. You can even stir it into a pot of beans at the end of cooking. Heck, you can dab it behind your ears, and it will be good!

MAKES 6 SERVINGS

1. Rub the skirt steaks with a generous amount of dry rub, then enough oil to make them shiny. Lay them out in a baking dish, pour the vinegar over them, and slosh them around a little. Let stand at room temperature, turning once or twice, for 30 minutes to 1 hour.

2. Heat a gas grill to high or build a charcoal fire and rake the coals into an even layer (see page 193).

3. Meanwhile, make the sauce: Stir the onion, parsley, oil, lemon juice, garlic, and salt together in a bowl. Cover until needed.

4. Grill the skirt steaks to your preferred doneness. If you use a grill pan indoors, cook over high heat. In any case, the heat must be very high. Skirt steaks give off quite a bit of liquid when you cook them, so you want to make sure that evaporates as quickly as possible. Cut the steaks in half crosswise. Plate them up and drizzle some sauce over each.

FOR THE STEAK

3 pounds skirt steak, trimmed of excess fat
Dry Rub, homemade (page 19) or store-bought
Olive oil
¼ cup vinegar

FOR THE SAUCE

½ large Spanish onion, finely chopped in a food processor
1 cup (packed) flat-leaf parsley
1 cup olive oil
Juice of 2 lemons
4 cloves garlic
Fine sea or kosher salt to taste

"FRIED COW" (TWICE-COOKED BEEF)

VACA FRITA

Mami had a friend, Matilde, a senior Cuban woman who escaped when Castro took power and still shed a tear whenever she spoke about the island. She would spend hours in Mami's kitchen telling stories about her *isla* and all the wonderful memories of her family. These stories were invariably full of food references, and my siblings and I were intrigued when Dona Matilde talked about *vaca frita*. What an extraordinary place this Cuba must be, we thought, a place where people could actually eat a fried cow!

Whatever the origin of the name, this beef is first cooked and steeped in broth, then seasoned generously and fried until brown and crispy. Marinate it the day before you serve it, if possible. It will really soak up the flavor that way. You might think this is not company fare, but as humble as it sounds and as much of a comfort food as it is, there is never any left over when I make it for crowds at my house.

You can serve the beef with chopped onion, tomato, and cilantro that has been given a quick toss in a frying pan kissed with a bit of olive oil. Heaven!

MAKES 8 SERVINGS

2 pounds flank steak
8 cups water
2 medium Spanish onions, unpeeled and left whole
1 red bell pepper, cored, seeded, and cut into quarters
2 tomatoes, cored and cut in half
6 cloves garlic
3 sprigs of fresh cilantro
3 sprigs of fresh parsley
2 bay leaves
1 teaspoon black peppercorns
Dry Rub, homemade (page 19) or store-bought
Canola oil

1. Put the flank steak in a heavy 5-quart pot. Pour in the water and then add the onions, red pepper, tomatoes, garlic, cilantro, parsley, bay leaves, and peppercorns. Bring to a boil, adjust the heat so the liquid is simmering, and cook, covered, for 2 hours. The flank steak will be quite tough, but the final cooking will tenderize it. Let the flank cool completely in the cooking liquid.

2. Once cool, strain the broth (with a handful of cooked noodles or rice it makes a nice soup) and discard the vegetables.

3. Pound the steak with a heavy mallet to about ½ inch thick. Season both sides generously with the dry rub. You can prepare the steak up to this point 2 days in advance.

4. Cut the steak across the grain into 1-inch strips. Pour about ¼ inch of oil in a large, heavy skillet and heat over medium-high heat until rippling. Add as many of the beef strips as will fit without crowding. Fry, turning only once, until crispy and well browned on both sides. Repeat with the remaining beef if necessary. Serve immediately.

STUFFED FLANK STEAK, COLOMBIAN STYLE

SOBREBARRIGA

My friend Miguelina has a deep appreciation for good food. This girl can find the best restaurant to eat any kind of food you're in the mood for, whether it is Colombian, Peruvian, Ecuadorian, or something else. I ate this dish of stuffed flank steak with Miggy at Pollos Mario's, a restaurant in the Jackson Heights section of Queens, New York. It was so good, I actually felt faint for a second. I'm not one to toot my own horn, so I won't say that my version will do the same to you, but I urge you to try it. You won't be sorry you did.

MAKES 6 TO 8 SERVINGS

1. Butterfly the flank steak: With a sharp knife, cut into the center of the steak along one of the long sides. Continue cutting until almost cut in half. Open the steak like a book and pound it with a meat mallet until it is approximately ½ inch thick. Rub both sides generously with the dry rub.

2. Using on-off pulses, chop the onion, garlic, and cilantro in a food processor. Spread the mix over the steak, leaving a 1-inch border. Starting at one end, roll the steak into a tight roll. Place it on the work surface, seam side down, and tie it securely with kitchen twine at 1½- to 2-inch intervals.

3. Heat the oil in a large, deep, ovenproof skillet or casserole over medium heat. Place the stuffed steak in the oil and cook, turning as necessary, until well browned on all sides, about 12 minutes.

4. Preheat the oven to 400° F. Transfer the steak to a plate and stir the onion and garlic into the pan. Cook about 2 minutes, just until the onion is wilted and starts to pick up color from the pan. Pour in the tomato juice, add the bay leaves, and bring to a boil. Return the steak to the pan, cover, place in the oven, and bake until the beef is tender when poked with a fork but not falling apart, about 3 hours. Carefully remove the pan from the oven and let stand 15 minutes.

5. Transfer the steak to a carving board. Cut off the strings and let the steak rest while you finish the sauce. Working carefully, skim the fat from the surface of the sauce. The sauce should be thick enough to coat a spoon; if not, heat the sauce to boiling and boil until it is.

6. Carve the steak into 1-inch slices, overlap them on a platter, and spoon some of the sauce over them. Pass the remaining sauce separately.

FOR THE STEAK

2 pounds flank steak
Dry Rub, homemade (page 19) or
  store-bought
1 Spanish onion, coarsely chopped
4 cloves garlic
¼ cup chopped fresh cilanto

FOR THE SAUCE

Vegetable oil
1 Spanish onion, chopped
4 cloves garlic, chopped
One 46-ounce can tomato juice
2 bay leaves

> **VARIATION:** *You could add chopped fresh tomatoes to the sauce. You can use parsley instead of cilantro. You can even toss a handful of raisins in with the bay leaves.*

"OLD CLOTHES"

ROPA VIEJA

This dish gets its name from the shredded texture of the beef, which resembles clothes so worn they're falling apart. If you're Cuban, please don't come after me for using chuck steak instead of the more traditional flank steak. Both are delicious, but I prefer the texture of the shredded chuck to that of flank. Other than that, this is a traditional version of a Cuban standard, and it tastes even better the next day.

Serve with white rice, little boiled potatoes, or Twice-Fried Green Plantain Chips (page 113).

MAKES 6 SERVINGS

1. Pound the chuck roast or flank steaks with a heavy meat mallet until about ½ inch thick. Season both sides of the beef generously with salt, pepper, and onion powder.

2. Heat the canola oil in a large, heavy, ovenproof skillet over high heat until rippling. Add the beef and cook it until well browned on both sides, about 10 minutes.

3. Preheat the oven to 350° F. Drain or spoon off most of the fat from the pan. Stir in the sofrito, 2 teaspoons salt, and the cumin, and bring to a boil. Depending on how much oil was left in the pan, you may have to add a little olive oil to give the mix a creamy texture. Stir in the tomato sauce, water, alcaparrado, and bay leaves. Bring to a boil, cover the dish, put it in the oven, and bake until the meat pulls apart easily with a fork, about 2½ hours. Let stand in the sauce until cool enough to handle.

4. Shred the meat coarsely by hand or use two forks. Return it to the sauce and add the celery and carrots. Bring to a simmer over low heat and cook until the vegetables are tender, about 10 minutes. Stir in the peas and cook a few minutes more. Watch the liquid as it cooks and add more broth or water as needed.

One 2¼- to 2½ pound chuck roast or two 1¼-pound flank steaks
Fine sea or kosher salt
Freshly ground pepper
Onion powder
3 tablespoons canola oil
½ cup Sofrito (page 6)
¼ teaspoon ground cumin
Olive oil, as needed
Two 8-ounce cans Spanish-style tomato sauce
1½ cups water
3 tablespoons alcaparrado or coarsely chopped pimiento-stuffed olives (see Daisy's Pantry on page 13)
2 bay leaves
4 celery stalks, with leaves, cut into ¼-inch dice
3 medium carrots, trimmed and cut into ¼-inch dice
1 cup fresh or frozen green peas

PUERTO RICAN POT ROAST

CARNE MECHADA

My dad is a real no-frills type in the dining room. He likes his food simple and tasty, nothing fancy. One of his favorite things in the world—to make and to eat—is pot roast. He is famous for his pot roast and quite proud of it. We all clamor for him to make it. He, however, waxes poetic about Mami's *carne mechada,* the Puerto Rican version of pot roast. He would pass over a lobster dinner or a filet mignon to eat *carne mechada.* I convinced Mami to part with her secrets.

MAKES 8 SERVINGS WITH LEFTOVERS

1. Grind the ham in a food processor until it is coarsely chopped; some larger pieces are okay. Set aside 1 cup of the ground ham and stir the olives and recaito into the remaining 2 cups. Take a look at the rump roast. You will be able to see the "grain" of the meat—fibers that run in one direction. You will slice the finished pot roast against the grain, so you want to make pockets of stuffing more or less diagonal to the grain, and then some of the stuffing will show in each slice. Make deep cuts about 1 inch apart and diagonally against the grain with a boning knife. To make the holes large enough to fill easily, wiggle a finger around in each cut. Fill each hole to about ½ inch from the opening. Don't overstuff, or when the meat shrinks, it will squeeze out the stuffing. If a little stuffing does get squeezed out during cooking, that's fine; it flavors the sauce. Season the outside of the roast generously with salt and pepper.

2. Heat the oil in a Dutch oven large enough to hold the meat and potatoes comfortably—a 5-quart Dutch oven works well—over medium heat. Add the roast and cook, turning it occasionally, until well browned on all sides, about 10 minutes. (A sturdy pair of tongs comes in handy here.) The oil will make the meat brown quickly, so keep an eye on it; lower the heat if the oil begins to discolor. Remove the beef to a plate and carefully pour or spoon off from the pan all but about 1 tablespoon of the fat. Add the red peppers and the reserved 1 cup of ham and stir until the little bits that are stuck to the bottom of the pot are loosened and the peppers start to soften, about 4 minutes. Stir in the tomato paste and cook for 1 to 2 minutes, stirring, so it doesn't stick and burn. Stir in the vinegar, bring it to a boil, and cook until the liquid is syrupy, about 4 minutes.

3. Return the meat to the Dutch oven, stir in the water, tomato sauce, and bay leaves. Bring to a boil and boil for 15 minutes, skimming off the foam and fat from the surface. Adjust the heat so the

1 pound smoked ham, cut into ½-inch cubes (about 3 cups) (see Note)
½ cup Spanish olives, pitted and coarsely chopped
3 tablespoons Recaito (page 99)
One 3- to 3½-pound rump roast
Fine sea or kosher salt
Freshly ground black pepper
¼ cup Achiote Oil (page 9)
2 red bell peppers, cored, seeded, and cut into ½-inch strips
¼ cup tomato paste
⅓ cup white wine vinegar
6 cups water or three 14½-ounce cans chicken broth
One 8-ounce can Spanish-style tomato sauce
2 bay leaves
4 large Idaho potatoes (about 2½ pounds)
Chopped fresh Italian parsley

NOTES: *You have a lot of wiggle room when it comes to the ham. You can use leftover ham from a roast, a piece of a packaged ham steak, or even sliced ham from the deli.*

liquid is at a simmer. Cover and cook until the meat is tender, about 2 hours.

4. Remove the meat to a carving board and cover it loosely with aluminum foil to keep it warm while cooking the potatoes.

5. Skim fat from surface of sauce and bring the sauce to a boil. Let it simmer while you peel and cut the potatoes into ½-inch slices. Add the potatoes and cook over low heat until tender, about 20 minutes.

6. Carve the meat against the grain into slices about ¼-inch thick—thick enough so the filling stays in place. Transfer the potatoes to a platter with a slotted spoon. Lay the slices of beef over the potatoes and spoon enough of the sauce over the meat to moisten it. Spoon the remaining sauce into a boat and pass it separately. Sprinkle the chopped parsley over the top of the platter.

BEEF BROTH

CALDO DE CARNE

MAKES 3 QUARTS

1. Preheat the oven to 400° F. Mix the bones, beef, onions, celery, carrots, garlic, and bay leaves together in a large roasting pan. Cook, stirring occasionally, until brown, about 45 minutes.

2. Transfer the contents of the roasting pan to a stockpot. Drain the fat from the roasting pan and pour in 1 inch of water. Heat over medium heat and scrape up the brown bits that cling to the pan. Pour the water from the roasting pan into the stockpot and add the cilantro and peppercorns and enough cold water to cover the bones and vegetables. Bring to a boil over high heat and then adjust the heat so the liquid is at a very gentle boil. Skim off any foam or fat that rises to the top.

3. Cook, skimming occasionally, for 90 minutes. Strain, cool to room temperature, and then refrigerate.

3 to 4 pounds beef soup bones
2 pounds stewing beef
2 large Spanish onions, cut into large chunks
2 celery stalks, trimmed and cut crosswise into 4 pieces
2 carrots, peeled and trimmed
6 cloves garlic
2 bay leaves
1 small bunch cilantro
7 black peppercorns

NOTES: *After you refrigerate the broth, the fat will rise to the top and solidify, making it easy to remove.*

• *Beef broth is perfect for freezing. You can freeze it in small quantities (about 1 cup). It is easier than taking a big block out of the freezer to defrost and using only a quarter of it.*

• *Use the beef from the broth to make "Old Clothes" on page 230. Skip the browning part, make the sauce, and add the beef to it. Simmer until the beef is very tender and proceed with the recipe.*

STEWED BEEF

CARNE GUISADA

Do you remember the commercial a few years back that had a little boy running home on Wednesday nights because Wednesday was spaghetti night at his house? Well, Wednesday was *carne guisada* night at the Martinez home. Mami would make it with a nice green salad and a pot of fluffy white rice. I loved to mash the potatoes with a fork and eat them with bits of beef and sauce.

MAKES 6 SERVINGS

1. Put the beef in a large mixing bowl, season generously with salt and pepper, and toss to coat. Sprinkle the flour over the beef and toss again to coat.

2. Heat the oil in a Dutch oven over medium-high heat and add as many of the seasoned beef cubes as fit without touching. Cook, turning, until lightly browned, about 8 minutes. Pay attention to the crust forming on the bottom of the pot; it should brown nicely but not scorch. Set the meat aside and continue with the remaining meat, adding more oil if needed.

3. When the last of the beef is browned, make sure that you have at least 2 tablespoons of fat. If not, add more oil. Stir in the sofrito, alcaparrado, and cumin. Return the meat to the pot and stir to coat with the sofrito. Stir in the tomato sauce.

4. Pour in the broth. Tie the bay leaves and cloves in a small square of cheesecloth to make it easy to remove them and then add to the pot. Bring to a boil, adjust the heat so the sauce is simmering, and cook for 45 minutes, skimming off any foam that floats to the top.

5. Add the potato and cook until the beef and potato are tender, about 15 minutes. Cover and let rest for at least 30 minutes. Remove and discard cheescloth bag of spices. You can make the beef up to a few days before you serve it. Cool to room temperature and then refrigerate, covered. Reheat gently over low heat.

2 pounds stew beef, cut in 1½-inch cubes
Fine sea or kosher salt
Freshly ground pepper
¾ cup all-purpose flour
¼ cup canola oil, or as needed
½ cup Sofrito (page 6)
¼ cup alcaparrado or coarsely chopped pimiento-stuffed olives (see Daisy's Pantry on page 13)
1 teaspoon ground cumin
½ can Spanish-style tomato sauce
4 cups Beef Broth, homemade (page 233) or canned
2 bay leaves
2 cloves
1 large potato, peeled and cut into 1-inch cubes

BRAISED OXTAIL

RABO DE RES

An oxtail is exactly what it sounds like. The Latin American food that I love most comes from very humble beginnings. When animals were butchered, for example, the "better cuts" went to the wealthy, and poorer people got things that took a little ingenuity to work with. From those simple beginnings came some wonderful dishes such as Black Beans and Pork (page 216) and this dish of braised oxtail.

There are days when I wake up and know I'm going to be in the kitchen all day. That usually happens when the weather starts to turn gray and cold. This is the kind of dish I like to make on days like that—something that feeds your body and soul and makes the kids say, "What smells so good?" when they come home from school.

I think the sauce looks much prettier and feels silkier on the tongue if you strain it. My husband waits for me to strain the sauce, and then he sneaks into the kitchen to nibble on whatever I removed from the sauce.

Mami likes to serve this with white rice, but I like it with egg noodles for a change sometimes. Either way, it is yummy!

MAKES 4 TO 6 SERVINGS

1. Season the oxtail pieces with salt and pepper. Roll them in the flour and tap off any excess. Heat the oil in a heavy, deep skillet over medium-high heat until rippling. Brown the oxtails, turning them to color evenly. Set aside.
2. Drain or spoon off all but about 2 tablespoons of fat from the pan. Add the carrots, celery, onion, and garlic, and cook, stirring, until soft and fragrant, about 5 minutes. Add the tomato paste, lower the heat to medium, and stir until the vegetables are coated. Pour in the cognac, bring to a boil, and cook until it has evaporated. Pour in the broth, stirring to incorporate the paste. Add the bay leaves and thyme. Return the oxtails to the skillet, adjust the heat so the liquid is simmering, and partially cover the pan. Simmer until tender, about 90 minutes, stirring occasionally. The oxtails should remain covered with liquid throughout cooking; if necessary, add more broth or water.
3. If you decide to strain the sauce, remove the oxtails to a dish and spoon the fat off the top of the sauce. Strain into a bowl through a fine sieve. Press on the solids to extract as much liquid as possible. Return the sauce and oxtails to the pan, and bring to a quick brisk boil.
4. Check the seasoning and then spoon the sauce and oxtails onto a serving platter. Sprinkle the chopped parsley over the oxtails and serve immediately.

3 pounds oxtail, cut into 2-inch rounds (about 10 to 12 pieces; see Note)
Fine sea or kosher salt
Freshly ground black pepper
½ cup all-purpose flour
3 tablespoons canola oil
2 medium carrots, peeled, trimmed, and finely chopped
2 stalks celery, trimmed and finely chopped
1 medium onion, finely chopped
3 cloves garlic, minced
2 tablespoons tomato paste
¼ cup cognac
3½ cups, or as needed, Beef Broth, homemade (page 233) or canned
2 bay leaves
1 sprig of fresh thyme
Chopped fresh flat-leaf parsley

NOTE: *Oxtails, usually cut between bones into about 2-inch lengths, are available in some supermarkets or by order from butchers.*

ROAST BEEF TENDERLOIN WITH BLUE CHEESE CREAM

LOMO DE RES ASADO CON CREMA DE CABRALES

My boys are pretty wary of blue cheese in general, but one taste of this sauce made them converts forever. Save this dish for a festive occasion because it's a rather large roast. Or you can buy individual fillets (a romantic dinner for two?), broil them, and serve with the blue cheese sauce. Either way you will fool your guests into thinking that you have been slaving over a hot stove all day!

MAKES 8 TO 12 SERVINGS

1. Dress the beef: Trim any silver skin (see page 206) and excess fat from the surface. Cut several lengths of kitchen twine and tie them tightly around the roast at 2-inch intervals.

2. Mix the salt, oregano, and peppercorns together in a small bowl. Rub the seasonings into the beef. Set it on a rack in a shallow roasting pan and refrigerate for at least 2 hours or, even better, overnight. Bring the beef back to room temperature for 1 hour before roasting.

3. Preheat the oven to 450° F. Roast the beef until an instant-reading thermometer inserted in the thickest part of the roast registers 130° F, about 7 to 8 minutes per pound, for medium rare.

4. About 30 minutes before your roast is ready, start to make the sauce. Bring the cream and thyme to a simmer in a small saucepan over medium-low heat, being careful not to scorch the pan. When reduced by half, add the cheese, stirring with a small whisk until all the cheese has melted and the sauce is smooth. Add the cider a little at a time, stirring, until incorporated.

5. Remove the beef from the oven and let rest for 10 minutes.

6. Remove the twine and cut the beef into 1-inch slices. Serve with the sauce on the side.

DAISY'S PANTRY *Hard cider is a dry, delicious fermented cousin of apple cider. You can find it in many liquor stores if you poke around the beer section or, around the holidays, in just about any Latin market. My mother bought a bottle of La Gaitera hard cider every Thanksgiving and every other major holiday. I remember the bottle looked like a champagne bottle with a cork that popped when you opened it.*

FOR THE BEEF

One 6-pound fillet of beef (or smaller if you prefer)
2 tablespoons kosher salt
2 tablespoons dried oregano
2 tablespoons crushed black peppercorns

FOR THE SAUCE

1 cup heavy cream
1 sprig of fresh thyme
½ pound blue cheese (try Cabrales if you can find it), crumbled
2 tablespoons hard cider or amber beer or sherry (see Daisy's Pantry)

VEAL CHOPS WITH LEMON

MAKES 6 SERVINGS

1. Make the dressing: Beat the mustard and a splash of lemon juice together in a mixing bowl. Slowly incorporate the oil with a whisk, alternating with the remaining lemon juice until it is absorbed. Add the basil, parsley, and salt and pepper to taste. Chill the dressing.

2. If you look at the chops, you will see the "eye" and a section of mostly fat that begins after the eye and runs to the end of the bone. Trim off all the fat and meat from the eye to the end of the bone. If you'd like to get very fancy, scrape the bone clean with the back of a knife. Place the eye of each chop between 2 pieces of plastic wrap and pound with a mallet to about ¼ inch thick. Season the chops with the oregano and salt and pepper.

3. Beat the eggs in a shallow bowl until foamy. Spread the flour and bread crumbs in separate shallow bowls. Coat the meat with flour and tap off any excess. Turn the chop in the egg until it is coated, then hold it over the bowl to let any excess egg drip off. Turn the chop in the bread crumbs, patting lightly, until coated. Set the finished chop on a baking sheet and repeat with the remaining chops.

4. Pour ¼ inch of oil into each of 2 large frying pans. (If you don't have 2 pans, heat the oven to 200° F and keep the first batch of chops warm while you fry the second.) Heat over medium heat until the tip of the handle of a wooden spoon gives off a lively sizzle when dipped into the oil. Fry the chops until golden on both sides, about 4 minutes on the first side and 3 minutes on the other.

5. Divide the tomatoes among 6 serving plates. Lay the chops on the tomatoes and drizzle with the dressing.

FOR THE DRESSING

1 teaspoon mustard
¼ cup fresh squeezed lemon juice
1 cup olive oil
I tablespoon fresh chopped basil
1 tablespoon fresh chopped parsley
Fine sea or kosher salt
Freshly ground pepper

FOR THE CHOPS

6 veal rib chops, about 13 ounces each
1 teaspoon dried oregano
Fine sea or kosher salt to taste
Freshly ground pepper to taste
All-purpose flour
3 eggs
Bread crumbs
Canola oil
6 plum tomatoes, cored, seeded, and coarsely chopped

VEAL CUTLETS WITH CHORIZO

FILETES DE TERNERA CON CHORIZO

Here is another example of the influence of Italian cooking on the cuisine of South America. You can make these with chicken or turkey cutlets, too. That isn't very Venezuelan, but it sure is deliciousl.

MAKES 6 SERVINGS

1. Heat the oven to 200° F.

2. Season the cutlets generously with salt and pepper. Dredge them in the flour to coat both sides, then shake off the excess. Heat 2 tablespoons of the oil in a large skillet over medium heat. Add as many of the cutlets as will fit without crowding. Cook, turning once, until well browned on both sides, about 4 minutes. Remove them to a baking sheet, keep them warm in the oven, and repeat with the remaining cutlets. Adjust the temperature under the pan as the cutlets cook so that the brown bits in the oil don't burn. Add a little more oil to the pan between batches if needed.

3. Wipe out the skillet with a wad of paper towels. Pour the remaining 1 tablespoon oil into the skillet and place it over medium-high heat. Add the chorizo and cook, stirring, until it takes on a little color and starts to render its fat, about 2 minutes. Add the yellow and red peppers and cook, stirring often, until wilted and crisp-tender, about 4 minutes. Season lightly with salt and pepper.

4. Transfer the cutlets to a serving platter and squeeze the lemon over them. Pile the peppers and chorizo on the cutlets and serve immediately.

2 pounds veal cutlet

Fine sea or kosher salt

Freshly ground pepper

All-purpose flour

3 tablespoons olive oil, or as needed

2 links chorizo, andouille, or any smoked garlicky sausage, cut in half lengthwise and then crosswise into thin slices

2 yellow bell peppers, cored, seeded, and cut into 2 × ¼-inch strips

2 red bell peppers, cored, seeded, and cut into 2 × ¼-inch strips

1 lemon, cut in half

HOME-STYLE STUFFED PEPPERS

PIMIENTO RELLENOS DE ABUELA

I like to play in the kitchen, taking dishes that I've had in restaurants or in friends' houses and making them my own. (My family loves when I play like this.) But some things, such as these peppers that my grandmother used to make, you just don't want to fool around with. Instead of using the tops of the peppers to cap the filling, Abuela soaked slices of bread in egg—like French toast—and folded them up to make little hats. As the peppers cooked, the top of the bread hats got crispy and golden brown and the bottoms soaked up the flavors and juices of the filling. I used to save the little hats for last. I still do, and so do my kids.

Serve these with boiled potatoes or yucca or white rice (even through there is a little rice in the filling).

MAKES 6 SERVINGS

1. Roast the peppers according to the directions on page 67. Scrape the blackened skin off the peppers but leave them whole. Cut around the stem and discard it; scoop out and discard the juices and seeds from inside the peppers. Set the peppers aside.

2. Make the stuffing: Mix the ground sirloin, sofrito, olives, rice, oregano, salt, and pepper together in a mixing bowl until the rice is evenly distributed throughout the mixture.

3. Beat the eggs in a shallow baking dish until foamy. Add the bread slices and turn them gently from time to time until they soak up the egg.

4. Using a tablespoon, spoon enough stuffing to fill the peppers halfway (you need to allow room for the rice to expand). Fold a slice of bread into quarters and use it to plug the opening of each pepper.

5. Sit the peppers upright in a flameproof casserole or Dutch oven in which they fit snugly. Pour the broth and tomato sauce into the casserole. Add the culantro, cover with aluminum foil, and bring to a boil over medium heat. Adjust the heat to very low and cook until the sides of the peppers feel firm to the touch and the bread plugs are cooked through and springy to the touch, 45 minutes to 1 hour.

6 large red bell peppers

FOR THE STUFFING

1 pound ground sirloin (at least 15 percent fat)
½ cup Sofrito (page 6)
⅓ cup chopped pitted green olives
⅓ cup long-grain rice
½ teaspoon dried oregano
Fine sea or kosher salt to taste
Freshly ground pepper to taste

3 large eggs
6 slices white bread

FOR THE SAUCE

1 cup chicken broth
½ cup canned Spanish-style tomato sauce
2 culantro leaves

> **VARIATIONS:** *You may bake the peppers in the same dish in a 350° F oven for about 1 hour. Cover the dish with aluminum foil.*
>
> *• Some people add a little chopped chorizo along with the rice.*

ABUELA'S STUFFED CABBAGE

ABUELA'S REPOLLO RELLENO

This was one of Abuela's favorite things to make for lunch on a cold Saturday. The funny thing is that she never had any trouble getting the kids to eat cabbage because of the delicious little "package" of meat on the inside of the cabbage leaf. She served it with a little white rice, and we would lick our fingers!

MAKES ABOUT 12 ROLLS, OR 6 SERVINGS

1. Peel off any yellow or discolored leaves from the cabbage. With a paring knife, carefully cut out the entire core. Choose a pot in which the cabbage will fit comfortably. Fill it halfway with water, toss in a handful of salt, and bring to a boil. Carefully slip the cabbage into the water and cook until the cabbage is softened but not mushy, about 15 minutes. Lift the pot to the sink and run cool water into the pot until the cabbage is cool enough to handle. Place the cabbage in a colander and let cool while you prepare the filling.

2. When the cabbage is cool enough to handle, carefully remove the outer leaves one by one, keeping them as whole as possible. Remove about 15 to be sure to have enough to wrap the filling. Cut out the thick part of the rib that runs up the middle of each leaf.

3. Place 2 to 3 tablespoons of the stuffing mixture in the center of each cabbage leaf. Fold the bottom of the leaf over the filling, then fold the sides of the leaf over that. Roll into a tight cylinder and place in a flameproof casserole dish or Dutch oven large enough to hold all the stuffed cabbages comfortably. (It's okay to stack the rolls one on top of the other.) Repeat with the remaining leaves and filling.

4. Pour the sauce ingredients into the casserole and bring to a boil over medium heat. Reduce the heat to very low, cover the pot, and cook until the cabbage is very tender and the filling is cooked, about 45 minutes. Taste the sauce and add salt and pepper if you think it needs it. Spoon the cabbages and some of the sauce onto warm plates.

1 head green cabbage (about 3½ pounds)
Salt
Stuffing and sauce from Home-Style Stuffed Peppers recipe (page 240)
Freshly ground pepper (optional)

VARIATION: *If you like, you can bake the stuffed cabbage in a 350° F oven until tender, about 1½ hours.*

MEATBALLS

ALBONDIGAS

I love traditional Italian meatballs simmered in old-fashioned tomato sauce, and so do my kids. But never one to leave well enough alone, I daisified spaghetti and meatballs, incorporating all the flavors I love. They became an instant hit. My kids will ask for spaghetti and meatballs Italian style or Daisy style. Just like the originals you love, these are tender, juicy, and delicious but with a little spin that will make you say, "Mmmmm." If you have kids in the house, you'll want to double this recipe to compensate for all the meatballs they steal while you are frying.

MAKES 20 TO 24 MEATBALLS

1. Make the tomato sauce.

2. With your hands, mix the ground meats, egg, yolk, and sofrito together in a large mixing bowl. Add the bread crumbs, dry rub, parsley, basil, and Spanish-style tomato sauce. Add the water, a little at a time, mixing after each addition. Pinch off a golf ball–size piece of the meat mixture and roll it into a ball between your palms. Repeat with the remaining meat mixture.

3. Pour 1 inch of oil into a large, heavy frying pan over medium-high heat. Add as many of the meatballs as will fit without crowding and cook, turning as necessary, until nicely browned, about 8 minutes. Drain on paper towels.

4. While the meatballs are browning, heat the tomato sauce to simmering if necessary. Slide the meatballs into the sauce and simmer until cooked through and seasoned by the sauce, about 30 minutes.

Tomato Sauce for Pasta (recipe opposite) or 4 quarts of your favorite tomato sauce

1½ pounds mixed ground meats (beef, veal, and pork are my favorites, but ground beef will do in a pinch)

1 whole egg plus 1 yolk

¾ cup Sofrito (page 6)

1 cup bread crumbs

2 teaspoons Dry Rub, homemade (page 19) or store-bought

2 tablespoons chopped fresh flat-leaf parsley

1 tablespoon chopped fresh basil

½ cup canned Spanish-style tomato sauce

¼ cup water

Canola oil

TOMATO SAUCE FOR PASTA

SALSA DE TOMATE PARA PASTA

When I make a pot of sauce at home, I always make enough for two meals. Constant juggling of five crazy schedules (not to mention my own) has taught me to cut a few corners whenever I can. If this means preparing two lasagnas instead of one or making a big batch of sofrito and freezing most of it, that's what I do. Here's a good example: Make a double batch of sauce, use half to cook meatballs, and freeze the other half to make a meal or turn into meat sauce next week. Feel free to halve this recipe, but bear in mind the saying about the birds and the stone.

MAKES ABOUT 4 QUARTS

1. Heat the oil in a heavy 6-quart pot over medium-low heat. Add the sofrito and cook, stirring, until the liquid has evaporated. Stir in the alcaparrado, culantro, and tomato paste, stirring constantly so the paste does not stick or burn. Add the oregano and cumin, and cook until fragrant.

2. Stir in the red pepper flakes, crushed tomatoes, tomato sauce, and bay leaves. Bring to a boil and then adjust the heat so the sauce is simmering. Cover and cook for 30 minutes.

3. Uncover and simmer 30 minutes more, or until the sauce is lightly thickened. Taste and add salt and pepper as you like.

3 tablespoons Achiote Oil (page 9)
1 cup Sofrito (page 6)
1 cup alcaparrado, coarsely chopped, or coarsely chopped pimiento-stuffed olives (see Daisy's Pantry on page 13)
4 culantro leaves or ¼ cup chopped fresh cilantro
2 tablespoons tomato paste
1 tablespoon chopped fresh oregano
1 teaspoon ground cumin
1 teaspoon hot red pepper flakes
Four 28-ounce cans crushed tomatoes
One 28-ounce can tomato sauce
2 bay leaves
Fine sea or kosher salt
Freshly ground pepper

VARIATION: *To make a meat sauce, brown 2½ pounds of mixed ground meats (see Meatballs recipe, page 242) or an equal amount of longaniza or Italian sausages, removed from their casings and crumbled. Add the browned meats to the sauce after it has been simmering for 30 minutes. If you like, remove 4 cups of tomato sauce from the pot before adding the meat to give yourself some meatless sauce.*

LASAGNA, *MAMI* STYLE

LASAGNA, ESTILO MAMI

I remember the first time I ever had lasagna. My cousin Lydia was a fabulous cook and would often have us over to her home for Sunday dinner with her family. I can remember arriving at her home, smelling something wonderful, but not being able to place it. I saw nothing on the stove top, which was very unusual in Lydia's kitchen! When she took the lasagna out of the oven, Mami said, "*Que es eso?*" One bite and none of us cared what it was, it was delicious! Lydia's lasagna had raisins in it, and Mami couldn't *wait* to get home and try to make her own version of lasagna. This is what she came up with.

MAKES 8 LARGE SERVINGS OR 12 REGULAR SERVINGS

1. Make the tomato sauce.

2. While the tomato sauce is cooking, remove the sausage from its casing and crumble the meat into a large skillet. Set the skillet over medium heat and cook the sausage meat, breaking up any large clumps with a fork, until browned and sizzling, about 10 minutes. Drain the fat from the browned sausage meat.

3. When the tomato sauce is done, ladle off 4 cups and set aside to pass at the table. Stir the browned sausage meat into the remaining sauce and simmer for 15 minutes.

4. Toss the eggplant slices in a bowl with a generous amount of salt (see Note). Set aside for at least 30 minutes or up to 1 hour.

5. Pat the eggplant slices dry. Coat a large, heavy, nonstick skillet with vegetable spray and heat over medium-high heat. Fry the eggplant slices in batches until soft. Set aside.

6. Bring a large pot of salted water to a boil and add the oil. Slip in the lasagna noodles and cook, stirring gently to keep the lasagna from sticking, for 3 to 4 minutes less than the package directions state. Drain and rinse under cold water.

7. Preheat the oven to 375° F. Spray the bottom of an 11 × 9 × 2½-inch-deep lasagna pan with cooking spray. Ladle in enough plain sauce to cover the bottom of the pan. You will be making 4 layers with your ingredients (and 5 layers of lasagna and grated parmesan), so make each layer accordingly. Don't worry if there is a slight difference between the layers; just don't run out of anything halfway through. Place a layer of lasagna noodles to cover the bottom of the pan, overlapping them slightly. Cover with a layer of meat sauce. Sprinkle the Parmesan over the sauce. Place the eggplant slices randomly over the cheese. Dot with ricotta and scatter with mozzarella. Repeat the process 4 times (or as much as your pan allows) and top

Tomato Sauce for Pasta (page 243)
2½ pounds sweet Italian sausage (or longaniza)
1 medium eggplant (about 20 ounces), stemmed, peeled, and cut into ½-inch slices
Kosher salt
Vegetable cooking spray
Splash of olive oil
Two 1-pound boxes curly-edge lasagna noodles
2 cups grated Parmesan, Manchego, or zamorano cheese
One 3-pound container ricotta cheese
2 pounds mozzarella cheese, preferably whole milk, shredded

NOTE: *Salting eggplant draws out bitter juices and makes the eggplant sweeter. Eggplant is a sponge; using vegetable cooking spray instead of oil makes a lighter lasagna*

with the last layer of pasta. Sprinkle any remaining Parmesan over the top. Cover loosely with foil and bake for 1 hour. Remove from the oven and let set for 1 to 2 hours. (I find that resting the lasagna and then reheating it helps the lasagna hold its shape when you serve it.)

8. To serve: Heat gently for about 30 minutes in a preheated 300° F oven until a knife inserted in the center feels warm. Just before serving, reheat the reserved tomato sauce and pass separately at the table.

VENEZUELAN LASAGNA

PASTICHO VENEZOLANO

My friend Carlotta worked as a cook in a restaurant on Marguerita Island off the coast of Venezuela. She tells me that this is one of the most requested dishes in the restaurant. What Venezuelans call *pasticho* is better known to us as lasagna.

MAKES 12 SERVINGS

1. Heat 3 tablespoons oil in a large skillet over medium-high heat until rippling. Add the onion and garlic, and cook, stirring, until the onion is translucent, about 6 minutes. Add the ground meat and cook, breaking up the clumps, until the liquid boils off and the meat is browned, about 12 minutes. Drain the fat from the pan.

2. Stir the tomato paste into the meat mixture until the meat is evenly coated. Add the tomatoes, bay leaves, and nutmeg. Season to taste with salt and pepper. Bring to a boil and then adjust the heat so the sauce is simmering. Cook, partially covered, for 30 minutes.

3. Preheat the oven to 350° F. Paint the bottom of a lasagna pan with the oil, using a paper towel or brush. Place a layer of meat sauce on the bottom. Top with a layer of lasagna and another layer of meat sauce. Spread the meat sauce with béchamel, sprinkle with ham, and dust with Parmesan cheese. Repeat until the dish is full, ending with a layer of lasagna noodles, béchamel sauce, and Parmesan cheese.

4. Cover the pan with aluminum foil. (Poking a few toothpicks into the top of the pasticho will prevent the foil from sticking to the top of the top layer.) Bake for 45 minutes.

5. Remove the foil and cook until the top layer is browned and the edges are bubbly, about 15 minutes. If the top is not sufficiently brown for your taste, you can run it under the broiler just before serving.

6. Let the pasticho rest at least 30 minutes before serving or up to a day before. Heat gently in a 350° oven until a knife inserted in the center is hot. (This probably isn't necessary if you have let the lasagna rest for only 30 minutes.)

Olive oil

1 large Spanish onion, chopped

2 cloves garlic, minced

2½ pounds ground meat (a mix of pork, veal, and beef is ideal)

3 tablespoons tomato paste

Two 28-ounce cans crushed tomatoes

2 bay leaves

Pinch of ground nutmeg

Fine sea or kosher salt

Freshly ground pepper

1½ pounds lasagna noodles (1½ boxes), cooked and drained

4 cups Béchamel Sauce (page 167) or 3 cups of your favorite tomato sauce mixed with 1 cup heavy cream

1 pound ham steak, finely chopped

2 cups grated Parmesan cheese

VEAL CANALONES

CANALONES DE TERNERA

Canalones in a Latin cookbook? Yes—another example of the Italian influence on the cooking of parts of South America. Close your eyes and think of your grandmother's (or favorite Italian restaurant's) manicotti, only filled with aromatic, sweet ground veal and topped with creamy béchamel sauce flavored with a kiss of ground nutmeg. Now you have the idea.

MAKES 6 TO 8 SERVINGS

1. Heat the oil in a large, heavy skillet or Dutch oven over medium heat. Add the veal and stir to break up any big pieces. Cook, stirring occasionally, until the water given off by the veal has evaporated and the veal starts to brown, about 10 minutes.

2. While the veal browns, chop the carrot in a food processor for a few seconds. Add the celery and then the onion, and process until finely chopped but not pureed. (It is best to chop the mushrooms by hand.) Add the vegetables from the processor and the mushrooms to the veal, stirring to incorporate completely. When the vegetables start to give off liquid, raise the heat to high and cook, stirring often to avoid scorching, until the liquid has evaporated. Stir the tomato paste into the mix and cook for 1 to 2 minutes. Add the sherry and cook until almost completely evaporated. Set aside to cool a few minutes, then add ¾ cup of the cheese. Check the seasoning, add salt and pepper to taste, and set aside.

3. Make the béchamel sauce, if using.

4. Cook the manicotti tubes in a large pot of boiling salted water for 3 to 4 minutes less than the package directions. They will finish cooking in the oven. Drain the tubes and rinse under cold water to stop the cooking.

5. Preheat the oven to 350° F. Generously butter an 11 × 14-inch baking dish. Coat the bottom with ½ cup of béchamel sauce or tomato-cream mixture. Using a small spoon, stuff each tube with about ¼ cup of the veal mixture. The tubes should be filled but not stuffed tightly. Place the filled tubes in the baking dish as you go.

6. Pour the remaining béchamel sauce or tomato-cream mixture over the canalones, cover with foil, and bake until the sauce around the edges is bubbling, about 30 minutes.

7. Remove the canalones from the oven and heat the broiler. Uncover and sprinkle the remaining ½ cup of cheese over the top. Broil until golden and bubbly, about 4 minutes. Serve hot.

3 tablespoons olive oil
2 pounds ground veal
1 medium carrot, peeled and cut into 1-inch pieces
2 stalks of celery, trimmed and cut into 1-inch pieces
1 medium onion, coarsely chopped
2 large mushrooms, finely chopped
2 tablespoons tomato paste
¼ cup fino sherry
1¼ cups grated Parmesan or Manchego cheese
Fine sea or kosher salt
Freshly ground black pepper
A double recipe of Béchamel Sauce (page 167) or 3 cups of your favorite tomato sauce mixed with 1 cup of heavy cream
14 packaged manicotti tubes
2 tablespoons butter, softened

VARIATION: *If you'd like to make canalones with fresh pasta, either home-made or store-bought, cut fourteen 5½-inch squares of fresh pasta dough and boil them for about 1 minute. Drain and cool. Spoon about ¼ cup of the veal filling along one edge and roll up the pasta into a neat little tube. Place the tubes in the sauce, seam side down, and proceed as in the recipe.*

HONEY-MARINATED FRIED RABBIT

CONEJO FRITO

You can find rabbit, cut into neat serving pieces, in the freezer sections of some supermarkets. If not, you can find fresh rabbit in upscale grocery stores along with, I hope, a butcher who will cut them up for you if that has not already been done. This is Peruvian street food, eaten out of hand all over the country, especially in Lima. Try it with a garlicky-spicy dipping sauce (Mojito, page 114). I love the hot/sweet combination.

MAKES 6 SERVINGS

1 cup honey
¼ cup white wine vinegar
1 tablespoon salt
2 teaspoons dried marjoram
1 generous teaspoon ground coriander
1 teaspoon freshly ground black pepper
½ teaspoon ground allspice
Two 3-pound rabbits, cut into 6 to 8 pieces each
Vegetable oil

1. Whisk the honey, vinegar, salt, marjoram, coriander, pepper, and allspice together in a large bowl. Add the rabbit and toss to coat with the marinade. Marinate at room temperature for 30 minutes or in the refrigerator for up to 1 day.

2. Pour oil into a deep, heavy pot to about 4 inches. Heat over medium-high heat until the tip of the handle of a wooden spoon gives off a lively sizzle when dipped in the oil (about 375° F). Carefully slip half of the rabbit pieces into the oil. Cook until the rabbit is deep brown and no trace of pink remains near the bone, about 12 minutes. Drain and repeat with the remaining rabbit pieces. Serve hot, warm, or at room temperature.

LAMB STEW

ESTOFADO DE CORDERO

Lamb stew was always one of my dad's favorite dishes. Mami used to make a big pot of stew, enough for leftovers for Dad the next day. I was never a big fan of lamb, though, and it wasn't until I went to cooking school that we made a Navarin of lamb, a very traditional stew of lamb and vegetables, and a little light went off in my head. Needless to say, I made my *estofado* for Dad to rave reviews. The savory chunks of lamb were melt-in-your-mouth tender, and they glistened with a satiny sauce redolent of aromatics and a hint of spice plus the caramel of the brandy. This is not your run-of-the-mill stew. It is certainly good enough for company and the good china!

MAKES 6 TO 8 SERVINGS

1. Trim the excess fat and silver skin from the leg of lamb. Cut the meat into cubes of about 1 inch, tossing them into a large bowl as you go. Season the lamb with salt and pepper, drizzle cooled achiote oil over it, and toss to coat.

2. Heat ¼ cup canola oil in a large skillet or Dutch oven over medium-high heat. Working in batches if necessary, add as much of the seasoned lamb as fits in the pan without touching. Cook, turning, until lightly brown. Remove to a bowl as they are done and replace with more lamb. Adjust the heat throughout so the little brown bits that stick to the pan don't burn.

3. When all the meat has been browned and removed, check to make sure that you have at least 2 tablespoons of oil left in the skillet. Add more canola oil if necessary. Over the same medium-high heat, add the roughly chopped celery, carrots, and onion, and the garlic, thyme, bay leaves, and cloves. Cook, scraping up any bits that have formed at the bottom of the pan, until the vegetables start to caramelize and are fragrant.

4. Add the tomato paste, reduce the heat to medium-low, and stir to coat the vegetables. Cook for a few minutes, stirring constantly to prevent the tomato paste from sticking to the bottom of the pan. Sprinkle the flour over the vegetables, reduce the heat to very low, and cook, stirring constantly for a few minutes, until the flour is well incorporated and no white remains.

5. Pour in the brandy, increase the heat to high, and scrape up any bits that remain on the bottom of the pan. Boil until the brandy has almost completely evaporated, then stir in the broth. Bring to a boil

One 5-pound boneless leg of lamb
Fine sea or kosher salt
Freshly ground pepper
2 tablespoons Achiote Oil (page 9)
¼ cup canola oil, or as needed
5 stalks celery, trimmed and roughly chopped
3 carrots, peeled, and roughly chopped
1 large Spanish onion, roughly chopped
4 cloves garlic, smashed
2 sprigs of fresh thyme
2 bay leaves
¼ teaspoon ground cloves
2 tablespoons tomato paste
¼ cup all-purpose flour
¼ cup brandy
7 cups Beef Broth, homemade (page 233) or store-bought (or lamb stock if you have it)

3 carrots, peeled and cut into ½-inch rounds
3 potatoes, cut into 1-inch cubes
2 cups diced celery root
1 cup green peas, frozen or fresh (see Note)

NOTE: *Cook fresh peas in boiling water for 2 minutes before using.*

and then adjust the heat so the sauce is simmering. Cook for 30 minutes, skimming off any foam that rises to the top. Strain the sauce and wipe out the Dutch oven.

6. Place the meat and the strained sauce into the Dutch oven and bring to a boil over medium-high heat. Adjust the heat so the sauce is simmering and cook for 45 minutes.

7. Add the carrot rounds and celery root, and cook for 15 minutes. Stir in the potatoes. Check the potatoes for doneness after 10 to 15 minutes. When the potatoes are tender, stir in the peas and cook just long enough to heat through, about 2 minutes. Taste and add salt and pepper if you like.

ROAST LEG OF LAMB (ON THE BONE)

PIERNA DE CORDERO ASADO

A whole leg of lamb on the bone always gets a gasp when it is presented at the dinner table. Usually people don't think of making a whole leg just for their family, unless, of course, you live in my house. If it's a weekend, Susan's boys, Gabriel and Luke, are at my house. If they're at my house, I'm making meat. And if by some luck their dad, Joe, graces my table, I'm making lamb—and plenty of it! With the sweetness of the cinnamon, the fragrance of the cumin, and the bite of the fresh black pepper in the rub of the lamb, this roast tastes so good that nobody even looks for the mint jelly.

MAKES 10 SERVINGS

1. Trim the excess fat from the surface of the lamb, trying to leave intact as much of the thin membrane around the leg as possible. This will actually help to hold the leg together.

2. Grind the salt, cumin seed, coriander seed, peppercorns, paprika, and cinnamon, using a mortar and pestle until the peppercorns are medium coarse. Rub the leg of lamb liberally with the rub. Marinate at room temperature for up to 2 hours or preferably overnight in the refrigerator. Be sure to bring the meat back to room temperature before roasting.

3. Preheat the oven to 425° F. Place the lamb on a rack set in a roasting pan. Roast until a meat thermometer inserted into the thickest part of the leg near the bone registers 130° F for medium-rare meat, about 1½ hours to 1 hour and 40 minutes. Check for doneness after 1¼ hours.

4. Let the meat rest for 15 minutes before carving. Follow directions for carving Puerto Rican Roast Pork Shoulder on page 212.

One 8- to 9-pound bone-in leg of lamb (without the shank)

FOR THE DRY RUB

1½ tablespoons fine sea or kosher salt
1 tablespoon cumin seed
2 teaspoons coriander seed
2 teaspoons black peppercorns
1 teaspoon smoked paprika
1 teaspoon ground cinnamon

VARIATION: *My butcher will cut the shank portion into 2 or 3 pieces, and I use these to make a simple gravy to serve with the lamb. Brown the meat on the stove top in a pan with some chopped carrots, celery, and onions. Pour in a little brandy to dislodge the brown bits from the pan. Add enough water to cover the meat and bring to a boil. Adjust the heat so the liquid is simmering, and simmer for 1 hour, then drain. I try not to make the gravy too potent because the meat's flavors are very assertive.*

LAMB SHOULDER ROAST WITH SPINACH AND PRUNES

HOMBRO DE CORDERO ASADO

I have to confess that I have not been a lover of lamb all my life. It seemed to me that lamb was a little more "gamey" than I liked my meat; this is kind of weird when you think that I never ate frozen chicken until my parents moved from Brooklyn, and fresh chicken has a much more pronounced flavor. That being said, my husband is a big fan, so I took to trying little bites off his plate when we went out to dinner and developed a taste for it little by little. Then I decided I would like to make lamb for my family, and after playing with a lot of lamb dishes, I came up with this recipe, pairing two of Jerry's favorites, lamb and prunes.

MAKES 6 SERVINGS

One 3½-pound boneless lamb shoulder, butterflied
Fine sea or kosher salt
Freshly ground pepper
2 tablespoons olive oil
1 small onion, chopped
3 cloves garlic, minced
One 9-ounce bag of spinach
8 prunes

NOTE: *Order butterflied leg of lamb from any butcher or some supermarket meat departments.*

1. Lay the lamb flat on your work surface. Cover with plastic wrap and pound with a kitchen mallet to a fairly uniform shape and thickness, about ¾ to 1 inch thick. Season generously with salt and pepper, and set aside.

2. Heat the oil in a large skillet over medium heat. Add the onion and garlic, and cook, stirring, until translucent, about 6 minutes. Add the spinach and stir until wilted. Taste and add additional salt and pepper as you like.

3. Preheat the oven to 425° F. Lay the lamb on a sheet of plastic wrap or a clean kitchen towel with one of the long sides facing you. Lay the prunes end to end about 2 inches from the edge closest to you. Cover with the spinach mixture. Using the towel to help you, roll the meat into a roll. Cut kitchen twine into 12-inch lengths and tie the roast at 2-inch intervals.

4. Lay the meat on a rack set in a roasting pan. Roast, turning once about halfway through, until a meat thermometer inserted in the thickest part of the roast registers 140° F. Let rest for 15 minutes after removing from the pan.

5. Carve into 1-inch slices and transfer carefully, to keep the filling intact, to a serving platter.

DESSERTS AND BEVERAGES

POSTRES Y BEBIDAS

Many times I think that most people are either sweet or savory. You can put me on the "savory" list, thank you very much. I would rather have a second pork chop than have a slice of cake anytime. My husband, Jerry, on the other hand, cannot get to sleep at night if he knows there is even one tablespoon of fresh ice cream left in the freezer. So even though I'll pass, there are enough family and friends on the "sweet" list to inspire me to make desserts on a pretty regular basis. This led me to develop a repertoire of simple, straightforward desserts that please. They are easy to master, and most should be made ahead. They will be as popular in your home as they are in mine.

Just because I don't have a sweet tooth doesn't mean I don't have a special place in my heart for desserts. Something as simple as a perfect piece of pineapple, delicate slices of ripe mango, or slices of banana drizzled with Dulce de Leche (page 270) would satisfy the "sweetest" person on your sweet list. I don't limit myself to fresh fruit, either. I can poach papaya in simple syrup scented with cinnamon and clove, place a lovely piece of cheese with it, and have a lovely snack or *merienda*.

Abuela loved to bring home two slices of *Brazo de Gitano* (my version is on page 260) from her shopping trips (baking was not her forte), and we'd sit in her kitchen at "the hour of coffee," *la hora del café,* sipping coffee, nibbling our cake, and talking about Abuela's childhood and her courtship with my grandfather, his white linen suits, which she kept pressed and starched for him, and their early life together in Puerto Rico. I would listen to her stories about my father and the family when they first came to New York. I felt as though I could have sat there forever listening to those stories.

Today I spend a lot of time in my kitchen, and I love to tell my children stories about Abuela, their grandparents, and my courtship with their dad. Most often Angela who is in with me, but sometimes I'll find her in the kitchen with her brother, David, making cookies, or by herself making coconut sorbet, and that gives me an incredible sense of accomplishment and the feeling that I'm passing down sweet traditions of my own.

You will need some kind of ice cream maker to make any of the following ice creams or sorbets. There are two types available: hand-cranked or electric models in which the container holding the ice cream mix is packed in ice and salt, and the newer models which feature containers for the ice cream mix that are frozen solid before churning. These newer models eliminate the need for ice and salt.

COCONUT ICE CREAM

MANTECADO DE COCO

Here's the secret to great ice cream: Start with crème anglaise, or custard sauce. Crème anglaise is one of those simple things that when mastered will raise your fabulousness index by fifty points. Serve the sauce warm (think chocolate cake!) or chilled. Or use it as I do here and in the following recipes for an unbeatable ice cream base.

Not being one to leave well enough, I whip the sugar and egg yolks before making the base to give the ice cream a smoother consistency. You can't rush the base. It takes time to gradually bring the eggs up to the temperature where they start to thicken the cream.

2 cups half-and-half
1 whole vanilla bean
8 egg yolks
1 cup sugar
½ cup (packed) shredded unsweetened coconut

MAKES ABOUT 5 CUPS

1. Pour the half-and-half into the top of a double boiler. Cut the vanilla bean in half lengthwise and add it to the half-and-half. Heat over medium heat until the half-and-half starts to steam.

2. Meanwhile, beat the egg yolks in the bowl of an electric mixer (or in a bowl with a handheld mixer) at high speed until very fluffy. With the motor running, add the sugar very gradually, stopping a few times to scrape down the sides of the bowl, until all the sugar is added and the mixture is very fluffy and pale yellow.

3. Fish the vanilla bean out of the half-and-half and let it cool for a minute. Scrape the seeds out of the pod; return the seeds to the half-and-half, and discard the pod.

4. Ladle about ½ cup of hot half-and-half slowly into the yolk mixture while whisking constantly. Pour the egg mixture slowly back into the half-and-half, whisking constantly. Stir the ice cream base over the simmering water until it thickens and coats a spoon. Be patient. This can take 20 minutes or so.

5. Pour the ice cream base into a bowl. Whisk in the coconut. (You'll get more flavor out of the coconut by whisking it into hot ice cream base.) Set the bowl in a larger bowl with 1 to 2 inches of water and several ice cubes. Stir the ice cream base until cool.

6. Freeze in the ice cream maker according to the manufacturer's directions. Pack into a container, cover tightly, and freeze for 4 to 5 hours, until well set.

ICE CREAM POINTERS

Whatever type of ice cream freezer you're using, ice cream should emerge from the machine soft and creamy, like soft-serve frozen custard. Pack it quickly into a container with a tight-fitting lid, cover it, and put it in the freezer immediately. Let it sit for 3 to 4 hours to firm it up and make it scoopable. (You can make ice cream up to a day or two before you serve it.)

Ice cream that you make at home contains less air than most commercial ice cream. Take it out ahead of time so it softens up a little. I take it out when I'm serving dinner.

ALMOND RUM ICE CREAM

MANTECADO DE ALMENDRAS Y RON

This is another approach to making ice cream, using just milk and cream without thickening them with egg yolks. It makes a lighter ice cream, that is not as rich, which seems to work well with the butteriness of the toasted almonds.

MAKES ABOUT 3 CUPS

1. Heat the cream, milk, almonds, sugar, and vanilla and almond extracts to simmering in a heavy saucepan over medium-low heat. Simmer for 10 minutes. Stir in the rum. Cool to room temperature, then refrigerate until chilled.

2. Pour into an ice cream maker and freeze according to the manufacturer's directions. Pack into a container with a tight-fitting lid and freeze for 3 to 4 hours, until firm enough to scoop.

1 cup heavy cream
1 cup whole milk
1 cup sliced almonds, toasted (see Note)
½ cup sugar
1½ teaspoons vanilla extract
½ teaspoon pure almond extract
2 tablespoons dark rum

NOTE: *To toast almonds, spread them out on a baking sheet. Bake in a 300° F oven, shaking the pan occasionally, until evenly light golden brown.*

CORN ICE CREAM

MANTECADO DE MAIZ

I first tasted this ice cream on a trip to Puerto Rico. There is an ice cream shop in Lares called Heladeria Lares that is famous all over the island for its variety of nontraditional ice cream flavors. They serve "rice and bean," "avocado," "turkey," and all manner of crazy flavors! I was anxious to visit as soon as my cousin Suzette told me about the place, and I was not disappointed. After gorging on ice cream I had the temerity to ask the elderly man behind the counter how he made the corn-flavored one. He told me that after trying all kinds of corn, he found that canned corn worked best. After a few attempts, I accomplished this good representation of the delicious one I tried in Lares.

MAKES ABOUT 5 CUPS

½ vanilla bean (see Note)
¾ cup sugar
Two 11-ounce cans corn, drained
2 cups heavy cream
2 cups whole milk
7 egg yolks

NOTE: *When you have supple vanilla beans, you can add them to the cream as in the recipe for Coconut Ice Cream (page 254). This method works wonders with less-than-soft beans.*

1. Split the vanilla bean down the center with the tip of a sharp knife. Using ½ cup of sugar, rub the inside of the bean to dislodge the vanilla flecks. Stir the vanilla sugar, corn, cream, and milk together in a medium, heavy saucepan. Bring to a simmer over medium-low heat. Simmer for 10 minutes. Let cool to tepid. (Never use a blender for anything hot. There is a real danger of blowing off the blender top and burning yourself, not to mention making quite a mess.)

2. Working in batches, liquefy the corn mixture completely. Pass it through a very fine strainer or a coarser strainer lined with a double thickness of cheesecloth. Press as much of the liquid out as possible. Clean out your saucepan and return the cream mixture to the pan. Bring to a simmer.

3. Beat the remaining ¼ cup of sugar and the egg yolks together until light in color. Gradually pour 1 cup of the hot cream mixture into the egg yolks while whisking. Return this mixture to the saucepan.

4. Cook over low heat while stirring, preferably with a flat-bottomed spatula. The custard will reach a point where you can run your finger down the back of the custard-coated spatula and leave a line. Watch very closely; if you overcook the custard, it will curdle.

5. Pass the custard once more through a strainer into a clean bowl. Set the bowl in a larger bowl half-filled with ice and water. Stir to cool quickly.

6. Once chilled, pour into the ice cream maker and freeze according to the manufacturer's directions. Pack the ice cream into a container with a tight-fitting lid and freeze until firm enough to scoop, about 4 hours.

MANGO SORBET

HELADO DE MANGO

My girlfriend Rosanne's favorite fruit in the world is mango. Recently I had her over for dinner, and since I was running late, I picked up some store-bought mango sorbet. Thinking I could pull a fast one, I served the sorbet for dessert and failed to mention it was store-bought. Rosanne busted me right away. I came up with this recipe to make it up to her!

MAKES ABOUT 1 QUART

¾ cup sugar
1½ cups water
One 14-ounce package (1¾ cups) pureed mango
Juice of 1 lime
¾ teaspoon fresh grated ginger

1. Dissolve the sugar in the water. Stir in the mango puree, lime juice, and ginger.
2. Pour into an ice cream maker and freeze according to the manufacturer's directions. Scrape into a container, seal tightly, and freeze until firm, about 3 hours.

DAISY'S PANTRY *Frozen mango puree in 14-ounce packages is sold in many supermarkets. I always keep a few on hand for this and other desserts. If ripe, juicy mangoes are available, you can certainly make your own.*

COCONUT SORBET

HELADO DE COCO

This recipe is so easy that my nine-year-old daughter Angela makes it by herself from start to finish.

MAKES ABOUT 5 CUPS, 4 LARGE SERVINGS

1. Heat the water and sugar in a saucepan, stirring until all the sugar is dissolved. If you are using solid cream of coconut, break it into smaller pieces and add to the syrup, stirring until dissolved. (If you are using liquid cream of coconut, remember to stir the contents of the can before measuring because it usually separates while sitting on the shelf.) Cool to room temperature and then refrigerate until chilled.

2. Freeze in an ice cream maker according to the manufacturer's directions. The mixture will be slushy.

3. Pour into a container with a tight-fitting lid and freeze at least 3 hours or until firm. Remove from the freezer 15 minutes before serving.

4 cups water
2 cups sugar
One 7-ounce block of creamed coconut (see Note)

NOTE: *Creamed coconut is a sweetened, condensed coconut paste that is usually sold in 7-ounce packages in Latin markets. It looks, truthfully, like a bar of soap but, thankfully, tastes a lot better. An equal measure of canned sweetened cream of coconut (such as Coco Lopez) can be substituted.*

A WORD ABOUT COCONUT

Coconut water, the liquid inside coconuts, is used in cooking and for drinks. Around the Caribbean, Spanish-speaking people buy a *coco frio* from vendors to beat the heat on hot days. Dotted along the highway are stands with coolers full of immature coconuts still in their husks. Vendors reach in, lop the top off one with a machete, and hand it over. Stick a straw in the coconut and sip the chilled coconut water. Heaven in summer.

One level up on the flavor scale is coconut milk, made by grating fresh coconut meat into the coconut water, simmering it, and then straining the liquid. I used to make coconut milk that way, but I don't anymore. Canned coconut milk is now widely available in the Latin and Asian sections of many supermarkets. Do not confuse canned coconut milk with sweetened cream of coconut, which is very sweet and is used to make drinks such as piña colada.

"GYPSY'S ARM" (JELLY ROLL WITH GUAVA CREAM FILLING)

BRAZO DE GITANO

I don't know how this dessert got its name, and to be honest, I think I'd rather keep it that way. This cake will be found in any and every Latin pastry shop, and in various flavors. This is my riff on that theme, playing around with another classic combination in the Latin kitchen: guava paste and *queso fresco*, a slightly tart cheese eaten fresh. In this filling the guava takes the form of store-bought jelly, and cream cheese lightened with whipped cream stands in for the *queso fresco*. I like it because it's simple, light, and refreshing. I can't tell you how proud I was the day I first served Abuela a piece of *brazo* that I had baked myself. The fact that she did not bake at all and that it was her favorite dessert (next to cheesecake!) added to my pleasure.

MAKES 10 SERVINGS

FOR THE CAKE

Vegetable cooking spray
¾ cup sifted cake flour
¾ teaspoon baking powder
¼ teaspoon salt
4 large eggs, at room temperature
¾ cup sugar

FOR THE FILLING

1 cup heavy cream
3 tablespoons confectioners' sugar
1 teaspoon vanilla extract
1 cup whipped cream cheese, at room temperature
One 17-ounce jar guava jelly or 2 cups strawberry jelly

Confectioners' sugar

1. Make the cake: Preheat the oven to 350° F. Coat a 13 × 18-inch jelly roll pan with vegetable cooking spray. Line the bottom of the pan with parchment paper or waxed paper. Sift the flour, baking powder, and salt into a bowl. Beat the eggs in the bowl of an electric mixer (or in a bowl with a handheld mixer) at medium-high speed until foamy. Add the sugar gradually in 3 batches and continue beating until very fluffy and pale yellow.

2. Add the sifted dry ingredients to the eggs in three batches, folding each one into the eggs with a rubber spatula just until a few streaks of white remain. Scrape the batter into the prepared pan and smooth it into an even layer, making sure to press it into the corners. Bake until the cake is golden brown and feels spongy, not tacky, to the touch, 14 to 16 minutes.

3. Make the filling: Beat the cream and sugar in the bowl of an electric mixer (or in a bowl with a handheld mixer) until fluffy. Add the vanilla and continue beating until the cream holds soft peaks when the beater is lifted from it. Add the cream cheese, half at a time, and beat just until blended into the cream. Scrape down the sides of the bowl.

4. Line your work surface with a sheet of waxed or parchment paper. Invert the cake onto the paper and lift off the pan. Peel the paper off the top of the cake. Spread the jelly in an even layer over the cake, leaving a ½-inch border around the edges. Do the same with the cream cheese mixture. Starting at one of the short sides, roll the cake up into a compact roll, working gently to avoid tearing the cake or squeezing the filling out. Set the cake, seam side down, on a serving platter. Cover with plastic wrap and chill for at least 2 hours or up to 1 day before serving.

5. To serve, sprinkle a dense coating of confectioners' sugar over the cake and cut it into 1-inch slices.

PLANTAIN CAKE

TORTA DE MADURO

This is another very traditional Dominican dessert. It tastes a little like banana bread but is a bit denser. I like to dress this up for company with chocolate sauce and some toasted almonds. It is perfect with a cup of black coffee.

MAKES 8 SERVINGS

1. Preheat the oven to 350° F. Grease 2 round 9-inch cake pans with butter.

2. Stir the flour, baking powder, nutmeg, ginger, and salt together in a medium bowl. Set aside.

3. In the bowl of a stand mixer using the paddle attachment (or in a large bowl using a handheld mixer), beat the sugar and 8 tablespoons butter together until light and fluffy. Add the eggs 1 at a time, mixing completely after each addition. Stir in the sour cream and vanilla.

4. Peel the plantains and mash them thoroughly with a fork or a potato masher. Beat into the batter and then fold in the dry ingredients and the almonds. Divide the batter between the prepared pans.

5. Bake until a knife or cake tester inserted in the center of the cake comes out clean, 50 to 60 minutes. Cool to room temperature.

6. Invert the cakes onto serving plates. Serve dusted with powdered sugar or fill and frost the cakes with the filling used in "Gypsy's Arm" on page 260.

8 tablespoons (1 stick) butter, plus more for the pans, at room temperature
1½ cups all-purpose flour
1 teaspoon baking powder
¼ teaspoon ground nutmeg
¼ teaspoon ground ginger
½ teaspoon salt
1 cup sugar
2 large eggs
½ cup sour cream
1 teaspoon vanilla extract
2 very ripe plantains (about ¾ pound)
1 cup chopped peeled almonds

VARIATION: *For a quick chocolate sauce that is delicious with the cake, stir ½ pound sweet chocolate, ½ cup heavy cream, and 1 tablespoon rum (if you like) together in a small saucepan over low heat until the chocolate is melted and the sauce is glossy. Use warm.*

ALMOND CAKE

TORTA DE SANTIAGO

It is said that the origin of this cake is the pilgrimage town of Santiago, a city in northwest Spain that is famous for the road where millions walked in pilgrimage to the burial site of Saint James the apostle (Santiago). Traditionally, this cake is sprinkled with powdered sugar stenciled onto the cake in the shape of the Saint James cross. You can simply sift some powdered sugar over the top or over a doily. I love to serve slices of this cake with crème anglaise and a few raspberries, which provide a fresh note to the buttery almond cake.

MAKES TWO 9-INCH CAKES

1. Preheat the oven to 350° F. Lightly grease 2 round 9-inch pans.
2. Stir the almond flour, all-purpose flour, baking powder, and salt together in a bowl. Beat the sugar and 8 tablespoons butter in the bowl of a stand mixer using the paddle attachment (or in a large bowl using a handheld mixer) on high speed until light and fluffy. Add the eggs, 1 at a time, and beat well after each addition. The batter should be light yellow and foamy. Add the zest and vanilla and almond extracts.
3. Fold the dry ingredients into the batter with a rubber spatula one-third at a time. Divide the batter between the prepared pans and bake until a toothpick inserted in the center comes out clean, 45 to 55 minutes. Cool completely.
4. Dust liberally with confectioners' sugar before serving.

8 tablespoons (1 stick) butter, plus more for the pans, softened
1 cup almond flour (see Note)
¼ cup all-purpose flour, sifted
¼ teaspoon baking powder
Pinch of salt
1 cup sugar
4 large eggs
Grated zest of 1 lemon
1 teaspoon vanilla extract
¼ teaspoon almond extract
Confectioners' sugar

NOTE: *Almond flour is sold in specialty stores and baking supply stores, or you can make your own. Start with blanched (peeled) almonds. Grind them, no more than 1½ cups at a time, in a food processor until powdery. Stop before the nuts become oily. Starting with chilled nuts helps avoid oiliness.*

PUMPKIN–SWEET POTATO PUDDING

CAZUELA

This past summer I had an opportunity to meet members of my father's family whom I hadn't met before. We got together in San Sebastian de los Pepinos, a charming little town reached by an adventurous route that takes you through the spine (cordillera) of the mountains that run along the island of Puerto Rico. It is a trip I wouldn't suggest if you're the least bit afraid of heights. But once we reached San Sebastian and my knees stopped knocking, I was happy I had made the trip.

I was thrilled to meet my cousins—first, second, and third—and to visit again with José Eliseo Martinez, my father's half-brother. We were treated like visiting royalty. Once I explained to my cousin Suzette that I was working on a cookbook, she insisted I speak to her brother Panchito, who is renowned in San Sebastian for his desserts. "Do you like *cazuela*?" she asked. When I told her I had never even heard of *cazuela*, she explained that it is a pudding made of calabaza (a hard, pumpkinlike squash), white sweet potatoes, and spices. As I later learned, no one can celebrate a birthday, holiday, or special occasion without one of Panchito's special *cazuelas*, which taste and look like a firmer version of pumpkin pie filling without the crust. Panchito graciously shared his recipe with me, and I am very happy to share it with you.

MAKES 12 SERVINGS

1. Bring a large pot of salted water to a boil over high heat. With a paring knife cut off the skin and stem, if any, of the calabaza and discard it along with any seeds. Cut the calabaza into 2-inch cubes. Boil the calabaza and sweet potato until soft, about 20 to 25 minutes.

2. While the vegetables are cooking, grease a 9 × 11-inch baking dish with 1 tablespoon of the butter.

3. Preheat the oven to 350° F. Drain the vegetables thoroughly in a colander and transfer them to a large mixing bowl. Beat them with a hand mixer at medium speed until they are the consistency of lumpy mashed potatoes. Beat in the remaining ingredients, one by one, including the remaining tablespoon of butter. Scrape the batter into the prepared dish and bake until a small knife inserted in the center of the cazuela comes out clean, about 1½ hours. Cool to room temperature.

4. Invert the cazuela onto a serving dish. (The easiest way to do this is to place the plate over the cazuela and, in one quick motion, flip the cazuela over.) Lift off the baking dish. Serve the cazuela at room temperature, chilled or rewarmed (see Notes).

1½ pounds calabaza or sugar pumpkin, peeled and cut into 2-inch pieces (about 4 cups)

1½ pounds boniato (white sweet potato), sweet potatoes, or yams, peeled and cut into 2-inch cubes (about 4 cups)

2 tablespoons butter

1 cup sugar

¾ cup canned unsweetened coconut milk

2 large eggs, beaten

1 cup rice flour

2 teaspoons vanilla extract

1 teaspoon ground cinnamon

½ teaspoon ground ginger

½ teaspoon salt

¼ teaspoon (or less to taste) ground cloves

NOTES: *To rewarm the cazuela, slide it onto a baking sheet and set the sheet in a preheated 300° F oven until warmed through, about 20 minutes.*

• Warm cazuela is delicious with store-bought dulce de leche ice cream. Häagen-Dazs makes a great one.

CHILEAN SANDWICH COOKIES

CHILENITOS

After a trip to Villa Colombia Bakery, a well-known bakery in the Elmhurst neighborhood of Queens, New York, I found myself trying to come up with a recipe for the classic Chilean cookie sold there. Juan Carlos Castro, owner of Villa Colombia (and its sister shop in Astoria), told me the secret of his light-as-air cheese bread was cornstarch. That inspired me to try it in cookies. Here are the fabulous results. Angela and I made up a plate of these and made the mistake of leaving the plate out while we walked our little dog, Chachi. When we got back we noticed that the boys had been home and not much more than crumbs were left of our plate of *chilenitos*. Luckily we had more dough and *dulce* in the refrigerator. We won't ever make *that* mistake again!

MAKES ABOUT 16 SANDWICH COOKIES

1. Stir the flour, cornstarch, baking powder, and salt together in a large bowl until well blended.
2. Beat the butter and sugar together in the bowl of an electric mixer fitted with the whisk (or in a bowl using a handheld mixer) at high speed until pale yellow and fluffy. Beat in the eggs and yolks one at a time. Beat in the rum, vanilla, and zest. Switch to the paddle attachment (or a wooden spoon if you're using a handheld mixer) and add the dry ingredients. Mix at low speed just until incorporated. The dough should form a soft ball but not be sticky or runny. If necessary, add a little bit of each of the flour, cornstarch, and mix.
3. Chill the dough until firm, at least 1 hour or up to 1 day. Let the dough stand at room temperature for 15 minutes before continuing.
4. Preheat the oven to 350° F. Divide the dough in half and roll each half out on a lightly floured surface to about ¼ inch thick. Cut into 3-inch circles and place them on a greased or nonstick baking sheet. Work in batches or use several baking sheets. Bake until the cookies are pale golden brown, about 12 minutes. Rotate the pans from shelf to shelf and front to back once as the cookies bake. Cool completely.
5. Make the Dulce de Leche. Use 2 cookies and about 1 tablespoon of the sweetened filling to make the sandwiches. The cookies will keep at room temperature for up to 3 days.

2½ cups all-purpose flour, or as needed
2½ cups cornstarch, or as needed
½ teaspoon baking powder
Pinch of salt
1 pound (4 sticks) butter plus more for the pans if necessary, softened
1 cup sugar
2 eggs plus 2 yolks
2 tablespoons Malibu rum
1 teaspoon vanilla extract
Grated zest of 1 lemon
Dulce de Leche (recipe on page 270)

VARIATION: *For decoration, press the cookie sandwiches lightly so the filling oozes out just a little. Set out plates with different "toppings" such as shredded coconut, salted peanuts, and cocoa powder, and have your guests roll the edges in them.*

MAMEY "PANNA COTTA"

TEMBLEQUE DE MAMEY

Tembleque is Spanish for quiver or shake, and that's what this dessert should do. In other words, it should be creamy and very lightly set, not at all firm. Every traditional Puerto Rican cook will tell you that you need cornstarch to make *tembleque*, but I took a page from Italian cooking and use gelatin to set the dessert, as an Italian would panna cotta—the classic dessert of "cooked cream." Feel free to make this with mango or passion puree or very finely grated coconut (see the Note) in place of the mamey.

I first made this with my hysterically funny brother Pete for a dinner party at my family's house. I'm surprised I managed to get a recipe down on paper, considering how hard I was laughing. That is usually the case when Pete and I get together in the kitchen. Thankfully, the results are still wonderful and yummi-licious!

1. Stir ½ cup cream, confectioners' sugar, mamey puree, and salt together in a small saucepan. Heat over medium-low heat until warm. Sprinkle the gelatin over the surface of the mamey mixture; sprinkle it evenly and lightly so it doesn't form lumps. Let stand for 1 or 2 minutes, until the gelatin is softened, then stir it into the mamey mixture. Stir in the lemon juice and heat just until a few bubbles form around the edges, but don't let it boil. Whisk the mixture very well and remove it from the heat.

2. Pour the mamey mixture into a heat-proof bowl and set that bowl into a larger bowl filled halfway with ice and water. Stir almost constantly until the mixture starts to thicken and is about body temperature. If you don't stir frequently, the mixture will set around the edges, and you'll have lumps in your finished panna cotta. Remove the bowl from the ice bath.

3. Beat the remaining 1 cup cream in a chilled bowl until it holds soft peaks. Stir the remaining ½ cup mamey puree into the cream. Fold the cream into the cooled mamey mixture with a rubber spatula. Cover with a piece of plastic wrap applied directly to the surface of the panna cotta. Chill until firm, about 2 hours, or up to a day in advance.

4. To serve: Place the bowl of panna cotta almost up to the rim in a sinkful of warm water for about 10 seconds. Remove and cover the bowl with a plate large enough to hold the panna cotta. Invert the bowl onto the plate, wiggle it gently, and lift slightly to see if the panna cotta has unmolded. If not, return it to the warm water and try again. Refrigerate until time to serve.

1½ cups heavy cream
1 cup confectioners' sugar
1 cup mamey puree (see Daisy's Pantry)
¼ teaspoon salt
1 envelope unflavored gelatin
Juice of ½ lemon

DAISY'S PANTRY *Mamey is a tropical fruit, roughly the size of a small cantaloupe, with orange-brown skin not unlike a sweet potato. The flesh also resembles a sweet potato when ripe. The texture is like a ripe pear, smooth and a little grainy all at once.*

VARIATION: *To make a coconut panna cotta, simmer 1 block of cream of coconut (see Note on page 258) or 7 ounces canned cream of coconut (such as Coco Lopez, stirred well) with the heavy cream for 1 to 2 minutes, then let it sit until lukewarm. Squeeze the coconut through cheesecloth or leave it if that texture doesn't bother you. Proceed as above.*

POACHED PAPAYA

DULCE DE PAPAYA

My cousins Judi and Maritza, who live in Puerto Rico, are terrific cooks. I can't even get through the front door without being fed—they usually meet me on the porch with plates of food, urging, "Try this." I don't mind one bit.

My cousins showed me how to make this incredibly simple and delicious dessert. They use papayas they pull off the tree in their backyard. You can treat mango the same way and it would be just as delicious.

You can serve this with ice cream, pound cake, crème anglaise (made by following steps 1 through 4 of the Coconut Ice Cream recipe on page 254), queso fresco, or cookies.

1. Cut the papaya in half lengthwise. Scoop out the seeds. Peel the halves with a vegetable peeler, then cut the halves lengthwise into wedges about 1½ inches wide.

2. Stir the water and sugar together in a large saucepan. Slip in the papaya, cinnamon, and ginger, and bring to a boil over medium heat. Adjust the heat so the liquid is boiling gently and cook until the papaya is tender but not mushy (a knife should slip easily into a piece), 10 minutes or more if your papaya is a little green.

3. Lift the papaya with a slotted spoon to a bowl and let it stand until cooled to room temperature. You have 2 options: Chill the papaya and serve it as is, saving the syrup to poach another batch of fruit. Or you can cool the papaya and syrup separately to room temperature, put the papaya in a jar, pour enough syrup over it to cover and chill thoroughly. In either case, serve it right from the refrigerator.

1 large or 2 small papayas (about 2½ pounds)
6 cups water
1½ cups sugar
1 cinnamon stick
One ½-inch slice peeled fresh ginger (see Note)

NOTES: *If you'd like only a hint of ginger, don't add the ginger until after you remove the pan from the heat.*
• The papaya should be just ripe, not soft. If yours is a little soft, make the syrup first and slip the sliced papaya into it.
• Papaya seeds are edible as well as pretty. Sometimes, when I make a fancy dessert and I have a papaya in the house, I sprinkle the seeds over the top.

VARIATION: *If you want to make this more exotic, add a star anise or two and a large pinch of whole cloves.*

AUNT MARIA'S RICE PUDDING

ARROZ CON DULCE DI TIA MARIA

My Tia Maria, Mami's oldest sister, always saved a piece of this rice pudding for "Chin" (my Papi's nickname) because she knew how much he loves it!

1. For the packet: Place the cinnamon, ginger, and cloves in a cheesecloth square and tie into a neat bundle with twine. Set aside.
2. In a medium pot, heat the oil over medium heat, add the rice, and stir to coat the rice with the oil. Add the packet, water, salt, sugar, vanilla, and cream of coconut, and bring to a boil. Adjust the heat to medium and cook until the liquid reaches the level of the rice. Remove the packet and add the raisins. Stir once, set the heat to very low, cover, and cook for 25 minutes.
3. Oil a pie plate or 9-inch cake pan and spoon the rice onto it. Cool and then chill at least 2 hours. Invert onto a serving plate and cut into serving pieces.

FOR THE SPICE PACKET

2 cinnamon sticks
One 1-inch piece fresh ginger
1 teaspoon whole cloves

2 tablespoons canola oil
2 cups medium-grain rice
5 cups water
1 teaspoon salt
½ cup sugar
1 teaspoon vanilla extract
4 ounces canned cream of coconut
½ cup raisins

DADDY'S RICE PUDDING

ARROZ CON DULCE DI PAPI

Papi loves rice pudding second only to bread pudding. In fact, he collects rice pudding recipes. When my parents got married, my father couldn't boil water, but after becoming a New York City firefighter, he turned into a very skilled cook.

MAKES 8 SERVINGS

1. Heat the milk, cinnamon, lemon peel, and salt in a Dutch oven or other heavy-bottomed saucepan on low heat until bubbles start to form around the edges. Add the rice and stir continuously for 5 minutes so that it doesn't settle to the bottom and clump.
2. Keep the heat low and stir the rice every 15 minutes.
3. When the rice has absorbed most of the milk and is tender, about 2 hours, stir in the sugar and brandy, and almond liqueur. Cook 15 minutes longer. Remove from the heat, stir in the raisins, stirring quickly, and stir in butter. Allow to cool.

10 cups milk
2 cinnamon sticks
2 strips lemon peel
¼ teaspoon salt
1 cup short-grain rice
1¼ cups sugar
1 tablespoon brandy
1 teaspoon almond liqueur (optional)
1 cup raisins
3 tablespoons unsalted butter

SWEETENED RED BEANS

HABICHUELAS CON DULCE

This is a very Dominican, very homey dish. My friend Miguelina tells me that traditionally this dish is eaten during Holy Week. Miggy is always on a quest for the perfect *habichuelas con dulce*. I'm not using the word "perfect," but I think I could have spared her a lot of running around. The flavors are unusual but work amazingly well together because the beans are bland and lend themselves beautifully to the coconut and spices

MAKES 8 SERVINGS

1. Pour the water into a large saucepan and add the beans. Bring to a boil over medium-high heat.

2. When the water comes to a boil, adjust the heat so the water is at a gentle boil. Cook, skimming any foam that rises to the top, until the beans are soft but not falling apart, about 2 hours. If the water level drops below the beans, add more water.

3. Meanwhile, cut a 6-inch double-thick square of cheesecloth. Place the cinnamon sticks, cloves, and ginger in the center and tie into a little packet.

4. When the beans are done, measure out 2½ cups of beans and 1 cup of the cooking liquid. Combine them in a food processor and process until smooth. Pour into a saucepan, stir in the salt, half-and-half, coconut milk, evaporated milk, sugar, and vanilla bean. Add the spice packet and bring to a simmer. Cook, stirring occasionally, for 15 minutes. Strain through a fine sieve, pressing down on the solids to remove as much of the liquid as possible.

5. Drain the rest of the beans and add to the strained bean-milk mixture. Taste and add a little more sugar if you like. Cool to room temperature, then cover and refrigerate until chilled. Ladle into shallow bowls to serve.

6 cups water
One 16-ounce bag red beans
1 large or 2 small cinnamon sticks
1 teaspoon whole cloves
One 1-inch piece of ginger, crushed
Pinch of salt
2 cups half-and-half
One 13½-ounce can unsweetened
  coconut milk
One 12-ounce can evaporated milk
6 tablespoons brown sugar
½ vanilla bean

VARIATIONS: *You can use coconut milk—the liquid from inside the coconut—or canned unsweetened coconut milk in place of some or all of the water to add another dimension of flavor to the beans. To enrich this a bit, use half-and-half in place of some of the water.*

• Sweet potato, peeled and cut into 1-inch cubes and then cooked until tender, makes a pretty addition to the finished dish. So does any type of crushed dry cookies, even vanilla wafers, scattered over the top.

DULCE DE LECHE

Long before the ice cream market got their hands on it, dulce de leche, a type of caramel made with sweetened milk, was a hit all over the Spanish-speaking world. Here is a very simple way to prepare it for yourself.

There is not much that you *can't* put dulce de leche on. Pour a teaspoon of it into your coffee. Drizzle some on pancakes, cheesecake, coffee cake, or apple pie. You can have it with ice cream or a smoothie or even on fresh fruit such as Granny Smith apple wedges or poached pears. You can eat it right off your finger if you like! It's *that* good!

MAKES ABOUT 2½ CUPS

Two 12-ounce cans sweetened condensed milk

1. Set a rack in the center position of the oven and preheat to 350°F. Place a shallow roasting dish on the rack and heat a kettle full of water to a boil.

2. Choose a shallow 9- or 10-inch baking dish. (A Pyrex pie plate or quiche dish works well.) Set the dish in the roasting pan and pour enough water from the kettle to come halfway up the sides. Pour the cans of milk into the pan, cover the pan loosely with aluminum foil, and bake without stirring until the milk thickens and turns a rich caramel color.

3. Scrape the contents of the dish into a bowl. While still warm, whisk the dulce de leche vigorously to smooth it out. Even after whisking you may have tiny lumps in the dulce. Don't worry, just enjoy. Eat warm, at room temperature, or cool.

LEMONADE

LIMONADA

This is a Brooklyn version of the kind of lemonade you find all over the Caribbean. It is made with yellow American lemons and is equally delicious. In Puerto Rico you would make this with *limones verdes*, the small, green, sweet lemons you find all over the island that are very much like key limes. If you ever go to Puerto Rico, have a limonada as soon as possible. In fact, I would make sure I didn't step out of the airport before finding one!

Roll the lemons on a hard surface, pressing down with the heel of your hand to loosen the lemons up and make them juicier. Cut the lemons in half and juice them, straining out the seeds if necessary. You will have about 1 cup of lemon juice. Pour the lemon juice and water into a pitcher. Stir in sugar to taste until dissolved. Stir in the vanilla. Serve over ice.

8 medium lemons
2 quarts water
½ to ¾ cup superfine sugar (see Note)
1 teaspoon vanilla extract

NOTE: *Latinos don't drink their lemonade very sweet, so add a little sugar if the smaller amount makes lemonade that is too tart for your taste.*

WHITE SANGRIA

SANGRIA BLANCA

Don't overthink the wine on this one. Pick a nice, dry white such as a pinot grigio. Peaches, nectarines, and strawberries all make fine additions to the citrus. My mood improves very quickly after a glass of this sangria, and I never regret it the next morning!

Stir the wine, brandy, and superfine sugar together in a punch bowl until the sugar is dissolved. Stir in the seltzer. Cut the citrus fruits in quarters. Squeeze each piece into the punch bowl and drop in the squeezed pieces. Leave at room temperature for an hour or two. Just before you serve, add a tray or two of ice and serve with additional ice if you like.

One 1.5-liter bottle dry white wine, such as Fontana Candida
1½ cups French or your favorite brandy
1 cup superfine sugar
1 liter or quart bottle seltzer or sparkling mineral water
2 lemons
4 limes
4 juice oranges

VARIATION: *You can also make a red sangria. Cut back a little on the brandy, though.*

PUERTO RICAN EGG NOG

COQUITO

It would not be Christmas for me without *coquito*. As a little girl I helped my Mami make it. I grated the coconut by hand and was rewarded for all my hard work with a taste of it before she added the rum. I felt *so* grown up.

Christmas on the island is the most joyous celebration I have ever experienced! I always tell my friends that Puerto Ricans love a good party so much that we start the day before. In the Latin community the night of Christmas Eve is the start of the celebrating. The aroma of *pernil* and *arroz con gandules* surrounds every neighborhood, and carloads of carolers, or *parranderos*, visit homes, knocking on doors and singing *aguinaldos*, our Christmas carols, with guitars and maracas in hand. Glasses of *coquito* are served to the revelers along with *pasteles*, *pernil*, and *arroz con gandules*. It is a blast!

After I introduced *coquito* to Jerry's family, they became fans as well. Today it is much easier to make *coquito* without sacrificing any of the flavor. It is always on my Christmas season menu.

Combine all ingredients in a blender and blend at low speed until smooth. Pour into a pitcher and chill. Serve in small glasses.

One 15-ounce can sweetened cream of coconut (such as Coco Lopez)
1½ cups white rum
One 12-ounce can evaporated milk
One 12-ounce can sweetened condensed milk
4 egg yolks or ½ cup egg substitute such as egg beaters
1 teaspoon vanilla extract

NOTE: *If you are concerned about eating raw eggs, you can use an egg substitute with wonderful results. Also, washing the shells well before using them may reduce any risk of infection. In any case, pregnant women and those with compromised immune systems should avoid raw eggs.*

ALMOND SOFT DRINK

HORCHATA

Stir the half-and-half, sparkling water, and almond syrup together gently in a 2-quart pitcher. Add enough crushed ice to fill the pitcher. Serve in tall glasses.

2 cups half-and-half
2 cups sparkling water
½ cup almond syrup
Crushed ice

NOTE: *Almond syrup can be found in Italian and Latin markets, as well as some supermarkets along with mixers and sodas.*

HOT CHOCOLATE

CHOCOLATE CALIENTE

I make this for my little Angelina Ballerina when her toes get cold in the winter.

MAKES 6 SERVINGS

1. Heat the milk in a 2-quart saucepan with the cinnamon sticks over very low heat. When it comes to a simmer, turn off the heat and set the pan aside to let the cinnamon steep for a few minutes.

2. Break up the chocolate bar, then chop it roughly in a food processor. Return the milk to low heat and add the chocolate to the hot milk in 2 batches, whisking well after each one to incorporate the milk into the chocolate. Watch the temperature very carefully because the chocolate will "seize" (turn hard instead of melt) if it gets too hot too fast.

3. Whisk the cornstarch into the water, then whisk the mixture into the hot chocolate, stirring until slightly thickened.

4. Pour into mugs and top each with a dollop of whipped cream and a dusting of ground cinnamon.

4 cups whole milk
2 cinnamon sticks
One 1-pound bar Cortes chocolate (or your favorite sweetened bar chocolate)
2 teaspoons cornstarch
2 tablespoons water
Whipped cream
Ground cinnamon

SPICED MILK

Mami's mother, Mama Clotilde, was Taino. She was a thin woman, her skin a copper color, and her hair the color of ebony. When she died at the age of eighty-three, she still had waist-long black hair, which she braided and wrapped into a bun. She was very well versed in herb lore and could pretty much cure anything with stuff growing in her garden. She was always making *teses* with this infusion or the other, for anything from a tummy ache to a fever to indigestion. I remember drinking a canela tea very much like this one for an upset tummy many times. I added milk, and my kids became hooked.

MAKES 4 SERVINGS

1 cup water
2 cinnamon sticks
½ teaspoon whole cloves
One 1-inch piece fresh ginger, smashed
2½ cups milk
1 tablespoon (or to taste) brown sugar
  or honey to taste
Ground cinnamon

1. Bring the water, cinnamon sticks, cloves, and ginger to a boil in a saucepan over medium heat. Lower the heat to a gentle boil and cook until the liquid is reduced by half.
2. Pour in the milk and bring to a simmer slowly. Cook, stirring occasionally, for 15 minutes. Strain.
3. Add the brown sugar, adjusting the sweetness to your taste. Serve in cups with a sprinkle of cinnamon on top.
4. After the kids are in bed, you can stir a little dark rum into a cupful of this and relax.

As a young woman Abuela had very long hair, and a lot of it. But as is often the case, our hair changes as we get older, and Abuela's hair thinned with age. I personally think that she missed the gorgeous braids and hairdos that she fixed herself, and she never really felt "dressed up" enough for special occasions without her hair all done up.

One of her nieces, a hairdresser, mentioned in passing that maybe she should consider getting a hairpiece. When Papi made the rank of captain in the Fire Department, Mami had a party in his honor in a lovely Italian restaurant. We invited family and friends, and I was to pick Abuela up at her home and drive her to the party. That afternoon I called her on the phone to let her know what time I was picking her up, and I asked her if she needed anything. She told me she was all set, and she was very excited because she had bought a hairpiece, or a *moño,* and was going to feel very glamorous going to the party.

With kids in tow, Jerry and I picked Abuela up at her house at the appointed hour, and she got into the car, all dressed up and looking very festive with her new "hairdo." We all made sure to tell her how beautiful she looked, and Jerry kidded her about getting a boyfriend. We took off for the party, and I started smelling coffee— I mean *strong* coffee—but I didn't say anything, thinking that maybe it was something we were driving through. The smell of strong coffee persisted throughout our car ride to the restaurant.

We were seated at the party, and Abuela was sitting between Mami and me. I still smelled coffee, so I said to Abuela, "Abuela, do you smell coffee? I can't seem to get the aroma out of my nose. I've been smelling it since we left your house." She looked at me out of the corner of her eye and said she didn't smell anything, but Mami piped up and said, "You know what? I smell it, too!" She leaned into Abuela and said, "Valentina, it's you! You are the one who smells like coffee!" Abuela looked a little sheepish and said, "Ay, Mija, you know what I think it is? I bought this new hairpiece, and I didn't want it to get crushed, so I put it in a coffee can to store it. Now my hair smells like coffee!"

That became one of my favorite "Abuela" stories. No amount of coaxing would make her change the storage container for her hairpiece, and after that, whenever Abuela got dressed up for special occasions, we knew that when she walked past, we would smell the aroma of Café Bustelo!

BREAKFAST COFFEE

CAFÉ CON LECHE

This always tastes to me like summer vacation. We always spent part of our summer vacation in Puerto Rico, visiting Mama Clotilde and the tias. Mama was always up at the crack of dawn, and everyone would have a breakfast of *café con leche, pan de agua* (simple country bread) with fresh butter, and fresh country eggs. Of course, there were always fresh mangoes and grapefruit from my grandmother's fruit trees, and the kids' *café* was more *leche* than *café*. But whenever I smell *café con leche*, I am in Arecibo, sitting on the *balcón* sipping my *café con leche* and sneaking bits of food to Mama's dog, Tokyo.

MAKES EIGHT ¾-CUP SERVINGS

Make the coffee. While it is brewing, bring the milk and cinnamon stick to a simmer in a small saucepan over low heat. When the milk is ready, skim off any skin that has formed on top. Pour ¼ cup of black coffee into your cup and then add ½ cup of milk. Sweeten to taste.

½ recipe for Puerto Rican Black Coffee
  (see below)
4 cups milk
1 cinnamon stick (optional)
Sugar

PUERTO RICAN BLACK COFFEE

CAFÉ NEGRO

Making coffee this way, bringing it to a gentle boil and then straining it, is one of the simplest and most delicious ways to prepare it. You will need a *coladór,* a strainer that looks like a very soft white flannel sock and is attached to a handle. They are sold in most Latin markets. I can't say I ever remember my mother's sister, Maria, eating anything. What I do remember is a blue glass bottle that she kept by the side of the stove, filled with *café negro*, which she would empty by day's end. Tia keeps her *coladór*—or, as my husband calls it, her coffee "sock"—hanging on a hook so it dries after she makes her coffee for the day.

MAKES ABOUT EIGHT ½-CUP SERVINGS (INGREDIENTS CAN BE EASILY CUT IN HALF)

1. Stir the coffee into the water in a medium saucepan. Bring the water to the brink of a boil, lower the heat, and simmer about 5 minutes (or more, depending on how strong you like your coffee).
2. Strain the coffee through a *coladór* into warm cups.

4 heaping tablespoons Puerto Rican
  coffee (Bustelo, El Pico, Goya, or
  other)
4 cups cold water

ACKNOWLEDGMENTS

I have heard that there are people who join contests for a living—that is what they do. They are inherently lucky, and so they participate in contest after contest. Unfortunately, I do not fall into that category of the population. I have won two things in my entire life: a basket of cheer at my niece's school picnic and a sword at a Web site that I support because I am a geek (go Tolkien!)

It is mostly for this reason that, when the opportunity to do this project (both the television show and this companion book) was given to me, I walked around sporting bruises on my arms from the pinches I gave myself. I feel very lucky to be able to give this obsession of mine a voice and a forum, but in doing so I have a long list of people to whom I owe much gratitude.

Throughout the series and this book, you will hear over and over the voices of two women and one man in my life who instilled in me the passion I have for the kitchen. To my mother, Conchita Martinez, and my grandmother, Valentina Martinez, I give the most heartfelt gratefulness. Thank you for teaching me the language of love through food, and I hope I can teach it to my family as well as you've taught it to me. For my father, Raymond Martinez, I have no words to express all that you've done and sacrificed for me, as well as the rest of your family. I stand before you humbled.

There never would have been a *DaisyCooks!* project without the vision of Geoffrey Drummond, president of A La Carte Communications, the company that has produced the show. Thank you so very much for giving me the opportunity to share this love of mine with your world. You, Nat Katzman, Hope Reed, Teri Meissner, her adorable daughter, Madison, and the rest of the wonderful staff at A La Carte have made my dream come true. When you handpicked the crew for the show, it was a crew like no other, and we all marveled at how incredible the energy and the chemistry was among all of us. First, Mark Solan, my set designer, made my kitchen look like a dream. Richard Dooley, my producer, knew what I wanted almost before I knew it. Herb Sevush, my director, brought out the best humor in me on a daily basis, even when I thought there was no more to be had. Dean Gaskill, director of photography and perennial boy, scared away the kitchen gremlins with his smile (and made me look good!), along with his two cameramen, Stephen (What's up, Doc?) Hussar and Mike McEachern. Joshua (Busta Move) Dreyfus, our grip, worked the lights to make everything sparkle, Decembe Bueno set my name to music!

The "invisible" crew in the production room were just as professional, but not so much as to be intimidating. Day after day video engineer Eliat Goldman, audio engineer Gilles Morin, and Brenda Coffey, who fussed over me with makeup brushes and hair gel (while keeping me in stitches), put in 120 percent of their expertise with good humor.

Miguelina Polanco, talent coordinator, production assistant, companion, friend, and car key finder, was my right hand. I'm sure that dousing anxiety attacks is not in the job description, Migs, but you certainly rose to the occasion and managed to do it all while teaching me the Miggy Dance!

Chris Styler. Whew! I think I'll need an entire chapter just to thank Chris. Not only did he pretty much give up his summer to test recipes with me, but he also inspired me, made me

laugh, held my hand, and snuck my little dog Chachi small pieces of bacon when I wasn't looking. Chris walked me through the entire book process and made it seem feasible when I was completely overwhelmed. His instinct, professionalism, compassion, friendship, and humor would have been amazing enough, but he went ahead and recruited my two kitchen ninjas, Angela (Ah-hee-see-toe) Spensieri, who also styled the food for both the show and the book, and Eve Formisano, both gifted chefs in their own right, to run the production kitchen. You guys rocked it!

Suzanne Nelson, wardrobe stylist, pastry chef, and beautiful spirit, worked indefatigably to shop for my "look." Who would have thought that you could hit the nail on the head even before you met me? Shelly Brafman coordinated all of my jewelry and accessories to put the finishing touches on my outfits. Buff Strickland took the beautiful photographs for this book. All of you ladies radiate beautiful light wherever you go.

A special thanks to my location crew in New York and Florida: Rod Lamborn, camera; Luciano Dias and John Austin, audio engineers; and Carolina Pinafiel, locations driver. Thanks also to the Miami Film Office and of course Miggy.

I want to give special recognition and sincere thanks to: the sponsors of my Public Television show, for their faith in me and my cooking, but more so for their faith in the vitality and passion of the Latino community; AllClad, for their terrific cookware; Brillo, for keeping it all shiny clean (along with my husband's golf clubs); and Marshalls, for making sure that my family and I all looked great for the book and the television series.

Also, I'd like to express my appreciation to Clarke Kitchens (Sub-Zero, Wolf, KWC) in Milford, Massachusetts, for creating and sharing such a terrific kitchen studio. To Tom Clarke, Jim Raftus, and their team, gracias. Thank you too to Olga Russo & Sons (great produce), Kitchen Aid (small appliances), The Pampered Chef, OXO, Jamon Redondo Iglesias, and The Homer Laughlin China Company.

There is no way that I can forgo mentioning and thanking Esmeralda Santiago, author and personal mentor, for being such an inspiration. For me, reading your words in a book was seeing the lives of the women of my family. Meeting you is a memory I will always cherish. Thank you.

I'd never forgive myself if I wrote one more word without thanking Will Schwalbe, my editor at Hyperion, for all his encouragement, generosity of spirit, and knowledge. Who would have believed that there actually was somebody who could get *more* excited about the book than me! It was truly a wonderful experience working under your guidance. Emily Gould, his assistant, deserves major props for all of her help, good cheer, and support throughout this project, and for facilitating the experience for me immensely.

A very large part of the *girl* inside Daisy is due to the company I keep. I would be remiss if I did not thank my girlfriends for their encouragement, critiques, laughter, warmth, and patience. I have made them sit through interminable dinners, testing innumerable recipes of them, and they did it all with graciousness and giggles.

Loni Shomstein, my neighbor and good friend of seventeen years, has sat through this with me offering encouragement, advice, and appraisal. I want to be just like you when I grow up! Violette Tonuzi, Latin cuisine *aficionada* and the first American girl I have ever met who made *pasteles*! You have a smile that melts frost and know my hair better than I ever have!

Jennifer Cohan, diva and stand-up comedienne (well, she's *not* but she should be!): Girl, just *standing* next to you makes me feel more fabulous! Two snaps up!

Rosanne Berardi, best friend since the second grade, and the strongest shoulder to cry on a girlfriend could ever hope for!

Miguelina Polanco: Honey, one more word about you and I'm going to have to change the title of this book! *Que bonita bandera!*

My brother Peter Martinez and his wife Rodale are both brilliant chefs and the two people that I have the most fun with in the kitchen. How is it we can make it sound like there is a party going on in the room whenever we occupy the kitchen?

A very, very special thanks goes to my children Erik, Marc, David, and Angela. You have filled my life and home with joy and laughter (and all of your friends!), and you are all still teaching me to be a better person by virtue of being your mother. I never thought myself capable of experiencing such happiness. You have given that to me, and more.

Last, but far from least, I thank Jerry Lombardo, husband, lover, partner, friend, and father of my children. Thank you for shoring me up, for letting me lean, for making me push, and for always believing. Thank you for being my prince. I love you.

DAISY MARTINEZ
March 2005

SOURCES

Achiote (annatto) seed
Amazon.com
deananddeluca.com or telephone 212-664-226-6800

Ajices dulces (cachucha peppers)
cubanfoodmarket.com

Banana leaves
amazon.com

Cheeses
  Queso Blanco (de freir)
  amazon.com
  mexgrocer.com

  Cotijo
  cheesesupply.com

  Spanish (Manchego, Zamorano, Cabrales)
  Tienda.com

  Valdeon
  cheeseandmore.com or telephone 201-445-1777

Chiles, dried
amazon.com
mexgrocer.com (dried chilies and chili paste)

Chorizo
amigofoods.com
cubanfoodmarket.com

Culantro, fres
Can be found in Latin markets. However, for the brave and not horticulturally challenged (like me) there is a website where you can order fresh culantro plants:
  mulberrycreek.com or telephone 419-433-6126

Epazote
amazon.com
mellisas.com or telephone 800-588-0151
penzeys.com

Latin American products from all countries
amigofoods.com

Media crema
mexgrocer.com
tienda.com

Paprika and smoked paprika
amazon.com
cubanfoodguy.com
deananddeluca.com

Piloncillo
amazon.com

Salt cod
elcolmadito.com (also carries adobo, mojo criollo marinade, achiotina)

Serrano ham
amigofoods.com
tienda.com

Tomatillos
amazon.com
mexgrocer.com
tienda.com

Vianda
cubanfoodmarket.com

White anchovies
deananddeluca.com

INDEX

Page numbers in *italic* refer to photos.